MACIEJ KRANZ

BUILDING
THE
INTERNET
OF
THINGS

IMPLEMENT NEW BUSINESS MODELS,
DISRUPT COMPETITORS, AND
TRANSFORM YOUR INDUSTRY

WILEY

Library of Congress Cataloging-in-Publication Data has been applied for and is on file with the Library of Congress.
978-1-119-28566-3 (hardback)
978-1-119-28567-0 (ePDF)
978-1-119-28568-7 (ePUB)

Printed in the United States of America

10 9 8 7 6 5 4 3 2 1

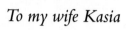

To my wife Kasia

Contents

Foreword

We are inundated with hype around Internet of Things (IoT) today. There is a need for a book like this—a practical guide that separates the hype from reality—to direct us to what's practical and immediately valuable about IoT and how we can start today and derive tangible benefits tomorrow.

Today's reality is that in a world of more than 7 billion people, there are 70 million who are joining the middle class annually. This growing middle class generates $8 trillion in consumer spending, and their demands require manufacturing companies to be more productive, more sustainable, more flexible, and more cost competitive. Manufacturers must also ensure global compliance and effectively manage enterprise risks while improving the connectivity across their business enterprises.

The Internet of Things will significantly impact and change how global companies conduct business. IoT technologies will transform the manufacturing environment; it will change more in the next 10 years than it has in the past 50 years. Cisco estimates there is $3.9 trillion of value in manufacturing alone for IoT, one of the largest sectors to benefit from this technology.

The convergence of information technology (IT) and operations technology (OT) has brought us to an inflection point for realizing a vision that we call The Connected Enterprise. The foundation of this vision is our belief that the future of manufacturing is based on standard unmodified Ethernet and open systems. The combination of information in the two worlds of IT and OT—seamlessly and securely connecting production data with business data and information—results in transformational benefits. And IoT accelerates The Connected Enterprise.

Manufacturers still have a long way to go to realize the full benefits of The Connected Enterprise and the fast-emerging IoT. In a January 2015 *Industry Week* survey of 581 manufacturing executives and managers, fewer than 28 percent said their plant floor was Internet-enabled. Only 8 percent of larger companies with sales over $1 billion described their organization as "completely ready" to benefit from the new IoT technologies. Thus, we need to accelerate the adoption of IoT technologies.

IoT starts with smart assets that are securely networked over an open, standard network (Ethernet). We realize the full value of IoT by complementing smart, networked assets with contemporary technologies such as scalable computing, information management, analytics, and mobility, to create high-value outcomes such as zero downtime and reduced energy consumption. The Connected Enterprise accelerated by IoT technologies delivers unprecedented benefits in productivity, sustainability, and global competitiveness.

Rockwell Automation is proud to be an early pioneer of IoT since 2005. Working with Cisco, we knew that this new technology would lead the industry through a major transformation, and we are committed to leading this transformation together. Through innovative collaboration on products, services, and educational initiatives, we are helping companies achieve successful convergence.

Our collaboration adopted a phased approach. In Phase 1, we initiated joint product development. So far, we have developed more than 50 products together. We joined forces to drive network migration to Ethernet/IP. We actively engaged with the standards bodies to chart the migration plans, combining the best of both IT and OT worlds.

In Phase 2, we worked on joint architectures—first a converged plant-wide Ethernet (CPwE), then more recently the Secure Industrial Network. In Phase 3, we moved to building joint solutions. Subsequent phases enabled new business models (CAPEX to OPEX), including pay-for-production performance approaches. Now we are working together to address the skilled workforce gap with joint certification programs. The history of our engagements alone present a good set of lessons learned for anyone working through the adoption of IoT.

Over the past 11 years of working with Maciej Kranz, Rockwell Automation and Cisco have successfully deployed joint products, architectures, and solutions to over 10,000 customers globally. In this book, Maciej has taken the lessons learned from our IoT journey and shares them with readers from all industries. Maciej, one of the pioneers of IoT, has masterfully captured best practices and combined them with practical guidelines to help readers begin their own IoT journeys.

Our customers continue to be inundated with IoT discussions. This practical guide helps differentiate the excitement from reality and provides pragmatic advice on starting your own journey along with advice on planning for the future. I recommend business and technical managers from every industry read this book to understand how to achieve faster innovation and higher productivity from a successful implementation of IoT.

Keith Nosbusch
Chairman, Rockwell Automation

PART 1

A Secure and Transformative IoT Now

1 | Beyond the Hype—All You Actually Need to Know About IoT for Business

Like it or not, the Internet of Things (IoT) will change your organization unlike anything before. It will change your organization more than business process reengineering (BPR), Six Sigma, lean manufacturing, agile computing, or any of the other business concepts that periodically pop up, experience success, and are forgotten when the next big thing arrives. Granted, to date most of IoT deployments have been incremental and evolutionary, streamlining an existing process here, cutting some costs or improving productivity there. That, however, is about to change as IoT ramps up, as standards are adopted, and as security is bolstered—all of which and more are in the works. So please don't misunderstand me. The Internet of Things certainly will be a big thing—an enormously big thing, actually. But it isn't *just* the next big thing. IoT is the future—your industry's future, your organization's future, and probably your personal future. Welcome to the future. It's spelled I-o-T. All this may seem like hype now, but it will prove in the end to be quite understated; IoT is very, very real.

You still are skeptical. The hype around IoT certainly has become deafening and distracting. Over the past few years, however, I have traveled more than a million miles meeting with people around the world to discuss IoT. Some of those people have actually done stunning things with IoT and wanted to show these off for me. Others were struggling with a problem IoT should be able to solve and wanted to know how their peers were doing it. Full disclosure: not every business problem, it turns out, lends itself to an IoT solution.

OK, so are there problems I wouldn't recommend an IoT solution for? Not many come to mind immediately. If you insist, for starters there is the connected home. At the Consumer Electronics Show in Las Vegas you can see home appliances from washing machines to coffee makers connected to the Internet and to each other. The problem: while I see value in connecting individual home devices to the Internet, the business case for connecting all appliances and devices to each other in the mainstream home is just not there yet. There are a few emerging use cases, for example, home security and elder care where specialized devices in the home have to be interconnected, but an immediate IoT payoff is still some distance away.

In truth, most of the current implementations of IoT are in the business-to-business (B2B) area and are focused on improved efficiency and productivity around existing processes. As I said, IoT gains are incremental at this point. The real payoff from IoT comes down to automating existing processes that have a large labor or time component and streamlining the related process in one way or another. The resulting improvements, despite having measureable business impact, are mostly evolutionary. Similarly, you, too, after reading this book, should focus first on streamlining and improving your existing processes, which will deliver your fast paybacks and set you on the path toward more revolutionary applications, new business models, and incremental revenue streams. For example, you might use IoT to automate a data collection process you now do manually or remotely monitor something that otherwise requires a person to actually visit. Such solutions are already well proven and documented. I do, however, expect that down the road many breakthroughs in IoT will also come from the B2B2C (business to business to consumer) domain, but today they are just starting to emerge, pioneered by early adopters: processes like mass customization, food safety, and even autonomic car or drone transportation/delivery (see Figure 1.1).

Figure 1.1   B2B and B2B2C Domains

In the meantime, manufacturing around the world, including in North America, is having a renaissance of sorts, and IoT is part of the reason. By converging previously siloed sensors, machines, cells, and zones, IoT-driven factory automation helps enterprises integrate production and business systems and then bring everything online over a single network. Organizations are gaining flexibility to quickly adapt to changes, whether for new product introductions, planned product line changeovers, or other adjustments. Each affected zone, from the enterprise to the plant floor to the loading dock, receives real-time alerts about changes through networked mobile devices, video monitors, and human-machine interfaces. The real-time information also links back to the entire supply chain, so each step in the manufacturing value chain, from supply through production to distribution, can respond as quickly as needed.

These represent evolutionary improvements that together deliver real business value. Similar gains are being achieved in transportation, utilities, agriculture, building automation, education, retail, health care, sports, and entertainment—even the military. Companies in these industries are taking first steps on their IoT journeys starting with low-hanging fruit. Still, the process improvements are real and the paybacks, the ROI, add up to serious money in the bank, as I will demonstrate in Chapters 3 and 4.

So this isn't theory. It's real, and it's working today. What a better example than a legendary American motorcycle manufacturer, Harley-Davidson Motor Company. The company was facing intense global competition while its core market was aging and new younger buyers wanted a different type of motorcycle.[1] It needed to get agile, to be able to respond to changes fast, and to be more efficient and productive. IoT gave Harley-Davidson the capabilities it needed. Here's how.

Harley-Davidson faced the familiar litany of problems encountered by many American businesses, especially large and market-leading companies or those with ambitions to be so in their industry. Labor was too costly. Production was not aligned with IT operations. Islands of incompatible data were everywhere. "You name it, we suffered from it," one former Harley manager told me.

So the company pulled together key people from both IT and operations (known as operational technology, or OT). In every industry and most businesses, IT and OT are notoriously uncooperative, almost as if IT, as the book title says, was from Venus and OT from Mars. We're not talking about a mass revolution here: more like a couple of people from different groups who got together by themselves and started actually talking to each other. Later they pulled in a few others and sat together in a room until they formed a unified team willing to communicate with each other and with other Harley-Davidson business units to gain the efficiencies IoT could deliver. The company converged its multiple networks into a single network and began consolidating data islands. As of this writing, one Harley-Davidson factory is fully IoT-enabled. The results are impressive. "What used to take a painfully long time to triage and troubleshoot now can be accomplished in a single morning," the manager said, an order of magnitude improvement. That alone led to increased productivity, efficiency, flexibility, and agility. The results have been so astonishing that other Harley-Davidson factories are clamoring to be the next adopters of IoT.

Moreover, those are just the operational results. Harley-Davidson's strategic business outcomes from the IoT-induced changes are equally impressive:

- Eighty percent faster decision making due to workforce enablement
- Dramatic reductions in costs and set-up time
- Continuous asset management, enabling even better decision making
- 6.8 percent increase in production throughput due to asset tagging
- Ten to 25 times improvement in build-to-order (BTO) cycle times (18 months reduced to two weeks)
- Seven to 12 percent increase in IoT automation-driven equipment utilization

All of this led to a profitability increase between 3 and 4 percent. And that was just one factory!

Harley-Davidson bet its future survival on IoT and, from its first IoT-enabled factory, it began paying off big (see Figure 1.2). This same future attracts what I refer to as Generation IoT everywhere.

Generation IoT Drives Business Survival in the 21st Century

If you look at the last 25 years of the tech industry, you'll see that change has been constant. Every three to seven years, organizations had to reinvent themselves. Companies that missed one technology transition could possibly recover if they scrambled to catch up. Those that missed two, however, most likely perished. Interestingly, according to The Boston Consulting Group, when you look at the roster of S&P 500 companies from 50 years ago, only 19 percent are still in existence.[2] The rest have perished.

As the S&P 500's mortality shows, we're so used to change that we barely notice it occurring. Remember tape recorders, CDs, VHS tapes, and answering machines? The advent of each changed society in substantive ways. When I asked my children about CDs and VHS tapes, I got blank stares. What about home telephones? I recently met a teenager who didn't recognize a telephone busy signal when she heard it; she had never experienced the phenomenon. When it was explained, she was baffled.

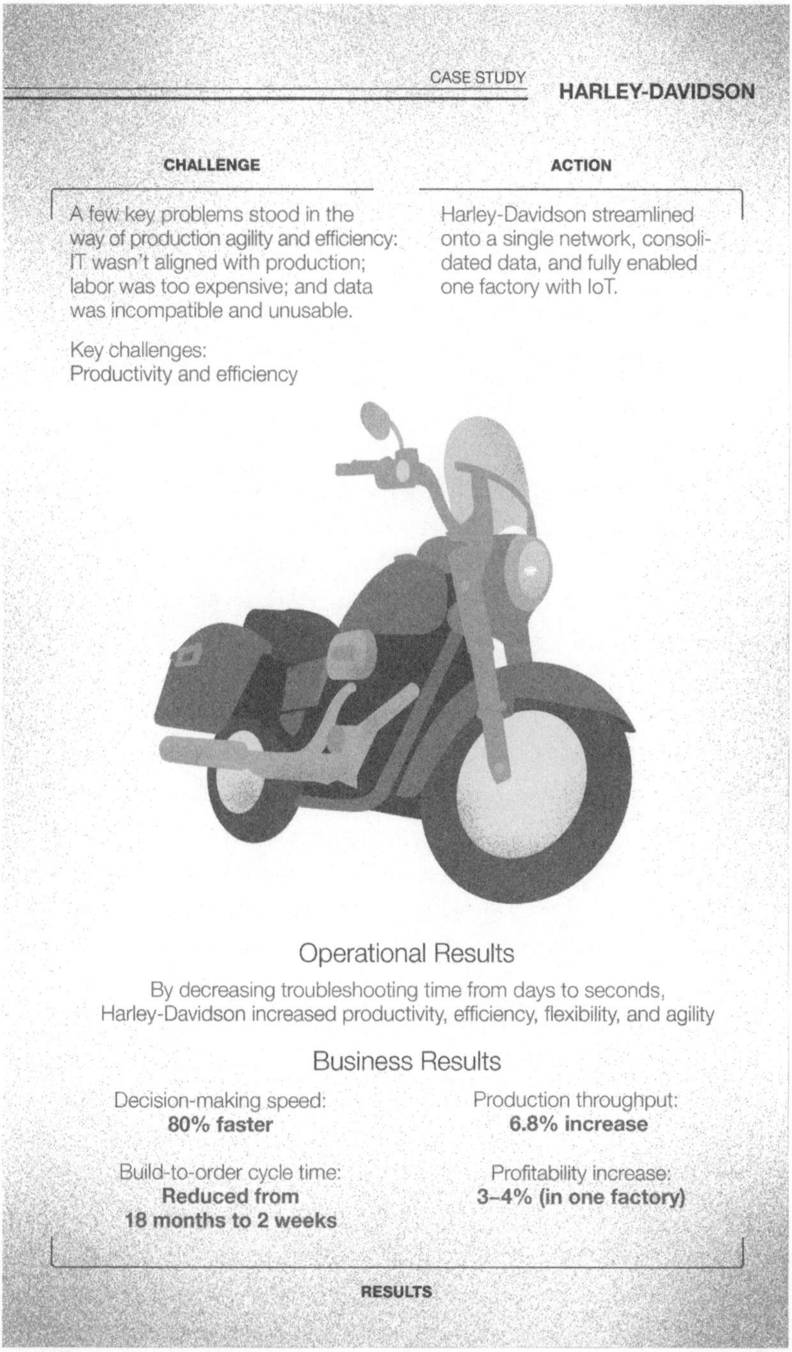

CASE STUDY   **HARLEY-DAVIDSON**

CHALLENGE

A few key problems stood in the way of production agility and efficiency: IT wasn't aligned with production; labor was too expensive; and data was incompatible and unusable.

Key challenges:
Productivity and efficiency

ACTION

Harley-Davidson streamlined onto a single network, consolidated data, and fully enabled one factory with IoT.

Operational Results

By decreasing troubleshooting time from days to seconds, Harley-Davidson increased productivity, efficiency, flexibility, and agility

Business Results

Decision-making speed:
80% faster

Build-to-order cycle time:
**Reduced from
18 months to 2 weeks**

Production throughput:
6.8% increase

Profitability increase:
3–4% (in one factory)

RESULTS

Figure 1.2   Harley-Davidson Case

Everyone has voicemail and call waiting, she insisted. Tape recorders, CDs, VHS tapes, and answering machines are maybe 30 years old, and yet they're not only obsolete but also now forgotten. Their replacements are now integrated into your smartphone. Society and business keep moving forward.

This is as good a point as any to tell you about me, your author. Obviously I'm a father with a bunch of kids, but what's important to you is my experience with IoT. My IoT journey started 12 years ago as a manager at Cisco when several of us flew to Cleveland and started working on industrial Ethernet switches together with Rockwell Automation. It was a challenging assignment for our team, encompassing a completely new set of requirements, certifications, and accommodating so many ruggedized systems versions, but we got things to work. A few years later, we decided that the time was right for Cisco to focus on the industrial networking segment, and we created the Connected Industries Group, which I ran. We also decided to adopt the IoT term to describe the phenomenon of everything connecting to everything. Anyway, this is how I started.

From there our plan for IoT was to expand our ruggedized infrastructure portfolio, develop vertical solutions expertise, build a partner ecosystem to augment our own skills—even then we realized that IoT would be bigger than any one organization could do on its own—and offer a platform for real-time analytics and vertical applications. We also evangelized IoT to the rest of the industry with the goal of getting them excited about its potential so that together we could turn the IoT vision into a huge market opportunity for everybody. Judging from the latest independent industry projections of billions of connected devices in just a few years and trillions in revenue, it has worked out pretty well to date. The important part, however, is that we have started to deliver on that promise. Now, if you haven't done so already, I hope that after reading this book you will join us as well by introducing your organization to IoT and participate in the IoT economy.

Today, the pace of change is more than a constant; it's the new status quo. The Millennials now entering the workforce know only unrelenting change. To them it's a way of life, one that will likely continue for the rest of their lives. But no matter our actual age, we are all part of a generation poised to encounter revolutionary change. That's why I call what we're experiencing in every business segment Generation IoT.

So how does your business survive in this environment? How do you avoid the mortality we've seen among the S&P 500? That's what this book is about—understanding this emerging change that has just begun to sweep over us and finding a strategy that will ensure your business and your career not only survive but thrive. The winners in this new era will recognize the changes occurring around us and be willing to adjust and re-learn, over and over again. They are Generation IoT.

So how do we spot these winners? You belong to Generation IoT if you embrace open standards, open collaboration, open communications, and open, flexible business models and you're willing to assemble a comprehensive partner ecosystem to build and deploy agile, flexible business solutions. The losers, however, will insistently stick to the old ways of doing business or try to do it all themselves. We've seen them many times in the past. They run their operations on proprietary or semi-standard technologies and adopt business models that lock in customers, ultimately destroying whatever value they initially delivered.

Need another example of IoT-led transformation? How about Ford Motor Company, a major U.S. automaker? It hasn't been long since the company together with its peers was on the ropes during the financial crises. Today, Ford has smartened up and changed processes. Of its 40 vehicle assembly plants, 25 now use IoT technology to speed communications within and between them. Plants around the world are now connected to the Ford enterprise network. Moreover, its next-generation automated vehicle scheduling system manages production in real time, handling more than 2 million variations. As a result, Ford is selling more cars than ever before. Thank you, IoT.

First Step on IoT Security Journey

The ability to deal effectively with security threats is the number 1 make-or-break factor for IoT adoption. Without it, companies will be reluctant to implement IoT and thus not benefit from the growing number of powerful use cases emerging across all industries.

The industry recognizes the challenge and is making it the top priority. IoT security is starting to be integrated into the very fabric of both industry and public infrastructure, including fundamental areas such as transportation and logistics, power grids, water supplies, and public safety. However, much more needs to be done. We still lack skills, education, and awareness. Many companies continue to be in denial, still relying on a discredited physical separation approach to securing their plants and infrastructure. The OT and IT divide prevents the companies from implementing modern and proven security best practices.

So how should organizations start to approach IoT security? According to Verizon's "2015 Data Breach Investigations Report," most security breaches exploit well-known vulnerabilities where companies have not applied available fixes. The first step, therefore, is to implement existing best practices by following these three sets of guidelines:

- **Adopt** a single policy-based security architecture built on an open, unified approach with automated, risk-based self-defense and self-healing capabilities.
- **Converge** around standards. Vendors and enterprises alike need to leverage IT industry standards and best practices in OT and to fill in the gaps between industry-specific and horizontal standards organizations.
- **Collaborate.** OT, IT, information security teams (CiSO), together with vendors and consultants, must work together on common architectures, incorporating not only OT requirements into the IT provider's product portfolio but also supporting form-factors, up-time requirements, and integration with legacy industrial protocols. Security isn't your differentiation; it's your foundation. Therefore, let's learn and share together.

Yes, IoT is different than IT in many ways: it is more distributed, more heterogeneous, and more dynamic. There are many new IoT scenarios that require brand new approaches to security. We will explore them in more detail in Chapter 9. But the first step on the IoT security journey is to leverage 30+ years of experience and best practices that IT security systems give us. So let's not reinvent the wheel.

A Revolutionary Economic Opportunity

Many of us view IoT as the next stage of the Internet/Web that uses the Internet protocol–based (IP-based) distributed cloud to connect anything to anything. According to Vernon Turner, senior vice president of enterprise systems and IDC Fellow for The Internet of Things, "Think of IoT as a network of uniquely identifiable things that communicate using IP connectivity without human interaction." Pretty straightforward, huh? Some people, including me, extend this definition into what some call the *Internet of Everything (IoE)*, a term first coined by Cisco, or even to the digitization of smart assets. IoE brings together the people, processes, data, and things that make networked connections more relevant by turning information into actions. For the purposes of simplicity and clarity, this book refers to both IoE and IoT as IoT—in effect, treating the two terms as synonymous.

Here's an easy way to think of what's going on: The first stage of the Internet connected people to networks, data, each other, and processes. With IoT, we're now connecting anything with anything—or, if you prefer, everything with everything. In short, anything that can be digitized can be part of IoT. The business impact of IoT makes it revolutionary; when everything can communicate with everything else, it essentially redefines and creates new business value chains (see Figure 1.3).

First, as Turner points out, IoT disrupts traditional value chains. This forces companies to rethink and retool everything they do, including product design, production, marketing, and after-sales service, while using analytics combined with security. That's essentially what happened at Harley-Davidson. From there, smart connected products expand traditional B2B channels and effectively demolish line-of-business (LOB) boundaries.

A decade ago, visionaries talked about mass customization—the ability to customize mass-produced products to each individual buyer's specifications. A few tried, but it proved very difficult to implement efficiently. The process had too much latency (delay), which added cost and slowed the results. However, IoT makes strategies like mass customization far more practical and cost efficient. Latency isn't a problem. Information can be shared in real time between every element in the supply chain. Buyers can click on the components they want. Suppliers and logistics providers

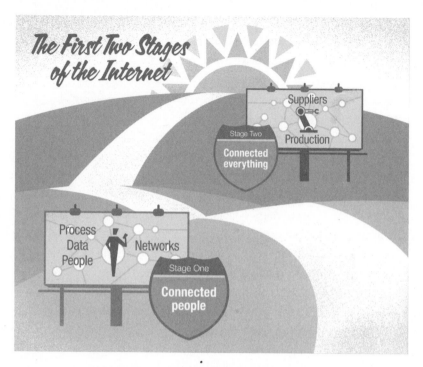

Figure 1.3   First Two Stages of the Internet

can see what components are being ordered, and with rapid systems re-tooling adjust their schedules appropriately—on the fly, if necessary. With the information flowing, the various players can ensure the desired components are at the production line when that customer's order is being assembled, whether it's a car or a three-piece suit. Customers order a car or a suit or anything else, specify the desired components, and have it built or assembled as ordered. Daihatsu Motor Company is already using 3D printers to offer its car buyers 10 colors and 15 base patterns to create their own "effect skins" for the car exterior. Each order rolls off the assembly line customized to that individual buyer. And it's no big deal. With IoT, mass customization is starting to happen.

Now imagine what's possible when you can connect anything with anything—production lines with parts and components, production lines with suppliers, products with service providers, logistics operations with transportation companies—and you can do it in near–real time. Designers could create products people really want and use, marketers could sell those products the way people want them, and service and support teams would know where potential problems are and address them before things break. Costs could be contained, and customer satisfaction would soar.

Or imagine if products you put out in the field could link back to you, signaling when a part starts to fail or a configuration isn't working correctly. You could effectively eliminate unplanned downtime. What could product managers do when they learned that customers were using the company's product in new ways the marketing teams didn't even imagine? The possibilities and opportunities are endless. Admittedly, not all of these concepts and value propositions are available at scale today, but there are plenty of mature, fast paybacks you can implement now.

At the same time, there is no magic here. That's right; *no* magic is at play, none, nada. We're talking about the same digitally connected world we know now, just more so. Essentially, we're using the cloud as we know it, plus an intelligent infrastructure within which every device is digitized and addressable over a common IP network. Yes, there are a few new innovations—such as fog computing, a form of cloud computing at the edge of the network for real-time data processing; blockchain technology, essentially a secure distributed log; and machine learning, the technology behind real-time predictive analytics—but none of these is magic either. These are concepts that industry is focusing on and implementing (if you can't wait to learn more about them, we will cover them in more detail in Chapter 10); nothing exotic, nothing magical.

IoT Background—A Brief History

For many people, the first time they heard about IoT was in the business media or at a business conference. But IoT isn't actually new. It has been around for years, in various forms. Banks run large, distributed automated teller machine (ATM) networks. Retailers operate large point-of-sale (POS) networks, as well as extensive deployments of radio-frequency identification (RFID) tags to track the movement of millions of inventory items. Manufacturers connect thousands of devices to monitor and manage production in machine-to-machine (M2M) networks. Utilities deploy connected sensors and meters to enable everything from customer billing to maintenance troubleshooting. Each network could amount to tens of thousands of connected devices.

Nobody referred to these initial networks as IoT, and there were significant differences. Typically, they dealt with only one type of connected device or one application, had a very limited and tightly defined set of functions, and often used proprietary protocols rather than IP or the cloud, which have become the dominant networking and computing options today. Still, these amounted to early large-scale attempts to connect devices with some level of built-in intelligence and communication for the purpose of managing critical business functions. They were the forerunners of what we think of as IoT today. As expected, not all initial IoT-driven efforts were successful. From the GE-Cisco Industrial Ethernet joint venture, to location-based digital advertising platforms, to active RFID implementations in retail, and to ambitious plans for smart cities, many concepts incubated in the early 2000s were for one reason or another ahead of their time. However, as IoT matured over the following decade, the more robust technologies, solutions, and business models were subsequently developed and increasingly adopted.

As I recall, an IoT term might have been coined in late 1990s to describe the emerging RFID networks. To be honest, six years ago, when Cisco was deciding how to best describe the trend of devices, machines, or things connecting to each other over the IP networks and, ultimately, to the Internet, it chose not to invent a new term. Cisco simply decided to adopt the original Internet of Things idea and apply it to the phenomenon we were seeing at the time. In effect, we morphed the IoT of yesterday to define the IoT of today—the next stage of the Internet.

The first generation of Internet adopters also didn't use the term IoT to describe the type of business transformations that are taking place now. Then, as I said, about six years ago things began to accelerate on the network connectivity front. The first stage of the Internet was in full swing, driven by the rise of cloud computing and the growing adoption of smartphones and tablets with the goal of enabling us to connect to each other, to the data, to the processes, and to the services we were using. The devices, however, were already pointing the way to the second stage of the Internet—the IoT we see emerging today.

We now have a robust standards-based global networking infrastructure and a myriad of connected devices from all sorts of sensors, meters, actuators, to cars, buses, robots, drills, MRI machines, office buildings, entire cities, even garbage cans—those assets can not only communicate but also generate and often process data and interface with a mind-boggling array of applications. And people have begun to adopt IoT terminology to recognize this phenomenon, the breadth of its scope and capabilities. IoT today is becoming pervasive.

You can clearly see a transformative power of IoT in the auto industry. Have you bought a new car lately? Well, the car is becoming a smartphone on wheels. Cars have long collected data from standalone subsystems and used processors embedded at various points to monitor and manage different functions. Car manufacturers are now installing standards-based high speed deterministic networks to connect all of these subsystems, the data they produce, and processing power into what amounts to a mobile datacenter. They're also connecting these mobile datacenters to the Internet. Pretty soon, every new car will be both smart and connected.

Remember when you bought a car based on its style or maybe key specs such as horsepower or its miles-per-gallon (MPG) rating? If you haven't bought a new car lately, your current car—I hate to tell you—is a dinosaur plodding along a path to extinction. If a car lacks even a Bluetooth interface, its trade-in value will be considerably lower. Car-buying criteria have changed completely for the majority of buyers. The electronics and device connectivity make a car appealing today. Similar changes are sweeping other industries. And it's due to the rise of IoT.

Now when we purchase a new car, we're actually buying, as I noted, a smartphone on wheels (Figure 1.4) and a mobile datacenter. Looks and style are important, of course, but for the majority of us speed and performance are secondary. What we really care about is how we interact with the car and how we automate tasks. We also care about how the car interacts with us—telling us when to change the oil based not on the mileage but on the actual use of oil. The car should warn us, and the dealer, that a part in the engine is about to break before it happens. And in the next few years we should expect an electric car to just pick us up and drive us wherever we want to go. Everything else becomes an afterthought.

Asit Goel, senior vice president and general manager at NXP Semiconductors, responsible for the firm's IOT solutions, summarized this new world well: "Ultimately, technology needs to replace or augment the

Figure 1.4   Smartphone on Wheels

senses of a human driver in a smart connected car. An army of sensors, radars, laser scanners, cameras, computing processors, wireless and cellular communications devices is needed to do this, to gain a 360-degree view of the car's surroundings and make critical decisions. The car isn't just a thing anymore; it's a system of things that delivers this hyper-connected experience with greater fluidity of service across my personal device, professional environments, and more."

Is the auto industry ready for such a dramatic transformation? Ford Motor Company's James Buczkowski, a Henry Ford Technical Fellow and director, Electrical and Electronics Systems Research and Advanced Engineering, has emerged as a thought leader on automotive electronics, including connected and autonomous vehicles. He assured me that the industry is comprehensively addressing smart mobility, which includes user experience, software, cyber security, data analytics and working toward new emerging mobility business models.

IoT Today—Digitally Transforming the World

Did the previous discussion about smart cars leave you disconcerted? Don't be. It's just the latest example of the revolution sweeping the world—and with it every industry segment. This new stage is transforming everything from the local pizza shop in Germany to a global Fortune 500 company in the United States; from an ice cream shop in India to brand new cities in China and Korea; from water pumps in Africa to wind farms in Europe. Businesses, governments, and nongoernment organizations are scrambling to figure out how they must adapt to thrive in this new world. That's the attraction—and payoff—of IoT.

So is adoption of IoT optional? Can you skip it or ignore it? For a while yes, but at considerable risk. Think of the horse and buggy industry at the start of the 20th century. The buggy and carriage trade survived for a couple of decades. Today it exists only for a few collectors and specialized use cases.

IoT is producing an economic tidal wave that will engulf everything in its path. Tim Jennings, chief research officer at Ovum, an analyst and consultancy firm that publishes the Machine-to-Machine and Internet-of-Things Contracts Tracker, told me that IoT is being adopted across many industries. Manufacturing, business services, and energy and utilities sectors are leading the way with most IoT deployments to date, with transportation, retail and wholesale, public sector, and health care industries being next in line. "As digital transformation accelerates across industry sectors, permeating deeper into the enterprise, the Internet of Things has become a key enabler of digital operations, with Ovum's research showing that deployment is occurring across a wide range of connected business processes," he commented. "An initial wave of adoption tended to focus on industry-specific use cases, but we are now seeing the emergence of cross-industry applications built on IoT platforms. Coupled with increased business awareness, we expect enterprises to take a more systematic approach to digitizing their processes and operations, and look for new opportunities to create business value from the Internet of Things," Jennings added.

We've already peeked at IoT in factories through Harley-Davidson. This book will also discuss other industries, focusing primarily on the B2B segment since B2B innovations are driving the transition to IoT today.

Moving forward, the research conducted by James Manyika and Michael Chui of the McKinsey Global Institute in July 2015 pegged the real dollar value of the global IoT market at potentially $11.1 trillion by 2025.[3]

Will this economic tidal wave hit your industry? Without a doubt. It will hit every industry and every segment sooner or later. McKinsey projected the first nine impacted industry segments as seen in Figure 1.5.

Ovum and McKinsey, of course, are not the only observers to weigh in with IoT status and projections. In May 2016, IDC's Vernon Turner predicted that the worldwide Internet of Things (IoT) market spending will grow from $692.6 billion in 2015 to $1.46 trillion in 2020 with a compound annual growth rate (CAGR) of 16.1 percent.[4] Furthermore, "We expect the installed base of IoT endpoints to grow from 12.1 billion in 2015 to more than 30 billion in 2020,"[5] Turner told me. In a July 2014 report titled "Hype Cycle for Emerging Technologies, 2014" written by Hung LeHong, Jackie Fenn, and Rand Leeb-du Toit, research and advisory firm Gartner put IoT at the top of the "hype curve,"[6] Gartner's terms for the blizzard of vendor hype that accompanies technology advances. Going forward, we can hope that the hype will start to subside as organizations embark on substantive IoT initiatives.

Why Now: Three Driving Trends

As previously noted, IoT isn't exactly new, having been around in different forms for more than a decade (think RFID, where every item sold at a retail store can speak with the supply chain). So why is it finally generating so much attention? I see three major trends coming into play:

- **The lines of business, as represented by the line of business (LOB) manager, are emerging as a major buying center for technology.** LOB managers are concerned with business outcomes and look for business solutions, especially those that reduce cost, increase productivity, and—most importantly—increase profitability. They look for the ways to improve overall equipment effectiveness, production delivery times and throughput, asset uptime and increasingly target specific sustainability metrics. Line of business managers weren't among the primary beneficiaries of the first stage of the

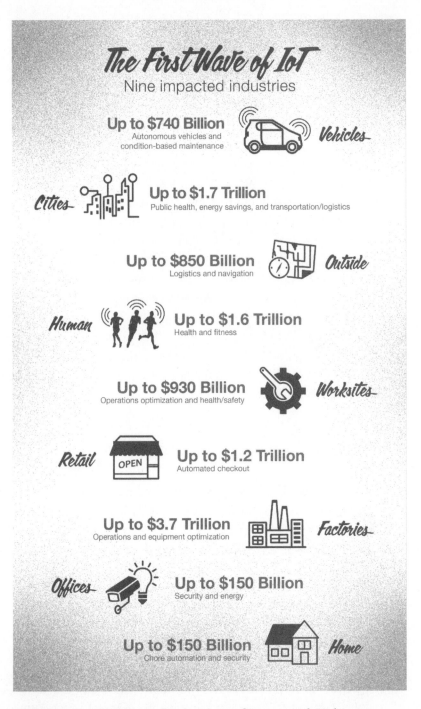

Figure 1.5   McKinsey Projection of Impacted Industry Segments

Internet, which focused on IT, service providers, and consumers. Today, however, LOB leaders are starting to harness technology to drive business outcomes. As a consequence, unlike the Internet's first stage, IoT promises not to be a technology-led transition; rather, it's a business-driven transition where technology is a tool to achieve specific business goals. Yes, LOB managers can create and spend budgets, but they're looking to increase both top-line and bottom-line results. For example, some manufacturing operations are reporting a 160 percent return on investment (ROI), a 20 percent reduction in cost, and a 75 percent reduction in network downtime from IoT. To LOB managers, such outcomes demonstrate a value proposition so compelling that they're willing to open up their wallets to fund such efforts.

- **The convergence of information technology and operational technology improving communication and efficiency.** Remember when millions of people read John Gray's book *Men Are from Mars, Women Are from Venus*? This best-seller suggested that the frequent misunderstandings between genders make it seem as though men and women are from different, alien worlds. But it's not just men and women who appear to be from different planets. Today, every organization that has begun an IoT deployment is bumping up against a fundamental disconnect between IT and OT. In many cases, these two groups are "alien" to one another—they have separate technology stacks, network architectures, protocols, standards, governance models, and organizations. IT/OT convergence is the solution, yet it didn't begin to happen until recently. Perhaps it takes a prolonged downturn, followed by a lackluster recovery, to make this happen. Alternatively, maybe the emergence of IoT multiplies the networked connections among people, processes, data, and things to the extent that it compels the worlds of IT and OT to converge out of necessity. The key driver, however (as shown in powerful use cases we will discuss later in this book), is the need for the data to flow between plants, enterprise infrastructure, and the cloud.

Such a need forces IT/OT convergence at the technological, architectural, and organizational levels. Of course, with this convergence comes a culture clash. Each organization has a long litany of complaints against the other. And each has completely valid concerns, all of which have to be resolved quickly. (As we mentioned, Harley-Davidson's solution to this challenge was to put representatives from both teams together in a room and not let them leave until all of their issues were resolved.) Despite the potential for a culture clash, over the past decade or so, OT and LOB functions have increasingly adopted IT-like technologies, such as Ethernet/IP and even cloud services. A 2014 Cisco study by Andy Noronha, Robert Moriarty, Kathy O'Connell, and Nicola Villa titled "Attaining IoT Value: How to Move from Connecting Things to Capturing Insights" found that both IT and OT leaders now recognize the need to share responsibility for IoT solutions, although they may still need to negotiate decision-making authority over each stage in the adoption process.[7] It also helps that increasingly IT organizations report to the LOBs, further aligning the technology and business agendas across the enterprise.

- **The proprietary/specialized technologies moving to open standards.** In the last two decades of the 20th century, the manufacturing industry went through the so called fieldbus wars, where several camps of vendors fought to establish their proprietary technologies as de facto communication or security standards for the industry. In the aftermath, a bunch of overlapping semi-standard technologies (including proprietary extension to open standards) was embedded into products locking customers into specific sets of vendors. Thus, despite the initial good intentions, the industry further diverged from common standards. Add to that a large number of existing single-purpose specialized or proprietary legacy protocols and the result was chaos, higher costs, little innovation, and Balkanized market. Since then, however, an increased number of vendors started to embrace standard and unmodified Ethernet and IP technologies and integrate them into their offerings. Today, most of the end-devices have Ethernet interfaces and the momentum is mounting to establish common truly open standards in the industry. We see the same transition starting to happen in other markets too, from transportation to healthcare to retail. The customers are increasingly demanding open standards and interoperability. In addition, the IT and OT vendors are joining forces to evolve existing horizontal standards to address the OT needs and are adopting open standards in vertical standards bodies and consortia. According to the Cisco report cited earlier, by year 2020, there will be as many as 50 billion connected devices.[8] Whether the actual number ends up being 50 billion, 30 billion, or even 7 billion, these are still staggering figures. Not long ago, on a typical manufacturing floor, there were just a few connected devices for every engineer; now there are dozens of these devices and soon there may be hundreds of them per every person working there. Converging all of these devices on one open unified standards-based network is not only a cost-effective and scalable way to get them connected but also a key to unlocking the revenue potential of IoT.

This book will discuss these three trends, as well as new value propositions such as connected operations, remote operations, predictive analytics and preventive maintenance. Because IoT is still a nascent discipline, industry segments have only begun to address related issues in the last few years.

A "Perfect Storm" of Technology, the Economy, and Culture

IoT is bringing together three key elements—technology, the economy, and culture—to form what can be popularly described as a "perfect storm." Whereas a lethal brew of elements is typically associated with a dangerous storm, IoT's wide open opportunities can be embraced by any organization that wants to be involved. In the process, we're all experiencing a massive rebalancing of key economic, social, environmental, and privacy/security priorities. Although the landscape is full of "900-pound gorillas," none has succeeded in dominating this issue. (Full disclosure: My own organization, Cisco, aspires to be an influential IoT leader.)

The truth is IoT presents an opportunity for every organization, not just a few chosen companies. Even small and midsize enterprises can participate. Winners will transform their businesses based on open standards and build ecosystems of partners to deliver vertical solutions based on horizontal capabilities. Meanwhile, losers will ignore these changes and stick to their old business models based on proprietary or semi-proprietary technology and ensure customer lock-in until those customers steadily abandon them. (With luck, some of these companies will realize the problem before it's too late. Others, sadly, never will. Remember the changes to the make-up of the S&P 500 over the past decades?)

In terms of *technology*, IoT is adopting cloud-oriented technology even as it drives an architecture shift to fog computing as an extension of the cloud to the edge. At the same time, IPv6-driven networking and nimble open technologies have been driving the corresponding application explosion. Fog computing, meanwhile, is removing latency and enabling real-time analytics and responsiveness while Time Sensitive Networking is offering real-time guaranteed latency for time critical traffic. Very quickly, you will see new technologies evolve to clearly distinguish IoT as the next stage of the Internet. I call them IoT-native technologies and applications—designed and optimized around everything connecting to everything.

With regard to *the economy,* the compelling benefits of IoT are leading LOB managers to welcome it. The expected result is a multi-trillion-dollar boost to the economy before the end of the decade.

As for *culture*, the opening of communications and collaboration between OT and IT as an extension of the popular DevOps trend, as well as the rise of LOB managers, highlight the changes underway.

There you have it: technology, the economy, and culture all coming together in a perfect storm that will do good things for those organizations open to change. Like every big storm, however, IoT will create dramatic impact—in this case, a massive rebalancing throughout the economy. Some of the early winners are already emerging, among them:

- Flexible business managers and LOB leaders, who can envision new business models and lead their organizations to new opportunities that arise when everything can communicate with everything. They must also be prepared to fully leverage the data, automation, and analytics that are key to capitalizing on IoT.
- Application developers and programmers, who will be in high demand as IoT brings about the API economy that will consume millions of apps, digital containers, and micro-services. IoT will also require large numbers of data scientists, data managers, and data analysts to create, deploy, manage, and leverage the automated data analytics that must make sense of and handle the massive volume of data as it's generated, collected, analyzed, or acted upon.
- Some economic sectors will experience a renaissance. Manufacturing and the rest of the "maker" movement is already an early beneficiary; for the first time in generations, young people—popularly referred to as Millennials—are being attracted to manufacturing. Never believed I'd actually write this: Manufacturing is cool again. Add to this 3D printing, drones, and all manner of new materials and network-connectable electronics and you start to get a picture. Other industries, such as business services, energy, utilities, transportation, retail, wholesale, public sector, and health care, will stand to gain big from IoT as well.
- Automation and analytics users are clear winners. The scale and volume of information creation and distribution requires automation and real-time analytics. People will set up the algorithms and rules, and then automation will have to take over. You can't operate fast enough

at this scale manually. As IoT ramps up, people will need to be aided by automation and analytics if they're to have any hope of keeping up with the volumes.

- New industries and opportunities, including real-time remote operations, smart (connected) cities and communities, and analytics–driven real-time security are all emerging.

The world after this perfect storm will be IoT-native, mobile-connected, automated, and driven by smart analytics. It will be real time, API-enabled, open, security-focused, and built around micro-services that can change virtually on demand.

Key Obstacles

This isn't meant to imply that IoT is inevitable and doesn't face hurdles. To the contrary, it faces significant obstacles in four broad areas: technical, security, organizational, and government.

- *Technical (privacy, standards/interoperability).* To deliver on its promise, IoT needs to assure privacy, the variety of connected devices needs to operate and interoperate seamlessly, and data needs to be exchanged in a fluid and understandable way. All of this requires truly open standards, industry-wide interoperability, and universal adoption of industry-accepted protocols. The traditional IT and OT standards groups are already tackling these problems, while new consortia are being created and old ones are being refocused. Semi-proprietary "standards" are starting to give way to those that are truly open. The industry knows how to do it; we did it for the first stage of the Internet and for the cloud. The current task at hand is even bigger and more complex, but the I know that the IoT community is up for the challenge.
- *Security.* To paraphrase real estate industry wisdom about the importance of location, IoT requires ironclad security, security, and security that management and users can count on. Many of the security components exist today, and many can be leveraged by extending current IT security architectures to OT. Plus, many new use cases such as vehicle-to-vehicle identity requirements, sensor swarms, always-on systems, and smart security paradigms are being addressed by the waves of new IoT security startups, academia, and established vendors. Companies like Harley-Davidson are deploying IoT without

undue risk. However, more must be done not only to reduce the number of security breaches but also to enable the early detection of cyber attacks and to minimize their impact on businesses while protecting the privacy of individuals. Equally important, self-reliant systems and devices that can continue to safely function even if under attack must be deployed. Smart analytics being built into IoT, especially with fog computing designed to deliver real-time processing, will go far in addressing a number of security gaps.

- *Organizational (cultural change).* This may be the biggest obstacle. Change is hard, especially for established organizations that, for decades, have been so successful with their existing business models, practices, and processes. It isn't easy for IT and OT to come together and cooperate, and it isn't easy for vendors to embrace common open standards but it has been done; the benefits are undeniable. Change is mostly a question of communication, leadership, retraining, and keeping an open mind. Opportunities as large as IoT provide a strong incentive for everyone to cooperate.
- *Government.* IoT benefits government in the form of smarter cities, like Barcelona, Spain, arguably one of the most advanced smart cities on the planet today. But in addition to adoption, government also has a role to play in regulating and agenda setting, ensuring that IoT develops and grows by applying regulations in some areas but also easing regulatory impediments in others to encourage new business models based on IoT.

These obstacles are far from insurmountable. Technical groups and industry and advocacy organizations are already working in various areas, hammering out standards and identifying best practices. Key components, similarly, are falling into place—from IP to cloud and fog computing to application development environments and real-time analytics. The common elements of IoT solutions, even at this early stage of maturity, reach across most industries and are being deployed by thousands of customers worldwide.

Scope of the Book

As noted above, I've traveled endless miles while meeting with business managers and discussing with them their challenges and questions about IoT. I wrote this book to help managers at midsize and large organizations understand what IoT is really about, why they need to adopt it for their businesses, and how they should go about doing this—specifically, how to start on an IoT journey. There is no reason, however, that smaller organizations can't fully participate in IoT; they already take advantage of cloud computing, IP networking, analytics, and the other core components of IoT. The book's focus on predominantly midsize and large organizations is the result of my personal IoT experience, which comes from that specific environment. However, a combination of the above core components, mature and proven fast payback use cases, and well-established integration channels should allow smaller organizations to fully embrace IoT, just as they embraced the Internet and the cloud.

Similarly, the book will primarily focus on B2B opportunities, with some B2B2C activity. IoT has a significant business-to-consumer component today, but that mostly falls outside the scope of this book. In the same way, this book will draw from key major vertical segments—primarily manufacturing, oil and gas, transportation and logistics, utilities, and government. It will also touch on retail, health care, agriculture, education, finance, and specialized situations like the connected car.

By reading this book, you've already started on the road to IoT. Figure 1.6 shows a recipe for IoT success. If there is one thing you take away from this book, this recipe is it. It summarizes what I believe are fundamental elements you should internalize and operationalize in order to effectively plan and implement your IoT efforts. I will elaborate on these eight points throughout the book.

In the meantime, if you're just taking a first step in your IoT journey, here are a few tips to begin:

- Begin talking about IoT in your organization, help people think about what might be possible when things can communicate with other things.
- Identify some operational and strategic goals for your IoT initiative—identify a problem to solve or an opportunity to grab. Have a big vision, but start small with low-hanging-fruit scenario.
- Introduce OT and IT team members and get them talking.
- Identify and secure a C-suite sponsor for your IoT efforts.

With IoT, you're embarking on a journey to the future. That certainly was the experience at Stanley Black & Decker, Inc., another early

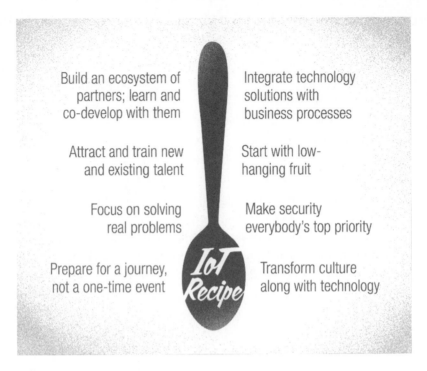

Figure 1.6   Recipe for IoT Success

IoT adopter. "We are on our way toward realizing our vision of a virtual warehouse and fully connected factory, with complete visibility and traceability," said a C-level executive at the manufacturer. Complete visibility and traceability. Would some version of that appeal to your organization? There's no reason it can't apply to your business, too.

How to Read This Book

Not every reader may feel the urge to read this book cover to cover. You are welcome to jump around following your particular interests and concerns and come back to a section that addresses a particular challenge you are currently facing. Use the following brief chapter descriptions as your guide.

Chapter 1, as you have just discovered, is an overview of what this book is about and introduces some of the basic concepts.

Chapter 2 looks at IoT adoption and puts the astounding growth projections into a meaningful perspective.

Chapters 3 and 4 address new business models and the business value proposition.

Chapter 5 provides a number of fast payback IoT models for readers who want to immediately start to benefit from IoT.

Chapter 6 explores the ways IoT impacts careers and workplace roles.

Chapter 7 looks at how IoT will change your organization.

Chapter 8 recognizes that IoT doesn't always deliver as promised and looks at common pitfalls and mistakes.

Chapter 9 provides an overview of the IoT security challenge and how it is being addressed.

Chapter 10 provides a similar overview of IoT standards and technology directions, the emergence of open IoT architectures, and ways to overcome integration issues.

Chapter 11 summarizes current state of the union of IoT, my vision of where IoT is going in the next 10 years and how you, the reader, can play a key role in charting the IoT future in your organization.

The next chapter discusses business change and transformation, which is what IoT is really about. It also looks at some quick paybacks—focusing on the low-hanging fruit—and some early success stories. OK, let's get started on your IoT journey.

2

IoT Is About Change and Transformation

Who is Generation IoT? No, it isn't some recently designated category from the U.S. Census or a new demographic classification coined by some researchers. It's how I refer to people like you, businesspeople who realize something very big may be happening as all types of devices get connected and who want to be part of it. Or it could be that you sense something different is happening—new business models suddenly appearing or competition suddenly doing something completely unexpected, either of which could pose a threat or an opportunity. If you're reading this book, you're already part of Generation IoT, whether you're looking to retire a few years from now, you are a newly hired Millennial, or somewhere in between.

Generation IoT really refers to managers who sense that this latest stage of the Internet is starting to redefine their businesses, industries, markets, and jobs. They also recognize both the potential for great opportunities and the significant threats in the resulting changes. On a personal level, these are people who welcome change (or at least aren't afraid of it) and see the opportunities it brings for business transformation.

For these people, adaptability and changeability are bywords as they move forward.

In the past few years, IoT has become a hot topic. But, to be fair, it isn't exactly new. Auto manufacturer General Motors (GM) has been talking for 10 years about a fully automated, robotized automobile manufacturing plant that can run without human intervention—that's IoT, machines talking to machines. GM credits its factory-of-the-future initiative for much of its more recent successes in the market. Today, there are numerous professional conferences on this very subject. One recent event, the January 2015 "Surface World" conference, promised attendees the possibilities of "lights-out manufacturing" for their businesses.[1] If you peel off the factory-of-the-future label, you'll quickly discover IoT at the heart. This is similar to what both Harley-Davidson and Ford are already doing.

In 2013, Cisco hosted the "Internet of Things World Forum" in Barcelona. It was the perfect location for this event, because the Spanish city had decided it wanted to be at the forefront of a new revolution and become the "edgiest" city in the world. The revolution, it turns out, was this: technology related to mobility, smart devices, and—mainly—the Internet. Part of Barcelona's vision included connecting, automating, and digitizing all key aspects of the city, which was one of the reasons Cisco chose this locale for its inaugural event. Now Barcelona is considered a leading example of an organization turning to IoT to digitize itself in a variety of ways while making the resulting benefits available to its citizens (see Figure 2.1).

As part of the event, city officials took delegates on tours of some of the installed connected infrastructure.[2] Much of it was energy and transportation related, including a digital bus stop that not only displayed digital advertising and real-time bus schedules but also offered tourist information and USB charging sockets and acted as a free Wi-Fi base station. Ah, yes, it would shelter you from rain, too.

Change as the New Status Quo

For Generation IoT, change is the new status quo. We don't fear or resist change; rather, we welcome it.

Figure 2.1   IoT World Forum in Barcelona

Just think, for example, about all the many ways you can buy a product today. Take something as simple and old-fashioned as a book. Years ago, you probably just walked into a bookstore or some other retailer and picked up a book right off the rack. Not anymore. Today, you can order a book online and have it shipped within a few days, overnight, or in some select markets, the same day—maybe even by drone one of these days. You can also download the book electronically and read it immediately on a wide variety of devices. Some books don't have to be purchased; many libraries lend electronic books free of charge, as long as you have a library card. And there are probably more ways to acquire books that I haven't even heard of yet. Similarly, the cost of buying a book varies widely, depending on where and how you acquire it and how urgently you need—or want—it. Hmm, even at this late date perhaps I should speak with the publisher about additional plans for delivering this book to the market, maybe even as part of an alliance with an IoT infrastructure vendor.

Books are one thing; a car is something else altogether. Have you considered how you'll buy your next car? The old way meant checking the ads, visiting one or more dealers to find the right car, and then negotiating the best price. The next time you buy a car, possibly just a few years from now, the process may not involve a traditional dealer at all. Even today, you can accomplish much of the process online—research, find, select, negotiate, finance, and buy—without walking into either a dealership or a bank. You could even arrange to test drive the car, but not necessarily at the dealership you may eventually buy from.

What if in a few years you want one of those newly emerging autonomous cars, where you don't even sit behind the wheel? Maybe a company will just let the car drive itself to you. It then takes you on a test drive and, if you like the car, you can close the deal on the spot. If you don't like it, simply direct the car to drive itself back to wherever it came from.

Still, there's one thing you can count on: The car will be completely IoT connected, both inside and outside, and all subsystems will work together. It will communicate with transportation systems and intelligent traffic lights at intersections, as well as with other cars, dealerships, manufacturers, insurance companies, and more. The car will form an integral part of IoT.

Consider this: In a few years, there may be no need for most people to own a car. Instead, cars from a fleet of autonomous vehicles will be summoned on demand, the same way you arrange for an Uber ride today. Pricing models can be dramatically different, too, as neither a driver nor anyone to tip is involved. The government might even subsidize your trip, if one of the administration's goals is to take individually owned cars off the road. At that point, only collectors and car aficionados may choose to buy and drive their own vehicles (see Figure 2.2).

Now think of your organization and its products and services. How do customers acquire them today? How did they receive them in the past? What other methods might they prefer to use in the future, and at what price? The entire value chains, from insurance providers to parking lot operators, will likely be disrupted; in the U.S., digital IDs (maybe based on blockchain) may replace traditional driver licenses as more and more people chose not to learn to drive. Are there any other ways a widespread IoT environment may affect your products and the way customers acquire them? If your product is actually a service, rather than a physical item, you

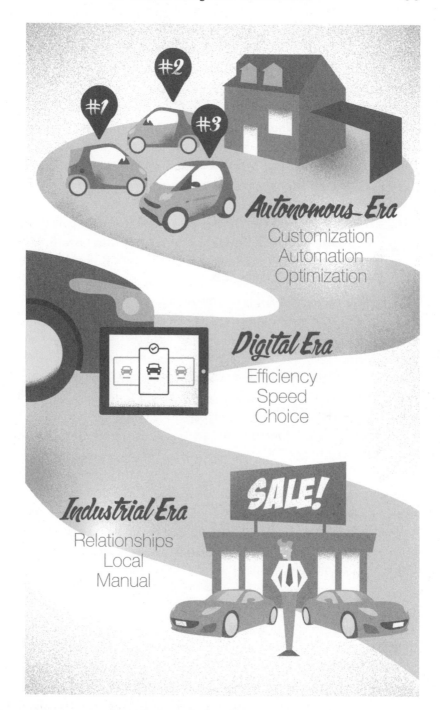

Figure 2.2 IoT Model for Automobiles

may face an entirely new set of delivery options beyond what you have traditionally used.

The point is, once change is constant, almost anything is possible. It becomes open season on how you go to market, price your products and services, and find and support your customers. Do you need to maintain that costly direct sales force or an extensive (and expensive) distribution network? You may decide that you do. But with change on the horizon, you're free to rethink any decisions over and over again, as well as to change, add, and modify your choices as often as you want and whenever it makes sense.

Different go-to-market models seem to crop up almost daily. Is there any product or service you cannot acquire in the cloud, from flowers to dog training? Whatever you seek you can find from industry leaders, young upstarts, innovative players with a radical approach, or others that offer only the basics. Just name it, and you can find it. And if it isn't immediately available, then simply wait a few months.

The same goes for pricing, billing, and payment. New options appear almost weekly. You can acquire anything, it seems, at a choice of pricing models: annual subscription, monthly rental, per usage, and more. For example, technology and consulting company IBM has started to offer mainframe computers on a monthly rental basis. It rents only the capabilities and capacity you think you'll need, and the service can be cancelled with minimum notice. Until now, this model was heresy in the mainframe market.

Look around. What's actually happening is that change and innovation are emerging as more than just the status quo. They have become survival imperatives. IoT, in effect, stimulates change and innovation. When everything is digitized and can communicate with other digital things, possibilities never previously considered open up. Everything is digital with IoT, so anything is feasible.

People, Process, Data, Things

IoT embraces much more than just technology. Ultimately, as important as it may seem now, technology will turn out to be the least of it. Data, meanwhile, will fuel the essential analytics and automation required to efficiently handle the massive volumes of expected activity that must be considered for fast, sound decision making. Already, the number of connected things is reported to be in the tens of billions and growing exponentially.[3] (The volume of revenue resulting from IoT activity is projected into the trillions of dollars, according to McKinsey Global Institute.[4]) It will quickly go beyond what even the best human workers and managers can absorb and handle manually.

This change will alter the makeup of the workforce. People who envision change and drive innovation will play a major role by reimagining processes and outcomes. We can expect increased demand for data scientists, data managers, process designers and modelers, networking communications professionals, and security experts. Demand will also increase for people who can implement and support new business models and processes, train others in new ways of conducting business, integrate diverse systems, and orchestrate complex processes. In addition, armies of programmers and developers will be needed to write the necessary software, build the applications to handle new business processes, and repeatedly write and maintain the APIs required to glue the entire IoT fabric together.

IoT is clearly changing the workforce, but this is nothing new. The automobile changed the face of the world, too. While horse and buggy workers lost work, gas stations and, eventually, car dealerships appeared everywhere. Remember when automated switching came to the phone industry? These switches eventually replaced the armies of human operators who manually processed calls. You can still dial 0 and an operator will eventually pick up. But younger generations, my children included, have never spoken with an operator and probably wouldn't know what to say if they did—unless it was a 911 emergency call.

I recently visited an oil refinery. Ten years ago, it employed several thousand people, and the average age of a control engineer was 57. As this workforce retired, the company wasn't able to attract new and younger workers. Systems and processes had to be redesigned to keep things running. Now, the refinery still employs 2,000 people but, due to automation and process reengineering, their jobs have changed dramatically.

Even in the context of the IT/OT convergence driven by IoT, those refinery jobs will need to be redefined. For example, control engineers need to be trained on IP and open systems. In addition, the IT people need to be trained on specific operational requirements in the plant—things like the elimination of the "Saturday night upgrade window," which is no longer necessary now that systems can predict when they'll need to be upgraded or maintained. Whatever is needed can be conveniently scheduled in advance and happen automatically.

These changes will create ample opportunities for those who accept this challenge. Many will eagerly learn or adopt new skills and ways of thinking and will reinvent themselves over and over again. Others will decide they don't want change and play out their time until they retire. Still others will resist change. None of these attitudes is new, and businesses know how to deal with all of them through training, education, communication, and change management. In the end, it's probably only nostalgia buffs who wish they could make their calls through live telephone operators.

New Conceptual Paradigm

IoT is forcing a new conceptual model. It will be a new paradigm for understanding this era, much like the factory assembly line in the Industrial Age and the Internet and the Web in the Information Age helped define those eras. So, too, will the emerging "Age of Connected Things" produce a conceptual paradigm that shapes our understanding.

It's too early to identify all key elements of this paradigm, but a shift from closed to open organizations will definitely play a key role (see Figure 2.3).

Unless you're ready to retire, IoT is too big and brings too much promise to ignore. In fact, ignoring IoT is a surefire prescription for business failure. Without a strategy and the desire to explore and adopt IoT concepts, you're assured of three outcomes, none of which you want:

1. Being surpassed by competitors with new approaches to business, new business models, and go-to-market strategies
2. Losing good people who, in effect, evacuate what they see as a doomed ship
3. Being abandoned by customers who are attracted to the value and advantages IoT brings.

Recent C-suite studies suggest that IoT is gaining traction faster than many observers previously thought. It has become a frequent topic of discussion among top management at larger companies. The challenge is to elevate that discussion with examples of strategic thinking, new business

Figure 2.3   Comparison of Directions

and go-to-market models, and different pricing approaches to produce previously unimagined business outcomes.

Operational Elements of IoT Success

First off, embrace the recipe for IoT success I included in the previous chapter. It's intended to start you thinking now, so you can consider how IoT can be operationalized. In addition, even at this early stage in IoT's maturity, certain operational elements have emerged as essential for success:

- *Start with strategy, planning, and preparation.* First things first. Lay the groundwork for change by envisioning and articulating ideas for possible changes and innovation to get things rolling.
- *Secure C-suite sponsorship.* You are embarking on a multi-year journey that will redefine your entire organization many times over. You need a top management champion to support your efforts starting from your first small IoT project.

- *Build a diverse team.* You will need all the help you can get. Your cross-functional team built right will provide critical skills, influence and access. Take time to include potential detractors.
- *Communicate and drive IT/OT convergence.* We spoke of this in the previous chapter. We all need to talk with each other and work collaboratively, especially those in IT and OT, but don't stop there. Every group or unit in the organization needs to become involved sooner or later.
- *Rethink operations from the ground up.* How can you do things more efficiently and effectively, faster, cheaper, and more richly when everything is digitized and can communicate with everything else? It may take several tries; this is new to everyone.
- *Design for flexibility.* Remember, you may need to rethink your business and operations every three to seven years.
- *Educate and train.* Your people won't automatically understand IoT. A few may intuitively grasp it (make them team leaders), but everyone else needs to be oriented, educated, and trained.
- *Revisit repeatedly.* IoT isn't a once-and-done effort or project. It's a dynamic thing, always changing and needing to be continually tuned and optimized.

Success, however, is possible and pays off big. Here are two inspiring examples.

As one of the world's largest tire manufacturers, Goodyear Tire and Rubber Company employs approximately 70,000 people and manufactures its products across 56 facilities in 21 countries around the world. However, the company's existing plant floor infrastructure was based on individually configured technologies that didn't connect to anything else. Goodyear wanted to, at a minimum, network its plant technology to make it easier to gather and analyze data.

The company deployed IoT technology that networks its systems together, enabling Goodyear to easily gather and analyze data from the factory floor while delivering advanced communications capabilities for a variety of plant solutions. It also simplified plant cabling, which made the effort even more economical by eliminating the need to run costly fiber to each machine. Goodyear's IoT effort proved a winner both strategically and tactically. The lesson: IoT delivers strategic and tactical benefits.

Metrolinx, a government transportation agency in Ontario, Canada, moves an average of 271,000 people a day via an integrated mass transit system. Its reach was expanded in June 2015 to connect via a new air-rail link—called the Union Pearson Express (UP Express)—Canada's busiest transportation hubs, Union Station in downtown Toronto and Toronto Pearson International Airport. From the start, incorporating digital technology was a priority in the design of this high-quality express rail service. UP Express's integrated technology strategy includes free passenger Wi-Fi, onboard infotainment, and onboard fare collection and validation. It has also integrated all passenger intercoms and public address systems. But that was just the start.

"We had an ambitious vision to be an undeniable symbol of Toronto prosperity, as well as an important strategy to help address traffic congestion and keep our region moving," said UP Express President Kathy Haley at that time. "UP Express was designed to meet the unique needs of travelers and change the way people experience our city. Not only is it the most efficient way to connect between downtown Toronto and the airport, but it is also a seamless end-to-end experience that anticipates and meets the needs of travelers through convenience and comfort."

The young system (see Figure 2.4) has been a success by almost every measure. It boasts a 97 percent on-time rate. Rider satisfaction is high, too: 87 percent say they recommend UP Express, while 90 percent report plans to use it again.

Seamless is also the goal for operations. The UP Express team is designing a full on-board, end-to-end network infrastructure to support all operational and passenger systems, including closed-circuit television (CCTV), public address, fare collection, infotainment, and visual next stop announcements. As part of the second phase of its digital transformation, Metrolinx is investigating the feasibility of implementing a private, carrier-grade fiber network infrastructure to support signaling, communications, passenger Wi-Fi, track-side telemetry, and supervisory control and data acquisition (SCADA) systems. The lesson: There are no limits to what you can do once you start digitizing and networking intelligent devices.

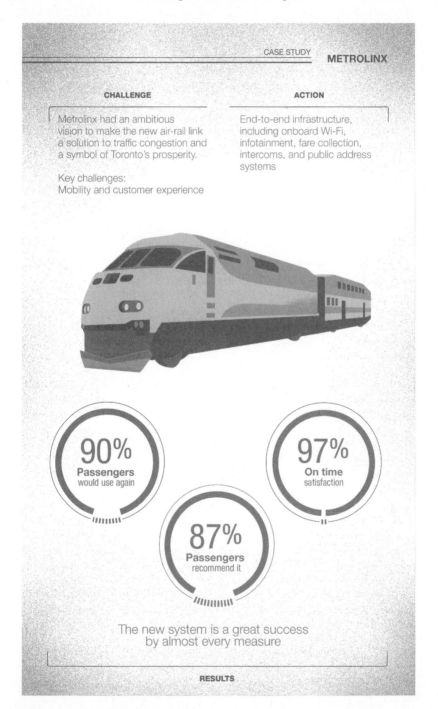

Figure 2.4 Metrolinx Case

Why Digital Adoption/Transformation?

In the natural world, living beings either eat or are eaten. In the business world, you could say organizations either transform or are disrupted (the corporate equivalent to being eaten). IoT is rapidly emerging as a major business transformation engine that can disrupt competitors, both known and unknown.

Although this won't happen overnight, you should start contemplating and envisioning the possibilities now. IoT is a learning experience, and not all ideas will work. Not every new business model or go-to-market strategy will prove to be a winner or a disruptive force, but some will. Of course, you won't abandon what's working until you have identified proven winners. Even then, you'll want to be ready to change again, and yet again, as the situation or environment changes. The only status quo in the IoT world, as I've noted, is change.

IoT has already demonstrated its ability to transform organizations, from General Electric to large public institutions like Metrolinx and the City of Barcelona. It doesn't even have to be complicated. In the case of both Barcelona and Metrolinx, one basic IoT infrastructure met multiple diverse needs. That's how you start small and keep it simple.

Every manager dreams of transforming the business. If the business is performing well, it can still get better. If it isn't performing up to expectations, then transformation of one sort or another should be a top priority. As we've noted, disruptive forces are popping up in every industry, fueled in large part by IoT. In that sense, either you need to harness IoT to transform your business and become a disrupter or you risk being disrupted by somebody else.

Figure 2.5 lists three reasons to consider IoT to power your organization's transformation.

Furthermore, every business can do three things to ensure that it's part of the IoT wave now and going forward, in whatever form it takes:

- **Collaborate.** Vendors and enterprises need to work together on common architectures, incorporating OT requirements into the technology provider's product portfolio by offering ruggedized versions and incorporating specific industrial protocols or up-time requirements. The collaboration should focus on a converged, standards-based

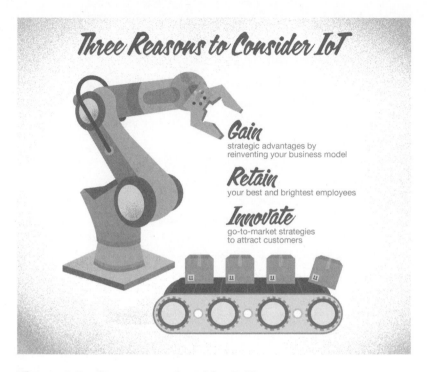

Figure 2.5   Reasons to Consider IoT

IT/OT technology and an open, validated policy-based security architecture.

- **Converge around standards.** Vendors and enterprises alike need to leverage IT industry standards and best practices in OT. As an industry we need to continue to bring OT use cases to traditional standards bodies and to fill in the gaps between industry-specific and horizontal standards organizations. (We will discuss standards in more detail in Chapter 10.)
- **Take an industry approach.** As part of an industry—any industry—organizations need to work together to address requirements for new IoT use cases. We must learn and share together. Existing industry players should also look for promising startups to fund, especially in the areas of vertical applications, real time analytics, and IoT security. (We will talk more about security in Chapter 9.)

IoT brings much to absorb, especially all at once. Fortunately, you don't have to. You can take it one step at a time. You can move at a pace that's comfortable for your organization and your customers, since you'll want to bring them along with you on this IoT journey. The important thing at this point is to take the first steps on this journey. Once you start, it will be the most exciting and rewarding journey your organization has ever embarked on.

The next chapter explores the promise of IoT and how it can transform your business. Among the stimulating examples are actual businesses that have, indeed, been able to transform themselves using IoT.

3

The Promise
of IoT Is Real

Imagine you're standing in a sprawling open mine (Figure 3.1). It's in the middle of nowhere, two miles across, and specked with 45 gigantic autonomous trucks hauling iron ore out of the pit. Each wheel on those trucks towers over a man standing on the ground, and each pair of tires costs $100,000. These trucks operate under extreme loads and in extreme conditions. The challenge is to keep these lumbering vehicles operating productively every single day. The solution is predictive preventative maintenance, but how—you're miles from anywhere. The answer is IoT.

Rio Tinto faces this scenario every day. The global mining operation, headquartered in London and with major operations in Australia and elsewhere, has the largest fleet of giant autonomous trucks in the world. Its vehicles have transported more than 200 million tons of materials across approximately 3.9 million kilometers. That's the equivalent of hauling approximately 3,500 Sydney Harbor Bridges or 540 Empire State Buildings to the moon and back five times.

The value of predictive preventative maintenance to Rio Tinto is fairly obvious, but it's even greater when you factor in the physical

47

Figure 3.1   Deep Open Mine

environments of its operations. Work happens within a huge, open-pit mine that's miles from the nearest place its trucks can even be serviced. Adding to that: Just getting a damaged truck out of the pit requires another equally costly truck. So immediately, the cost of the problem doubles. It could, however, be even more expensive than that, depending on how long it takes to get the parts and then fix the damaged truck. Imagine having two vehicles out of service for two, or very probably more, days at a cost of $2 million per vehicle per day. This is not trivial.

Open-pit mining is a formidable environment. It's isolated, desolate, and has a one-mile deep and two-mile wide hole in the middle. The giant trucks used in these operations are barely specks along the sides of the open pits, which are themselves an inhospitable and dangerous place for even the biggest, toughest vehicles. Blasting is a constant threat. Getting a broken vehicle out for service seems next to impossible. That's why IoT-based preventative maintenance with predictive analytics is so critically important. It enables mining companies to fix vehicles onsite, before they fail, or at the very least drive a vehicle out under its own power.

At a different but similar location to Rio Tinto's operations, another mining company implemented an IoT-based predictive preventative maintenance program. The results: It could anticipate failures with 80 percent accuracy up to three months in advance. Each failure it could anticipate and prevent saved the company millions in out-of-pocket costs, as well as millions more in delays and lost production time.

The problem was a little different at Goldcorp's Éléonore gold mine (Figure 3.2) in northern Canada, as documented recently by Cisco. Here, the work takes place not in an open pit but underground. More than 1,000 people work far beneath the frigid soil mining 3,500 tons of rock a day in search of gold. Committed to continuously seeking improvements in safety and efficiency, the company turned to IoT to create what it calls a "connected mine." As a result, Goldcorp is able to efficiently manage its communications and mining operations on one multiservice, secure IPV6 network. Built to withstand harsh conditions, the solution delivers unified, secure access from any device and any location.

Specifically, IoT helps Goldcorp achieve real-time visibility, monitoring, and ventilation control for a ventilation on-demand system over a single, multiservice IP network that provides wireless connectivity in the most demanding of environments. The company's connected mine also leverages RFID to enable live tracking of all people and assets anywhere in the mine.

The payback proved significant:

- Ventilation on demand reduces energy costs between $1.5 and $2.5 million per year.
- Improved tracking enables the mine to locate employees instantly in the event of an emergency, 45 to 50 minutes faster than before—incredibly important for safety.
- Enhanced asset tracking for near-real-time insight into the status and location of equipment for safer and more efficient operations.

For mining and related industries, IoT has proven to be a business savior. The same can be said of other vertical industries. Paradoxically, as we talk about these "vertical" industries, what's saving these companies

CASE STUDY   **GOLDCORP**

CHALLENGE	ACTION
Goldcorp's Éléonore gold mine is deep underground. The company must make constant improvements to ensure the safety and efficiency of more than 1,000 miners. Key challenges: Safety and efficiency	A "Connected Mine": A multiservice network, allowing for real-time visibility, monitoring, and ventilation control

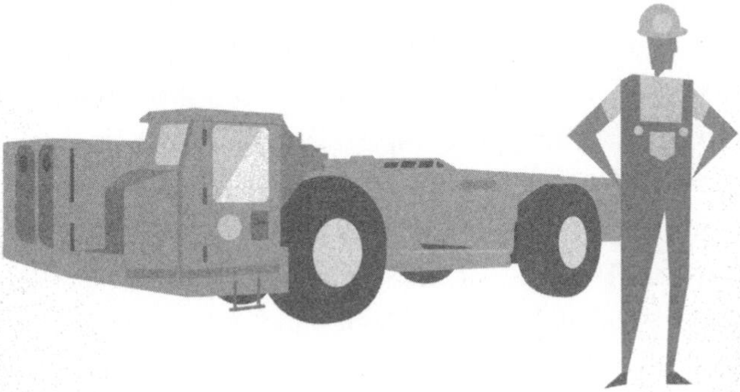

Energy cost reduction:
(from on-demand ventilation)
$1.5–2.5 million per year

Employee detection:
(from improved tracking)
45–50 minutes faster

Location and equipment tracking:
Near real time

RESULTS

Figure 3.2   Goldcorp's Éléonore Gold Mine

are a few critical "horizontal" capabilities—sensors, networks, real-time analytics, application development environments. All of these horizontal sets of capabilities are being deployed across a number of vertical segments to produce stunning results.

IoT Creates Opportunities

Despite the hype around IoT, the concept is real, already proven, here to stay, and growing as you read this book. The dynamics of IoT, however, vary by industry and use case. As a result, IoT is neither one market nor one opportunity; rather, it's a series of opportunities across different vertical markets, each with myriad business cases, time frames, and payoffs. These varied opportunities are proving to be winners, and they share some common use cases.

Preventive predictive maintenance, for example, is a horizontal use case that pays off big in transportation-related industries—much the same as it did for Rio Tinto in mining. At Rio Tinto, remember, each day the company avoids a vehicle going out of service for repair saves $2 million. That's not chump change, even to a large global operation.

The following examples (Figure 3.3) describe a proven IoT use case in transportation and logistics, oil and gas exploration and extraction, and smart city initiatives.

Transportation and Logistics Use Case: Preventive Predictive Maintenance

Sensors throughout the fleet's vehicles continually report on the state of each vehicle. When sensors indicate signs of a likely problem, such as suddenly dropping oil pressure or heat buildup in the engine, dispatchers and drivers are alerted to the problem and can take corrective measures. Vehicles spend less time off the road and get back on the road faster, without a major disruption to delivery schedules. That means vehicles spend more time generating revenue and less time out for repair. Just the reduction in operational disruption and logistics can virtually pay for the IoT investment.

IoT solution
Sensors in vehicles report on the state of each vehicle

PAYBACK

COSTS
Reduced truck operation and delivery system costs

EFFICIENCY
Reduced delivery disruptions, increased on-time delivery, and optimized logistics systems

IoT solution
Sensors placed throughout an oil rig enable operators to identify problems before they occur

PAYBACK

SAFETY
Increased safety with earlier and more reliable warnings

EFFICIENCY
Real-time alerts, reduced time to oil extraction (faster to revenue), 4x the asset utilization, and full data use with near real-time analysis

IoT solution
Connected devices improve a multitude of city services

PAYBACK

REVENUE
Increased 20%+

COSTS
Reduced operational expenses by 30%+

EFFICIENCY
Increased planning efficiency and optimized personnel with more data

Figure 3.3   Examples of Proven IoT Solutions

Payback in this use case comes from:

- Reducing truck operations costs
- Reducing delivery disruptions
- Increasing on-time delivery
- Reducing delivery system costs
- Optimizing logistics systems

Oil and Gas Exploration and Extraction Use Case: Smart Analytics

On oil rigs, which are complex factories and cities fused together and precariously planted in the middle of an ocean, smart analytics can be a lifesaver.

As in the transportation and logistics example, lots of sensors, as many as hundreds of thousands of them, are placed at appropriate places throughout an oil rig. One class of these sensors, called distributed acoustic sensors, that are cemented into the wells, can generate an astounding amounts of data—up to 2 terabytes of data per day. This myriad of sensors collect readings and analyze all kinds of data, enabling operators to optimize the use of resources (for example, by reducing the amount of water, sand, or proppant needed) or to identify problems sufficiently in advance to initiate remediation or trigger critical safety procedures in time to save lives and minimize damage. In such cases, IoT literally saves lives and property. Furthermore, by reducing time and cost to oil extraction, companies speed time to revenue realization, increase margins, and accelerate ROI as a result of IoT.

Compared to the pre-IoT process, this is a vast improvement. Then, the rig drills collected data, the data were put on a tape which was flown by helicopter to the shore for analysis. The drills, meanwhile, waited. Only after the data were analyzed in the datacenter located on the firm ground could instructions be sent back to the rig. Now, with IoT, once the rig is connected to the fog computing system and the network, the data from the sensors can be accessed and analyzed simultaneously by multiple parties and decisions can be made in real time. The result is a two to three times increase in the rig's utilization.

Payback in this use case comes from providing:

- Real-time alerts
- Increased safety through earlier and more reliable warnings
- Full data utilization with fast, near-real-time analysis
- Two to three times the asset utilization
- Reduced time and cost to oil extraction, which translates into faster time to revenue and higher margins

Smart City Initiative Use Case: Open Platform, Data Analytics, and Flexible Services

Another increasingly popular horizontal IoT use case is smart cities. This proved true in Barcelona, a leader among the world's smart cities from an IoT standpoint. Here, the goal was to connect a variety of devices for the purpose of delivering different services in areas as diverse as energy consumption, transportation, municipal services, and law enforcement.

Every week, it seems, another city is stepping forward to deploy an IoT-based smart city strategy. But there is much more to the smart city IoT story. At a time when the general public is demanding more and better services from government, often in the form of an efficient way to create and deliver varied services customized for each city and its constituents, IoT offers an attractive solution at the right cost.

Let's look more closely at Barcelona.[1] The city wants to efficiently provide services at multiple levels to all of its citizens and businesses by harnessing information and communications technology (ICT) through development and implementation of the Barcelona Smart City Model, essentially an IoT model. It identifies 12 areas under which smart city projects are initiated: environmental, ICT, mobility, water, energy, matter (waste), nature, built domain, public space, open government, information flows, and services.

Currently, Barcelona has 22 major programs and 83 separate projects that fit into one or more of these 12 areas. Some of the projects include smart initiatives in lighting, parking, and water and waste management. Today, Barcelona has more than 500 kilometers of fiber-optic network, development of which began more than 30 years ago when the city networked two municipal buildings with optical fiber. Its smart city efforts are built on this initial network.

In 2012, the city government structured its smart city projects under the umbrella of "Smart City Barcelona." In addition to implementing smart technologies, the city uses its connectivity projects to deliver coordinated services across departments. This, in turn, helps to further eliminate departmental silos and to improve the resident experience for people living in Barcelona. The Municipal Institute of Information Technology of Barcelona (IMI) played a key role in the initial organizational formation, which emphasized the involvement of government, residents, and the business community in developing and shaping the city's technological initiatives.

Barcelona also initiated what it calls a "City OS," an operating system that will sit atop its established network of sensor technology to collate and analyze data collected across the network. City officials envision this OS as an open platform working across the various specific smart technology projects operating in Barcelona. They also see this platform as the key to unlocking IoT benefits associated with data analytics and predictive modeling.

The goal of Barcelona's smart city program is to provide city services at multiple levels to all citizens based on the use of Internet and telecommunications technologies. The strategy underlying its approach is that the city functions as a network of networks that connects all of its different affiliated networks—for example, transportation, energy, and technology.

Barcelona's City OS amounts to a unified network of what otherwise would have been different, possibly incompatible networks. In terms of payback, Barcelona reports saving $58 million annually using smart water technology and increasing parking fee revenues by $50 million annually with its smart parking technology. Overall, its smart city efforts have created 47,000 new jobs. With results like these, Barcelona's administration and its citizens at large are more than satisfied.

But where, exactly, does this payback in a smart city come from? Let's drill down a bit. Parking is typically a second- or third-tier revenue source for most cities, which means it's very important. The IoT parking system is a win–win for both the city and the user. Here's how it works: Drivers use a mobile phone to find and reserve a parking spot, thus saving time. The city better utilizes available parking spots and can apply variable pricing, which increases revenues (a reported 20 percent). For example, the city could increase the price of parking just before and during a rock concert, and then go back to its usual (probably lower) pricing model when there is no sudden big demand. The payback: more money and lower expenses (a reported 30 percent).

Lighting is another money saver in cities. In the United States alone, the ROI from installing light-emitting diode (LED) systems has been around 18 months. Now it's possible to install sensors on top of these systems that turn on street lights only when there is traffic or other movement on a street. Should a pedestrian or vehicle appear, the lights would immediately go on. Given the cost of energy, it makes no sense to light streets when no one is using them. Even with the recent drop in the cost of energy, it still isn't free. The ability to efficiently and automatically turn lights on and off will still save money, wherever the cost of energy goes. Cities and communities that implement such smart lighting solutions report savings ranging from 30 percent all the way to 80 percent.

Another example of savings may catch you by surprise: commercial garbage collection. Think about the current system. The garbage truck has a set route it goes on to collect garbage, regardless whether the bins are full or not. Now imagine that the city can adjust collection schedules and routes dynamically so that only bins that are full or almost full are emptied. The implementation is fairly straightforward. You install fill-level sensors in garbage containers, connect them to the IoT system that manages the collection trucks routes, and voilá, the routes can now be optimized. Besides Barcelona, such systems are already operational in many cities in Europe, North America, and Asia and bring in a minimum of 20 percent cost savings.

Here is the final example of emerging use case in smart cities and transportation: mobile advertising in buses. There have been several attempts over the years to deploy location-based advertising services, but both the technology and business models proved to be too challenging. However, as the transportation sector moves from paper advertising to digital screens placed in the interior and exterior of buses, taxis, and shared vehicles, there is a real need for solutions that can push rich content onto this new class of moving billboards.

Although many content management systems exist for online advertising and fixed screens, the market for ad placement platforms specific to intelligent transportation systems is still looking for solutions. But

Veniam, the provider of mobile mesh networks for vehicles in the cities, are planning to change that. Their mobile advertising platform, which is provided as a managed service with a monthly fee or revenue sharing model, fills this gap in an ingenious way. After the advertisers or their agents upload their content and define their target audience via a cloud-based portal, their solution chooses the best vehicles, locations, and times for displaying each particular ad and proceeds to orchestrate the entire delivery by leveraging their vehicle-to-vehicle and vehicle-to-infrastructure communication. Vehicles distribute the content among themselves in a wireless mesh and cooperate to send key audience data back to the cloud. Since every vehicle knows its position and types of passengers at any point in time, each campaign can be managed in a fine-grained way. For example, Veniam's system can flash a given promotion when the taxi is within half a mile of the shopping mall running it or show a specific ad in all the buses of a city at the same time to mark the launch of a new product the minute it is presented to the world. "Veniam's mobile advertising service is only one of the many new use cases and business opportunities that present themselves when we enable vehicles and other moving things to communicate with each other, acquire relevant context information and make local decisions that generate the global behavior we target, in this case delivering the right ads to the right passengers at the right location and in the right time," commented João Barros, CEO of Veniam.

At a time when people around the world are demanding more and better services from their governments, IoT offers a solution that actually pays for itself. It also brings greater efficiency and the ability to address critical issues, such as energy, transportation, public safety, and civic processes, among others. IoT provides an effective, cost-efficient way to create and deliver varied, customizable services for each city and its constituents.

Payback in this scenario comes from:

- Realizing new revenue increases of 20 percent or more
- Reducing operational expenses by 30 percent or more
- Increasing planning efficiency, due to the availability of more and better information
- Increasing productivity of the personnel, again due to the availability of more and better information
- Improving the citizen experience by conveniently and efficiently delivering more services

- Improving safety and security by tying police and other emergency responders into the same sources of information

The Growth of IoT

A few years ago, the numbers around the growth of IoT were so large that I even hesitate to recite them. Some projections of market impact were as high as $19 trillion. However, as the IoT revolution progressed, they have gotten much more precise and grounded. That said, I'll provide a few figures you can use if you're called on to justify your interest in exploring IoT at your organization. If you do use them, please run an online search to get the latest numbers. Undoubtedly, there will be updates.

Here's a widely used number: 50 billion smart objects by 2020. Those that aren't classified as "smart" will account for billions more. All this means is that IoT has emerged as a massive opportunity, and it continues to grow. By the way, the population of Earth is currently less than eight billion. In 2012, we had 12 billion connected devices and approximately three billion connected people. That means four devices per connected person. Moving forward, the number of connected devices per person analogy will lose its meaning as the role of connected devices evolves from enabling humans to connect to each other and to the data, to enabling machines to connect to each other and to the networks. The 50 billion number is about the various sensors and devices organizations are embedding in factories, vehicles, oil platforms, assembly lines, retail stores, hospitals, and other "things." But we still can't forget all of the consumer-oriented things, such as appliances, TVs, and the like that are also being connected. The point to keep in mind: Your organization will never have to deal with 50 billion devices, or even one billion devices, or possibly even one million devices.

Rather than just the number of connected devices, a more informative metric may be the revenue associated with IoT. Here is the recent estimate from IDC[2]: The worldwide Internet of Things market spend will grow from $692.6 billion in 2015 to $1.46 trillion in 2020 with a compound annual growth rate (CAGR) of 16.1 percent.

But the actual numbers aren't what counts. By the time you read this book, any market size numbers will have changed. What's more important is that these numbers show how quickly IoT is gaining traction. It's clear that we're only in the first phase of the IoT revolution, and yet some initial improvements are already changing industries. The numbers also suggest the likelihood that investments made in IoT will achieve the market revenue to support a sufficient payback.

IoT is a diverse opportunity that touches various vertical markets. Its many use cases, including preventative maintenance, remote operations employee training and productivity, energy management, supply chain management, and customer experience, are common across industries. Preventative maintenance, for example, applies to mining, manufacturing, and transportation and logistics, among other industries. Remote operations provides value anywhere organizations have facilities or devices that need to be watched and operated but don't want to absorb the cost and inefficiency of dispatching staff to perform these tasks. And although we've been focusing on vertical segment use cases, IoT deployment at this point follows a remarkably horizontal approach.

The good news is that in addition to productivity and efficiency improvements and cost savings we discussed earlier, IoT is also enabling new value propositions for customers. We discussed how Harley-Davidson was able to embrace mass customization in an efficient and cost-effective manner. Other customers are using data coming from their products to provide instant feedback on how these devices operate and how they can be improved. They are also shifting to offering business outcomes and experiences rather than the product and its functionality. By signing up for the service rather than buying a product, the customer can expect continuous improvement of service and upgrades that are built into the contract.

IoT is also transforming the value propositions and business models for vendors. It allows them to move to recurring business models, for example charging customers for time of operation of the machine versus the traditional approach of selling the device itself. It creates new revenue streams by allowing the manufacturers and service providers to monetize the data and enhance existing offerings with new service level agreements (SLA).

These attractive new opportunities prompted many large companies and startups to also pursue the IoT platform approach. Out of this race a few open platforms embracing diversity of end-devices and application ecosystem are likely to emerge, but I expect that most of the device vendor-specific offerings will struggle. Why? When you operate a fleet of airplanes, how many IoT platforms would you want to use for your preventive maintenance and data analytics? Would you want to use a separate platform for an engine, for the cockpit, for the brakes, for the wings? In addition, customers are looking for vertical solutions based on horizontal capabilities that can solve their specific business needs. That means a general horizontal solution with minimal overlay of industry functionality, perhaps nothing more than industry-specific labeling and some customer-specific customization.

Many companies with successful IoT deployments adopt an architectural and partner ecosystem strategy. They're essentially breaking down silos with a holistic view of the enterprise. The result produces a truly organizational and cultural transformation as much as a technological advance. This strategy calls for what I refer to as an "architected approach to IoT deployment." You follow a standard deployment pattern, making small modifications based on your particular situation and the specifics of the problem you're addressing. You also avoid assembling, deploying, and maintaining multiple slightly different versions for each business problem you want to address with IoT.

If, for example, inventory management is a problem, you might use RFID for a connected device that can be scanned at various points, such as warehouses, loading docks, and checkout terminals. In the office or retail store, you would use Wi-Fi or Bluetooth low energy. But when it comes to transportation issues, connected devices might use a global positioning system (GPS), a dedicated short range communication (DSRC) capabilities, or other location technology to pinpoint an exact location. These devices might also use any of a dozen other sensors to measure a vehicle's mechanical performance. In an architected approach, you can minimize the number of variations you need to deploy and manage. You just design an overarching organizational—or enterprise or city—architecture that enables you to leverage seamless integration while reducing costs. Otherwise, the growth of IoT might drive you crazy and, as a result, you may hesitate to deploy it despite this or that proven benefit.

Barcelona's City OS is another example of the architected approach. Although it had, at one point, 22 major programs and 83 separate projects going, the city really had only one network. The approach simply enabled Barcelona to avoid implementing IoT separately in hospital, office building, roadway, parking, stadium, and every other setting where the city might find things it wanted to connect.

IoT Is Just the Beginning

We're clearly only at the beginning of the IoT journey. New technologies, such as wearables, 3D printing, drones, connected and autonomous vehicles, and many others, together with new business models, will transform virtually all of today's industries as well as create new industries and segments we haven't even envisioned. Just think what may evolve out of the combination of IoT and blockchain technology mentioned in Chapter 1. In 10 years, your business will look completely different. But by sticking with an architected approach based on open industry standards, you will build the foundation for your IoT journey and most likely be able to accommodate changes as they happen.

Also, don't be intimidated by the huge numbers researchers and vendors throw around. They don't matter to you. Instead, just pursue your vision of what you could do with IoT in your business. There's no reason to wait for more technologies to mature before starting an IoT journey; new technologies will continue to emerge for as long as we live. The ones we have now are already working and delivering results. As long as you stick with an open, standards-based architected approach (yes, I know I sound like a broken record), and integrate your technology solutions with business processes, you won't get left behind regardless of what else comes along. With fog computing, analytics, and tested applications as the foundation, you'll find many proven ways to put your IoT ideas to work, improvising as you go if it's required. Try it, and if it doesn't work exactly the way you want, make adjustments and try again. That's the path to success.

The Internet of Things World Forum meetings are a good proxy for the state of the industry. The first meeting in 2013 in Barcelona was about the excitement, the inspiring vision, and aligning the industry around the common purpose. The main theme of the second meeting in Chicago was joint framework and sharing the best practices. I still remember the buzz that the Rio Tinto main stage presentation created (I shared some of their story earlier in this chapter). And then the World Forum in Dubai in 2015, where we presented business cases and demonstrated real-life solutions. Let's take a look at a few examples of customer IoT implementations that Cisco documented recently (Figure 3.4).

CHALLENGE
Monitoring costs and
theft, safety concerns

ACTION
1.9 million smart meters

RESULTS
Lower costs, faster response time

**BC
HYDRO**

**ANGLO
PLATINUM**

CHALLENGE
Process-control and decision-making systems

ACTION
Converged platform: IT and OT to customer

RESULTS
Cut network cost by half of industry average

CHALLENGE
Factory inefficiencies

ACTION
Automated, self-running plants

RESULTS
Faster and more efficient operations

BENTELER

FANUC

CHALLENGE
Lack of product feedback

ACTION
Secure hybrid cloud

RESULTS
Data collection and analysis that
reduced cycle time, enhanced product
quality, and improved efficiencies

Figure 3.4   IoT Cases

BC Hydro, Canada

This electric utility wanted to improve visibility, manage costs, reduce theft and technical losses, and provide greater safety and reliability to its customers. After deploying 1.9 million smart meters, the company created an IPv6-capable network that provides advanced metering, real-time outage notification, wide-area monitoring, and grid automation. A fog computing architecture enables data analytics and applications to run locally at the edge of the network, leading to improved power management and predictive maintenance. With real-time visibility into all of its customers' meters, BC Hydro has lowered both costs and its response time to problem resolution.[3]

Anglo American Platinum, Ltd., South Africa

Over the years, the process control systems at the world's largest producer of platinum-group metals grew from several small, isolated networks to large, complex, multilayer networks with multiple connections to the outside world. As it managed a full range of mining operations and engaged in both greenfield projects and joint ventures, the company realized that its key challenge was bridging the gap between on-site process control systems and business-critical IT decision-making systems. Anglo American Platinum developed a strategy to integrate its IT and OT networks into a secure, standards-based platform for enterprise-wide visibility and decision making. By transforming from a complex, nearly unsupportable operational environment to a converged, centrally supported architecture, the company has cut its network cost of ownership to one-half the industry average, while still providing higher systems and support availability, as well as comprehensive visibility and reporting.[4]

By the way, the convergence of IT and OT should be one of the first steps you take when starting the IoT journey. That's how Harley-Davidson started, as we discussed in Chapter 1. More on this topic in Chapter 7.

Benteler Automobiltechnik GmbH, Germany

A manufacturer of components for nearly every major automaker in the world, Benteler embarked on a comprehensive effort to make its factories more agile and efficient through IoT. The company created a fully modular production environment of automated, self-running plants. Every aspect at each factory is connected, and operations are managed from a central location. Through an ecosystem of partners, Benteler has built applications that run seamlessly from fog computing to the cloud. It has also integrated hardware and software components to provide an easy-to-manage solution that will deliver better business outcomes, faster changeovers, and increased operational efficiencies.[5]

FANUC, Japan

In the past, this maker of industrial robots for manufacturing companies shipped robots out but had no feedback about robot usage unless there was a problem and downtime. By building a highly secure hybrid cloud to extend its existing datacenter to its customers' premises, FANUC can now extract data from its robots and connect the units with people, processes, and things. The company analyzes data to gain visibility into robot performance. This information also helps in predicting a problem before it impacts production and avoiding knee-jerk reactions. Not surprisingly, such data insights contribute to reduced cycle times, enhanced product quality, and improved process efficiency. We will discuss the "near-zero downtime" solution in more detail in the follow-on chapters.[6]

Emerging IoT Ecosystem

I've said it before and will continue to say it throughout this book: You can't do IoT alone. This is why I placed the *"Build an ecosystem of partners; learn and co-develop with them"* as the first item on my recipe for IoT success in Chapter 1. No single vendor can deliver a complete IoT solution for every customer. Similarly, it doesn't make sense for an organization to develop a custom IoT solution for itself. You'll burn too many resources reinventing multiple wheels that have already been invented. At a minimum, you're better off developing your vertical solution based on proven horizontal modules, architectures, or platforms that you can readily adapt. Going it alone is too costly, too risky, and pushes any acceptable payback far into the future.

That's the message of noted venture capitalist Whitney Rockley, principal at McRock Capital. "Most needed now are partnerships in the ecosystem," she said. There clearly is an abundance of startups, because the "younger generation goes into these companies. However, they lack domain experience," Rockley continued. Companies considering an IoT initiative can partner with these young startups and apply their domain knowledge to the startup's advanced technical capabilities to the benefit of both.

In short, IoT is best delivered through a set of partners, each of which contributes its particular capabilities to the complete solution—including your contribution. It has become increasingly clear that user organizations should no longer accept the 20th century model of one vertically-integrated vendor providing end-to-end proprietary solutions. Most have heard that message loud and clear. Even vendors realize they can't do it all alone, much as they might wish they could.

Due to IoT, the industry is rapidly evolving into a world of partnership ecosystems and customer co-creation. Many companies are working together with customers to develop optimal solutions with horizontal reusable modules that are both open and interoperable. This is a complex and strategic transition for both vendors and users of technology-based solutions. The result will be an open ecosystem of standards-based contributors to IoT solutions. I call this trend *co-economy*.

Imagine what it would take for a company like Cisco to provide a complete solution. Even working in management at the company, it's immediately clear to me that going it alone simply isn't practical. But by partnering with key players that complement each other in terms of technology and market knowledge, cost-efficient solutions can emerge and arrive faster. For example, Cisco provides technology know-how in IT infrastructure, security, and collaboration and market knowledge of the IT industry.

Industrial automation and information provider Rockwell Automation, meanwhile, brings technology know-how in manufacturing automation and market knowledge in manufacturing, transportation, mining, and oil and gas segments. FANUC's contributions complement both Cisco's and Rockwell Automation's. If a major element is still missing, then perhaps an eager startup can fill the gap. Once the partners providing key building blocks are in place, you can add vertical specialists and vertical integrators who can pull together elements provided by multiple vendors and combine them with existing or new customer business processes into a cohesive business solution. Before long, you will have created a logical ecosystem of complementary skillsets and know-how. As you work through several projects together, the initial loose cooperation may soon evolve into alliances, then a set of strategic partnerships, and eventually into a symbiotic IoT ecosystem.

"IoT is not a solution in a box. You can't buy it off the shelf. No one company can implement IoT end to end; not us, not Cisco, no company," said Sujeet Chand, CTO at Rockwell Automation. And everyone will be better off for it in the long term. Vendor lock-in was only the most obvious drawback to the single-vendor solution. Slower innovation, higher costs, and inconsistent service are other, now widely recognized drawbacks to the proprietary vendor approach.

In terms of benefits, here's one example: When a tier-one automotive supplier decided to jettison its proprietary in-car IoT technology in favor of standards-based systems that will interoperate with competitors' IoT applications, it also enabled the company to build an extensive ecosystem of applications and partnerships. This manufacturer recognized the larger opportunities of a wider playing field, especially as the IoT market expands at the astounding rate various leading analysts report.

In another example, a transportation company wanted to help transform a client's railway value chain. At that time, the client company was forced to build complete rail stations with just one of three vendors—a situation almost as constraining as having a single vendor. So the transportation company began development of an open IP architecture that would enable the mixing and matching of not only the various solution pieces from the three vendors available to the client company but from other vendors as well. The resulting open ecosystem won the day.

So now you, the manager of a company considering a possible IoT deployment, have to assemble an ecosystem or find a lead vendor or consultant who can help assemble one for you. Keep in mind that you'll probably want to set aside some pieces for yourself, where your unique expertise and valuable domain knowledge will bring extra dividends.

Let's take a look at what the main categories of this ecosystem exist today.

Figure 3.5 gives you a sense of the breadth of the emerging IoT ecosystem. You can use it as a template to start assembling your own network of partnerships.

Startups Join IoT Ranks

The speed at which the IoT market is growing means that you'll inevitably be dealing with young startup companies. According to Cisco, the number of B2B IoT startups has multiplied, from some 100 in 2013 to more than 1,000 in 2015. (Expect many more by the time this book reaches bookstores.) Ravi Belani, founder and managing partner at business incubator Alchemist Accelerator added: "There is an important role for startups in the IoT ecosystem. Their job is to push the ecosystem even faster. Plus, there will always be a few renegades who will dash ahead rather than waiting for the consortia." As a business manager considering your first IoT initiative, how do you handle this flood of startups?

The good news is that many of today's key IoT challenges are being tackled by the startup community. Real-time analytics, IoT security, visualization, orchestration, and vertical applications are just a few areas in which startups are innovating today. Many have intense vertical focus, while some develop horizontal elements of the stack that can be integrated in multiple solutions. The most successful startups target use cases that can be implemented across vertical markets.

One of the most prominent categories of startups, however, is going after low-hanging fruit, which means connecting various sensors—probably specialized for one industry or another—and providing an abstraction layer and development environment for the applications. I mentioned them earlier in this chapter: They call themselves "IoT platforms." Dima Tokar, CTO and head analyst at MachNation, a specialty IoT and digitization research firm, has identified two types of start-up IoT platforms.[7] The first is an IoT application enablement platform—a horizontal,

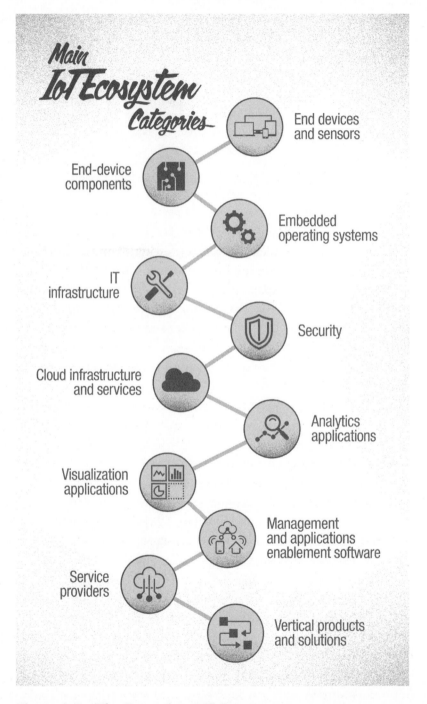

Figure 3.5   The Emerging IoT Ecosystem

best-of-breed, industry-agnostic middleware core for building a set of IoT solutions. The second is an IoT platform-enabled solution—a vertically specific, solution-centric offering optimized to reduce the time to develop an IoT solution.

If one of these startups focuses on your industry and its solution is what you need right now, certainly take advantage of it. However, many of these "platform" startups are solving a similar problem: Every sensor vendor currently has proprietary interfaces. The industry has understood the critical need to solve this issue comprehensively. It is working to standardize the interfaces and formats among sensors, actuators, and other sources of data and the infrastructure (including the fog nodes) at the device, data, and management levels. Granted, even when these standards are finalized, the implementation and interoperability will take time. But make sure that any "platform" startup you speak with is aware of these larger industry efforts and is participating in them. Then insist that the startup guarantees that any product you choose will comply with whatever standards eventually emerge and ensure that the company has a plan to transition your chosen product to that compliant environment. Otherwise (yes, you guessed it), you'll surely face a prescription for vendor lock-in.

Startups desperately want to work with you. These companies need to get established in the market as quickly as possible. Having real customers is the best way to do that. In the process, startups will gain an understanding of an industry's pain points and may be willing to co-develop solutions. In fact, seeking out a startup is a good plan if you're looking to develop an IoT solution and have a functionality or skills gap. Either way, both sides benefit. According to MachNation's Tokar: "These IoT startups can also provide access to their partner ecosystem. The best IoT startups have pre-integrated their technology with relevant partners' technologies. That can really reduce the time and costs required to deploy your IoT solution and reduce deployment risks, since some of the technology work has already been done." You'll likely have to agree to act as a reference, but for most companies that's a trivial commitment. Ideally, you'll entice your entire ecosystem of partners/suppliers to develop a solution with a startup. In the emerging collaborative world of IoT, this is how everyone gains. Yes, IoT is simply too big for any one company to do it alone.

If your problem is particularly challenging and specific to your industry, consider crowdsourcing a solution. This method can be very successful when the results benefit the entire industry. You can start by running a contest to attract entrepreneurs and startups to meet the challenge. You'll have to stake a sufficiently large award for the winner or winners. You might even be able to work out a revenue-sharing arrangement with the winner, if the solution is that good.

Does IoT Need Service Providers?

I remember a few years ago when we at Cisco decided to embrace and drive this new phenomenon of everything being connected, we had a fierce debate whether to call this trend Internet of Things or Machine to Machine or M2M for short. Service providers (SP) had been focusing on M2M for a few years by then. One SP told me at that time that they were shocked to discover that one-third of subscribers on their 3G network were M2M devices. According to Steve Hilton, president of MachNation, an analyst firm specializing in IoT and digitization research, "It was at this point that service providers realized there was a bigger opportunity in store for them and started paying conscious attention to these new types of connections." Mobile operators got an early start in M2M with connecting cars and early IoT solutions as mundane as optimizing pizza delivery. Their challenge turned out to be less about technology and more about the business model. They built their mobile businesses based on a relatively high average revenue per user or unit (ARPU) that smartphones delivered. Thus, they were looking for IoT solutions that could deliver similar ARPU. Unfortunately, most of the M2M services such as remote monitoring and maintenance delivered a monthly dollar ARPU in single digits. There was also a question of credibility with enterprise customers. I heard from many enterprise customers that SPs were just "providers of pipes" and could not be trusted with enterprise SLAs and complex solutions.

But since then SPs have evolved: Some chose to invest in internal capabilities to develop vertical expertise and IoT services; some created ecosystems of partnerships; some attempted to buy their way into telematics capabilities and IoT platforms; some considered operating dedicated IoT networks using older generation mobile technologies; many created dedicated divisions (separate from their wireline and wireless operations) focused on M2M, vertical IoT solutions and managed services with some becoming $1B+ businesses; several mobile virtual network operators (wireless services providers that do not own the underlying network infrastructure), either independent or divisions of larger operators, started to offer vertical and horizontal IoT services as well. "In order to take advantage of the opportunities in the market, SPs focused on changing five key areas of their businesses: organizational redesign, partnerships development, technology portfolio enhancement, network development, and market messaging," said Hilton.

Today, most major SPs have a strategic focus on IoT. They are designing and implementing the latest wireless networking technologies such as 5G or LoRa with IoT use cases in mind (more on that in Chapter 10). They have developed and matured vertical businesses and IoT business models going beyond connectivity (for example, they are pursuing several distinct profit pools in the connected vehicle domain, each with an additional ARPU), including four categories of IoT solutions we will discuss in more detail in Chapter 5. Almost every week, we see an announcement of an IoT partnership between an SP and an enterprise. As the smartphone market becomes saturated in the United States and Europe, connected cars and connected things have become a bright spot and a high-growth area for the operators. Many of these services now deliver a relatively high ARPU through the combination of connectivity and managed services.

So yes, SPs, after a few years of trial and error and some failed attempts and early starts, are playing a key role in the IoT ecosystem; many of them are worthy of your consideration as well.

Collaborate at the Next Level

Now let's take this collaborative work a step further. It isn't enough to simply connect devices and have them communicate with each other. That's just a first step, an enabler. You really want applications and data analytics that will add business value. You might even say that applications and analytics are the reason we connect things and collect data from those things. So we need more than open APIs. We must make it easy for an application to obtain the data it requires from the infrastructure in a standardized and interoperable format.

Developers also need different APIs and standards so they can build the right intelligence into the applications that do "smart" things with the connectivity you just painstakingly cobbled together. That means applications need to also respond to the changing ways people want to interact with devices at the edge. Whereas a process engineer might control or program a production line using a fixed human-machine interface (HMI) screen physically attached to production machinery, the need for remote and mobile interface capabilities is growing. This is especially true among the increasing ranks of Millennials, who want to use iPads and other mobile devices to interact with production machinery and IoT systems. Therefore, it's important to have a consistent IoT application development environment across the network, from the cloud to the edge. This gives developers the flexibility to implement their applications in the cloud, in the fog, or in the end-device itself or use a combination of all three, depending on the use case.

By the way, a number of vendors already offer IoT application enablement capabilities that combine cloud-based asset management and business intelligence (BI) services. One such vendor is Davra Networks, which combines cloud-based asset management and BI services with an IoT fog controller. It enables local analytics, local decision making, and effective sensor-based data collection with cloud policy and visualization (we will come back to Davra Networks in Chapter 5). Another vendor is azeti, a company in Berlin that built its business around remote asset monitoring and management software. It started with a focus on service provider towers, building its IoT application development platform modules based on the needs of this specific vertical industry. It has since extended the application to substations, banks, and oil rigs. Cisco has recently acquired Jasper, whose Control Center software helps companies launch, manage and monetize their IoT services in all major industries and markets. For example, if you drive a connected car, its IoT services are most likely operated using Jasper's Control Center software. Expect many more such vendors to emerge.

Whatever enablement solution you choose, the goal is for an application to use fog, end-device and cloud computing capabilities, as appropriate, to combine local presence with remote expertise. In this way, for example, a production line engineer can take a picture of a broken tool on an assembly line using a mobile device, send the image to a remote expert, and then get live help from that expert to diagnose and fix the problem fast—ideally without stopping production.

The next chapter takes up the justification for the IoT projects and provide a template for a model ROI justification. This should make it easier for you to build a business case for IoT in your organization.

4 | Understanding the IoT Business Value Proposition

I've visited dozens and dozens of customers in every corner of the world to understand and experience firsthand how enterprises are deploying IoT, how they're achieving a payback, and how much that payback is. Because IoT is still a fairly new phenomenon, at top of the Gartner hype cycle,[1] I expected customers to be early in their IoT adoption. And yes, I often came across customers, even executives, who have never heard of IoT. But I was also surprised to discover how many organizations in a variety of vertical segments are already achieving significant paybacks from IoT without having to wait years.

Take PepsiCo, for example. As one of the leading soft drink makers and bottlers, PepsiCo turned to IoT for the most basic of reasons and found an efficient solution. Like many enterprises, the company had inefficient and ineffective IT and OT infrastructure, as well as limited IT and OT resources available inside its plants. It also suffered from server sprawl, where each server supported a very small portion of the production load. PepsiCo essentially incurred high costs to purchase and support an ever-expanding infrastructure of underutilized servers, operating systems, and networking assets. The resulted: highly inefficient use of capital—at a minimum. Even worse, its inefficient network hindered the collection of data that would ordinarily drive plant productivity.

When PepsiCo decided to leverage IoT, it partnered with Rockwell Automation to replace its existing infrastructure and create what amounted to an Infrastructure as a Service (IaaS) model. The company adopted virtual industrial servers and a standard network infrastructure, coupled with round-the-clock centralized expert support. Based on a pre-engineered, scalable server infrastructure, its solution includes all hardware, software, and network connectivity preconfigured specifically to support PepsiCo manufacturing. It also improves the reliability of plant manufacturing systems and reduces both downtime and support costs.

IoT enables the support staff to communicate with all components of the infrastructure through continuous remote monitoring. This enables highly skilled technicians to proactively react to any issues *before* they even have a chance to impact production. Whenever a plant requires tech support, a manager dials the 24x7 call center and receives a response within a guaranteed 10 minutes. With this level of support, each PepsiCo plant essentially has a highly skilled manufacturing-aware team at its disposal, ensuring downtime or technical challenges are addressed quickly and effectively, thereby minimizing any impact on production schedules.

The payback from all of these changes was almost immediate, according to Rockwell Automation's "PepsiCo Infrastructure as a Service" profile.[2] For one monthly leasing fee, PepsiCo now has a unified, fully supported platform that runs all of its manufacturing applications. It's simple, flexible, and worry-free (Figure 4.1).

At Harley-Davidson, which we discussed in the first chapter, the IoT payback came down to resolving what turned out to be a straightforward issue: lowering the hours per unit (HPU) to build motorcycles. It was just too high, but to lower it the company had to change its manufacturing culture and processes. It needed to adopt new technologies similar to those used at other world-class manufacturers.

To justify the effort to top management, Harley-Davidson's IoT team brought in a third party to provide outside restructuring data and cost estimates. Meanwhile, the internal team prepared a side-by-side cost estimate based on what its members knew about building new facilities, new model ramp-up, cultural transformation, and similar functions for which

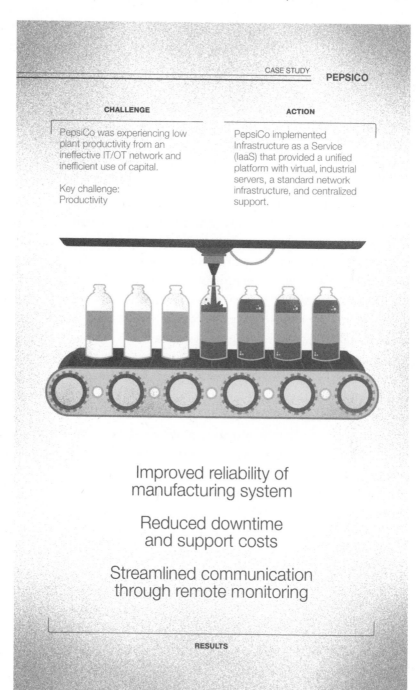

Figure 4.1 PepsiCo Case

the company already incurred costs. Management went for it, which probably saved an iconic American motorcycle company from being acquired or going out of business.

Delivering Payback and Business Value

When it comes to IoT implementation, every manager wants to know the ROI. Unfortunately, in most cases the answer is specific to each organization, the issues it's trying to address, and its starting point. "Take the problem of asset downtime," said Sujeet Chand, Rockwell Automation's CTO. "A 10 percent improvement projected nationally translates into billions of dollars of productivity across the United States. Or optimization of energy consumption; if I can measure energy at many points using IoT, I can know where energy is being consumed and detect unexpected spikes." Knowing this will help the company take steps to remediate the problem and reduce energy consumption. In both of these use cases—asset monitoring to avoid asset downtime and energy monitoring to reduce consumption—Chand added, "IoT can provide pragmatic solutions."

Exactly how much any company gains will depend on how it responds to what IoT reveals. Still, the ROI is there; you just have to dig it out. The areas of impact—especially positive paybacks—have turned out to be surprisingly comprehensive, covering pretty much all operational aspects.

Here are just a few of the paybacks I've seen while visiting companies deploying IoT:

- Reduction in costs
- Revenue generation
- Streamlined business processes
- Increased uptime
- Design and creation of new business models
- Implementation of new go-to-market strategies
- Development of new product and service delivery options
- More efficient ways to service and support customers
- New insight into product usage and customer information
- Speedier service and delivery

Predictive maintenance, for example, lowers cost through reductions in unplanned downtime. You can also view it from the other side of the coin: increased uptime. Either way, it boosts production and efficiency. New business models can attract more and different revenue-generating customers, while new service delivery options boost customer satisfaction and convenience and lower support costs. Remote service and support both increases efficiency and lowers costs. New go-to-market strategies can open markets you previously couldn't effectively address. The wealth of information, about your products and your customers' use of those products, collected through IoT can help you develop new and much improved offerings and attract more and different customers. Some of this knowledge, as well as the data itself, can generate revenue, as partners and even customers are increasingly willing to pay for pertinent, timely, and actionable information as a service.

The most compelling business case for IoT today is predictive maintenance, observed John Berra, principal at the namesake John Berra Consulting and past chairman of Emerson Process Management, an automation and engineering services provider. "Discrete and process manufacturers, for example, use thousands of motors, pumps, and compressors," he explained. "All of this rotating equipment is subject to frequent breakdowns, which interrupt production, raise costs, and create unsafe conditions. IoT gives an early warning system, which enables operators to take action before a problem becomes serious. Predictive intelligence is also valuable at the individual equipment level. IoT is used on farm equipment, medical equipment, and more. The downtime cost of an MRI scanner, for instance, is huge."

With IoT, the idea of a traditional manufacturer building out a service model for its business is one that suddenly seems to be taking hold. It's emerging as an important revenue consideration, as well as a strategy for growth in an age of connected devices and digital information. A November 2015 survey of hundreds of senior manufacturing decision-makers from both industrial machine builders and end-user manufacturers by Cisco titled "The Digital Manufacturer, Resolving the Service Dilemma" makes this point: 86 percent of respondents view the transition from product-centric to service-oriented revenue models as a core part of their growth strategies.[3]

IoT makes possible the profitable transition to a service model and the corresponding ability to digitize the production environment. A digital model can vastly facilitate the service model, and the payoff can be tremendous. According to the same Cisco survey, an economic analysis for an average $20 billion manufacturing company that digitizes its environment typically shows profits rising 12.8 percent over three years and 19 percent over 10 years. (See Figure 4.2.)

Our survey respondents aren't, however, naïve. They're well aware of the digital disruption they face. When asked which technologies would most change how they manage production over the next three years, the top three responses were cloud computing (37 percent), the Internet of Things (33 percent), and big data analytics (32 percent). We will be discussing all three in the context of IoT use cases throughout this book.

Dundee Precious Metals is a great example of such transformation. In an effort to increase production quality and output and to improve miner safety while minimizing costs, the company initiated an IoT effort to track the location of miners and vehicles, monitor vehicle status, and automate building controls. The payoff was stunning:

- Production quadrupled from 0.5 million to 2 million tons annually (versus 30 percent original goal).
- The company saved US $2.5 million in long-distance communication costs over two years.
- Miner safety was improved by connecting the blasting system with the location-tracking system.

Suddenly, management could see exactly what was going on inside the mine as it was happening. Specifically, supervisors could see into shift changes, miners' locations, the number of buckets filled and transported, and vehicle status. Supervisors could even send an instant message to a driver to adjust the route to pick up more ore. Talk about payback; instead of leaving its vehicles idle as they had done in the past, the company was able to redeploy them to get closer to 100 percent utilization.[4]

PepsiCo and Dundee illustrate just two of the ways IoT can deliver business value and a business payback. In many cases, you will start collecting that payback soon after you deploy IoT. Sometimes all it takes is analyzing the data you just collected through remote monitoring. With IoT, companies can now understand what their operations looks like on

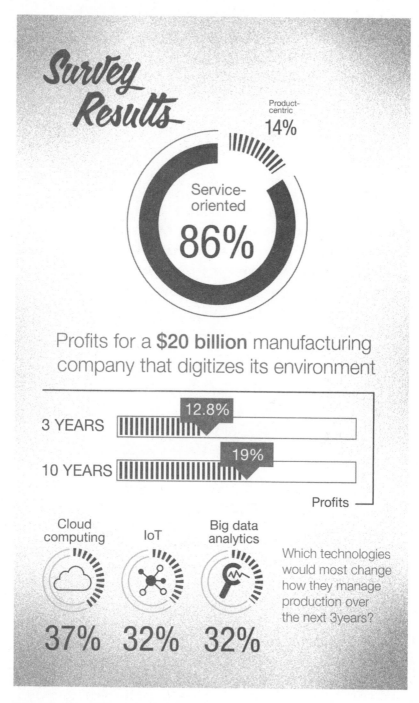

Figure 4.2 Cisco Survey Results

a global basis. They can maximize the use of their equipment to get the most out of it. But that wasn't all. Ultimately, thanks to digitization, IoT, and analytics, these companies and many others like them expect to redesign their businesses from the ground up.

Building an IoT Cost Justification

As we've discussed, IoT varies by industry—happening first in manufacturing, transportation, utilities, smart city initiatives, and handful of other market segments. Just as important, IoT payback is industry- and use-case-specific. In his keynote at the 2015 Automation Perspectives, Keith Nosbusch, the chairman of Rockwell Automation, cited the following examples (see Figure 4.3) of industry-specific gains:

- Brewer increased capacity 25 percent and cut brew cycles 50 percent, among other savings

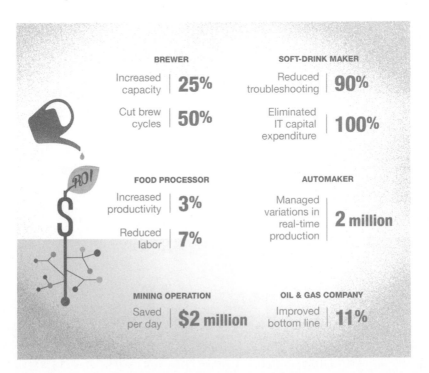

Figure 4.3   Gains from Using IoT

- Soft drink maker reduced troubleshooting 90 percent and fully eliminated IT capital expenditure (100 percent)
- Automaker managed more than 2 million variations in real-time production
- Food processor increased productivity 3 percent and reduced labor 7 percent
- Mining operation saved $2 million each day per broken vehicle through predictive preventative maintenance
- Oil and gas company improved bottom line 11 percent—a three-fourths cost reduction and a one-fourth revenue increase

At this point, there's no generic IoT magic number or rule of thumb that will tell your business it will save X percent or generate Y in new customers or Z in added revenue. Instead, you're going to have to put together a cost justification the old-fashioned way, using the few hard data points specific to your organization and any other data you can pull from a variety of disparate sources. The goal isn't to create the *perfect* ROI model or cost justification. Instead, you want to collect credible data that you can then use to assemble a *plausible* cost justification for solving a given problem using IoT.

Start by identifying the problem you want to solve. Be sure to resist the cosmic temptation of some grand challenge the company faces. That can come later. For now, focus on a specific problem you know you have that IoT can clearly fix now. Take the problem PepsiCo wanted to fix: an inefficient and complex technology infrastructure that was costly and hindered productivity. The company chose one of the most compelling and mature IoT solution categories—remote operations and then deployed and connected the right set of smart things to enable remote experts to see what was happening and fix any problems over the network. The remote operations use case can be applied to almost any organization, and it should deliver a fast and attractive payback.

Next, pull together the data you'll need. Look for the parameters that describe the scope or extent of the problem, the amount of resources currently focused on dealing with it, the time you now spend on the problem, and any other data points that will give you an objective sense of the issue and its ramifications. Much of this information is likely available in a number of your organization's systems. You may need to dig for them across your systems or reach out to a few people.

After that, look at what you can glean, in terms of industry data, from industry associations, professional groups, seminars, and IoT events. This data won't be specific to your company and situation and sometimes may even come from other industries, but it should provide both a general approximation and a good sense of where your peers are focusing. You're looking for industry rules of thumb, averages, and published benchmarks. You can pick up some of this data at industry conferences just by chatting with the people around you.

At this stage of IoT's maturity, the productive areas you can tackle fall into four basic categories:

- *Information collection.* Pulled from the heterogeneous intelligent and interconnected devices with unique identities that interact with other machines/objects, infrastructure, and devices in the physical digital environment, you sift and sort the information, and then take action based on the inputs you receive or the devices' own rules and policies. This is how you do remote monitoring and remediation with IoT.
- *Predictive analytics.* Data-driven systems leverage the data collected from or generated by the things you have connected, and then thoroughly analyze, digest, and take action based on the results. This is where you perform fraud detection, reduce account churn, and so on.
- *Application-specific issues.* For example, connected health care wearable devices and analysis of the massive amounts of data in both electronic medical records and the vast health and medical database archives.
- *Consumer-related IoT activities.* These are driven by consumer products, which are increasingly being embedded with processors and communications capabilities, ranging from connected and autonomous cars, refrigerators, and garage doors to home security and home entertainment systems.

Given the business scope of this book, it will focus primarily on the first two areas (*information collection* and *predictive analytics*), with only rare digressions into the second (*application-specific* and *consumer-related* issues and activities).

John Berra offered one final piece of advice on calculating the ROI of an IoT investment: It's a business challenge. Most organizations don't have good baseline data on their current state and so would have great difficulty proving the positive impact of an IoT project. Organizations can say what they want in words but have difficulty translating that into numbers. Suppliers should help with this. "IoT suppliers need to have testimonials with quantified business results and also offer templates to assist their customers in preparing an ROI analysis," Berra said. That's another reason to seek out appropriate IoT suppliers as partners.

Components of IoT Payback

IoT already has a number of proven patterns that can help you avoid reinventing the proverbial wheel when building your solution. A number of these are readily available and can be adjusted to suit your organization's specific problem and situation, including:

- *Connected operations:* when you need to connect the intelligent things the networking industry continuously develops and enhance patterns for connecting and communicating among those devices in an IoT solution. Of course, there's IP networking and cloud computing, not to mention the emerging fog computing and blockchain. Expect even more moving forward.
- *Remote operations:* when you need to distribute people to one or more remote sites and keep them there for a period of time. IoT can efficiently address these always costly situations. Once equipment is instrumented, relatively few situations can't be handled remotely.
- *Predictive analytics:* when you have more data than you can manually absorb, the data change at a rapid rate, or—in the reverse case—the data change infrequently and you want to be notified only when it changes. Predictive analytics enables a remote staffer to identify, understand, and quickly take the right action on this data.
- *Metering and measurement:* when you need to monitor and measure things. Meters and measurement devices can be connected with a variety of controllers. They not only capture readings but, in conjunction with controllers, do calculations and make basic decisions based on the information, such as identifying thresholds.
- *IoT-as-a-Service:* when you seek opportunities to leverage IoT to create new business models that shift the focus from standalone products to service-based offerings. The results are better engagement with customers and fueling additional revenue streams.

- *Remotely controlled machines and equipment:* when you benefit from avoiding the need to staff costly locations; reduce worker travel time, fatigue, and exposure to dust, vibration, or other conditions; and prevent accidents, injuries, and other risks. This pattern involves not only the devices but a variety of controllers and robotics, depending on what actions need to be taken.
- *Industrial control zones:* when you wrestle with controlling activity at multiple manufacturing sites or utility substations and when employees, contractors, and equipment vendors require access to these sites and the local network. Access can be restricted to valid personnel, to only certain equipment in the area for which employees are authorized, or to resources residing in the enterprise network.
- *Smart environments:* when you're considering cities, communities, campuses, factories, industrial or business parks, and designated zones for various types of use. This pattern is for areas connected to and populated with a variety of devices and controllers to enable a wide range of actions, from managing parking availability to conserving water or energy to policing and emergency services.

New patterns will continue to emerge as IoT is applied to an ever-widening array of problems.

As you look for IoT payback options, take the data you've gathered and see whether it applies to any of the patterns described above. Then look for payback in the following key areas:

- Labor efficiency:
  - Increase productive time on the job (efficient delivery of information)
  - Reduce or eliminate travel time (remote monitoring)
  - Speed troubleshooting and problem resolution (predictive analytics)
  - Remote service and support
- Streamlined business processes:
  - Efficient, real-time data capture
  - Remote monitoring
  - Predictive analytics
- Revenue enhancement/new opportunities
  - New go-to-market strategies
  - Remote service and support
  - Data as a service
  - Increase uptime/continuity of operations

Helpful Hints

When building your IoT cost justification, here are some questions and answers I've found to be helpful when working with business managers like you.

What IoT Project Gives You the Fastest Path to Payback?

We will discuss fast payback areas in more detail in the next chapter. As of this writing, remote operations, especially remote monitoring and control, similar to what PepsiCo did, is one of the most mature and well-established examples. It eliminates the need to keep highly skilled people onsite at all times. You may only need to send them there occasionally, if at all. Once you've instrumented all of the devices you're concerned with and connected them to the network, you can keep your highly skilled experts in whatever location is convenient for them and cost-efficient for you. Doing it remotely is much more efficient and far cheaper, by any measure, than sending expensive resources onto the site weekly, monthly, quarterly, or even annually.

John Berra is convinced that remote asset management, which is closely related to remote monitoring, is also one of the top payback areas. He cited the experience of a two-unit refinery. Asset management was deployed in one unit, and in the other unit asset management package was postponed for two years. Data from those two years showed that the unit with asset management was twice as reliable as the one that remained untouched. Both units were built at the same time and had identical equipment. The only difference was the asset management system. You can draw your own conclusions.

Which Vertical Markets Deliver the Largest ROI?

I'm tempted to say the markets that have the most at stake. In that case, the largest and fastest ROI might be in manufacturing, as we saw in the PepsiCo and Harley-Davidson examples. Next is the oil and gas industry, where IoT can deliver tremendous automated efficiencies, especially if you're concerned about the cost and risk of maintaining large teams on oil rigs at sea. Another big payback comes from the mining industry, which, following the slump in prices of raw materials, is now focusing more on cost, productivity and efficiency. As we saw in the previous chapter, just blowing out a tire can have huge financial ramifications. But the good news is that your peers are realizing positive ROIs in almost any industry and geography. Look to the next chapter for more examples.

Which IoT Process Has the Biggest Payback?

Here I have to vote for predictive and preventive maintenance. Once you've instrumented and connected your devices, the ability to avoid mechanical failures through a combination of predictive analytics and preventative maintenance generates a potentially huge payoff. And I'm not just thinking about oil and gas or mining operations. Imagine a transportation and shipping operation with thousands of shipments always in transit and huge pressure to meet overnight, two-day, or whatever-day service commitments. Every unplanned breakdown avoided through well-instrumented vehicles and predictive preventative maintenance can save a bundle. Related to this example are predictive analytics applications in food and food safety, retail, agriculture, and even sports and entertainment.

What Is the Largest Expense in Setting Up an IoT Initiative?

The answer depends on where you start. Obviously, building a modern IPv6 network from scratch can be expensive if you don't already have an IP network in place. Similarly, if you're deploying a lot of devices and haven't instrumented any of them, that can be a large expense. You should also pay attention to the costs of the different pieces of IoT software and middleware you'll need, ranging from predictive analytics to security to visualization. Finally, one of the major buckets of costs are integration services, including technical integration of various components into well-functioning solutions as well as integration of technical solutions and business processes. However, as we will discuss more in Chapter 8, there are other less obvious cost elements you should seriously consider as well—project delays, cost overruns, lower than predicted ROI. These are mistakes that can cost you a bundle and also the costs that can be avoided with proper planning, careful vendor and integrator selection, and applying the learnings from your peers.

How Can an Organization Save Money When Deploying IoT?

If you've kept your technology infrastructure—networks, servers, storage, and applications—up to date, you should be able to leverage much of what you already have with some modest infrastructure upgrades: more ports, more memory, and more storage here and there. If you haven't kept your infrastructure current, you can still use what you have, but performance and scalability may become problems at some point. As far as assembling your IoT ecosystem, remember that everything is negotiable. Vendors are eager to have referenceable customers. New players to the IoT market, especially startups, may be willing to partner with you in exchange for your use-case domain expertise. It's very exciting when IoT ecosystems start to come together. Be prepared to take advantage of that to control costs.

One last suggestion: Don't try to do too much all at once. As I stated in my recipe for IoT success in Chapter 1, *"Start with low-hanging fruit,"* a preferably small IoT project that solves a worthwhile problem in one plant, store, or refinery. Get yourself a fast win, and then move on to more ambitious problems. Starting small is also a good way to manage costs and risks. Such an initial project should also provide you with your own ROI and TCO data that would aid you in developing the business cases for the next phases of your IoT journey. And remember that technology and a business case are just a small part of your overall challenge. You'll be dealing with huge organizational and cultural issues, so starting small and getting quick wins will help your build credibility, convert at least some of the naysayers, and position you for the success in this transformational journey (more on this in Chapters 6 and 7).

Data Data Everywhere

I borrowed and adopted the ROI model in Figure 4.4 from Cisco. It's simple, but it should help you start. Of course, you'll want to modify it to reflect your specific situation. In general, feel free to use any of the materials, checklists, models, and so on presented in this chapter (or in this book) as you build your IoT business case and assess the ROI of your project. Think of these materials as examples or templates and modify them to reflect your business, market, and situation.

This is a standard table. Simply plug in your actual numbers or estimates. Feel free to use ranges, if necessary.

In short, you can leverage IoT in numerous ways to generate or create revenue, reengineer industry segments, and streamline business processes. Rio Tinto in mining, Metrolinx in transportation, and PepsiCo in process manufacturing are all examples. Companies like these use IoT to reduce costs and streamline processes. Along the way, they're also disrupting their industries to one extent or another.

It's important to explore numerous opportunities to use IoT to save money, reduce costs, increase uptime and efficiency, speed processes, and improve customer service/customer experience by deploying predictive analytics, remote management, remote predictive maintenance, and remote service.

As we previously discussed, the following new IoT technologies are helping to drive new business models, payback, and opportunities:

- Fog computing, real-time fog analytics
- Blockchain (secure audit-level tracking)
- Machine learning and self-learning networks (combination of networking, deep machine learning, and cognitive analytics on edge devices)

But please be thoughtful about when, where, and why you would choose to deploy these technologies. There are many examples of use cases where they may not be needed. For example, if you need to analyze 30 years worth of seismic data, you can do it in the cloud. Similarly, if you are connecting basic vending machines that require little bandwidth and do not need real-time analytics, you can connect them to the cloud directly. However,

Build Your Own ROI Worksheet

Downtime (operations)

Cost reduction (operations)	Downtime reduction (operations)	Your numbers here
Average cost of downtime operations ($/minimum)	$5,000	
Average downtime duration operations (minimum)	45	
Number of downtime incidents operations (annually)	100	
Average reduction in number of downtime incidents with IoT (%)	50%	
Average change in downtime cost (annually)	4%	
Average change in downtime duration (annually)	10%	
Average change in downtime incidents (annually)	10%	
% Realization in average reduction downtime incidents with IoT in (Yr1)	70%	
% Realization in average reduction downtime incidents with IoT (Yr2)	80%	
% Realization in average reduction downtime incidents with IoT (Yr3)	90%	
Downtime cost reduction (operations) (Yr1)	$7,875,000	
Downtime cost reduction (operations) (Yr2)	$11,325,600	
Downtime cost reduction (operations) (Yr3)	$16,033,652	
Downtime cost reduction (operations) (Yr1–3)	$35,234,252	

Figure 4.4   ROI Model

if you are considering connecting vehicles or plants or oil rigs to run data analytics or predictive maintenance, yes, fog computing will be vital.

Once you know what's happening in near real time and apply analytics to that information, you can:

- Make better decisions
- Forecast capacity and resource needs
- Better allocate resources
- Reduce hard-to-predict costs and delays
- Increase management efficiency
- Boost customer satisfaction
- Meet or beat service-level agreement (SLA) commitments

The chart in Figure 4.5 indicates which areas tend to generate the most payback and the form it takes. Again, this data is based on a manufacturing

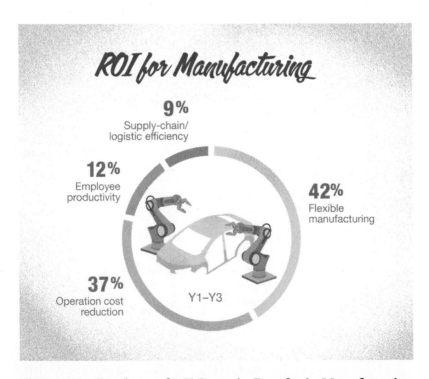

Figure 4.5   Breakout of IoT Domain Benefits in Manufacturing
Source: Cisco, 2015.

operation. You will want to modify it for your industry, specifics of your use case, and project.

Most importantly, my hope is that IoT will change the way you think about your business and how you design, plan, develop, and deliver products and services, go to market, and interact with customers. It's an opportunity to radically transform your organization and put it in the right position for the future.

I've talked about understanding the IoT payback in a general way. The next chapter introduces four fast paths to an assured payback. This is the information C-level executives will want to see first.

5 | Four Fast Paths to an Assured IoT Payback

Prudent business managers won't invest in IoT before they see tangible evidence that IoT pays off. And not just pays off, but demonstrates the type of payback an organization can achieve fast, as in almost immediately. The four categories detailed in this chapter do just that. They've been proven by your peers. The technologies and best practices are fairly mature. They do, however, require some investments, such as the need to connect existing devices and, in some cases, upgrade or replace a few of them. Still, the ROI can be quite high. And it can be achieved much sooner than you would typically expect.

Before we jump right in, let's take a moment to recap how you can generate quick returns. As I stated in my recipe for IoT success, you should *"focus on solving real problems."* This is where your fast paybacks come from. These are the organization's pain points, and they're often well known. As we discussed in the previous chapter, the first step is to arm yourself with your organization's current data, benchmarks, and goals. From there, we start with the basics. If you can get IoT to enable a few devices to communicate and it removes or lessens a pain point, you stand to collect a significant payback without breaking the bank or a much sweat. It may, for example, take only a few temperature gauges that automatically alert someone to something getting too hot or too cold. Yet, having that information sooner, rather than later, could avoid a host of related problems and the costs that would follow. Often, these types of solutions don't require purchasing and deploying new devices and systems. They may very well be things the organization already has but haven't connected for this purpose.

Another potential early win involves remote operations. How often do you have processes that require someone to stop by and shake a door or check a meter? With IoT, you can monitor processes like these, perform the required action, and avoid dispatching a person to do the job. You collect your payback every time somebody *doesn't* have to perform these tasks, because an IoT connected device enables you to do it remotely. Similarly, many industries have a common practice that calls for people to work in pairs, driven mainly by safety concerns. IoT technologies reduce the need for the second person—or even the first, most likely—thus dramatically increasing workers' productivity.

To sum it up, you would see fast payback in the following five areas:

- *Reduced labor.* Wherever IoT can perform a task that somebody otherwise would have to do, you have an immediate win that compounds itself every time you avoid using a person.
- *Lower costs.* Wherever devices can connect and communicate to automate a process, you stand to lower your costs. This is the automation payback.
- *Increased productivity.* Whenever you can use devices that connect and communicate over IoT to reduce the human labor involved in a process or, similarly, speed up the process, you will achieve a productivity boost.
- *Improved quality.* Wherever you can use intelligent devices connected and communicating through IoT, you can avoid or at least reduce errors, which will increase process quality.
- *Better decision making faster.* Whenever you take the information your devices are collecting and communicating through IoT, your staff are positioned to make better decisions. If you add some analytics or predictive analytics into the equation, more and better decision making can be done even faster. Your managers need only pay attention to the exceptions.

OK, so how do you get there? I promised you four fast paths to IoT payback (Figure 5.1), and we've reached them within the first two pages of this chapter. Is that fast enough? Here they are.

Connected Operations

Join/link devices, sensors, meters to a network

Remote Operations

Monitor, control, asset management

Four Fast Paths to the Internet of Things

Predictive Analytics

Identify, understand, and immediately take best actions

Predictive Maintenance

Increase uptime and productive hours

Figure 5.1   Four Fast Paths to IoT Payback

Connecting Devices, Sensors, and Meters to Each Other and to a Network

Any business facility with devices that either are already capable of connecting directly or indirectly to the company's IP network or can be retrofitted to do so using enterprise-grade technology and architecture can be networked together. Such connected operations start realizing benefits immediately. So your first IoT payback begins by connecting your existing devices (that are either not connected today or are connected to a myriad of specialized incompatible networks) to your existing IP network and adjusting your existing business processes to take advantage of things now being connected and inter-connected.

The following example comes from the oil and gas industry, but the oil rig the company connects could be any factory, facility, branch office, or vehicle. As we've discussed, oil and gas has achieved substantial payback by connecting the multitude of devices on an oil rig and then metering those devices. Not only does this deliver a substantial financial payback, it can actually save lives—which, in turn, generates another set of paybacks, some that are literally priceless.

Specifically, when the devices on an oil rig—or in any facility—are networked, the entire facility becomes an IP platform with sensors placed at appropriate spots throughout. These sensors collect readings and analyze the data, enabling operators to identify problems sufficiently in advance to initiate remediation or trigger critical safety procedures in time to save lives and minimize damage. Furthermore, by reducing time to oil extraction, the company speeds time to revenue realization, which further accelerates ROI as a result of IoT.

Rockwell Automation (Figure 5.2) gives us another example. The company is a leading provider of manufacturing automation solutions, so it's no surprise that Rockwell deployed IoT extensively in its own manufacturing facilities. By connecting assembly lines and operations in its manufacturing plants, and then connecting those plants to each other and to its connected enterprise infrastructure, Rockwell achieved a fast initial payback. Even though the process involved 20 plants scattered across the globe, the results are startling. Five years ago, the operation was saddled with a 120-day inventory cycle and achieved only an 82 percent time-to-want customer experience (essentially, on-time delivery). Once

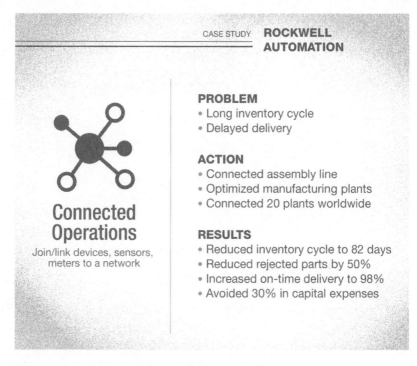

Figure 5.2 Rockwell Automation Case

it had everything connected, Rockwell reduced the inventory cycle to 82 days and increased time-to-want to 98 percent. Specifically, the company managed to cut in half the number of rejected parts, effectively avoiding 30 percent in capital expenses. Rockwell credits these gains entirely to connecting all of the devices throughout its plants.[1]

Steps in Starting an IoT Project

The good news is that you don't have to start with such a comprehensive project involving many plants across the globe to realize a fast payback. As we discussed, your first IoT project can and should be small. I have seen many of your peers implementing connected operations in manufacturing in several steps:

1. Connect devices within a standalone island with Ethernet and open protocols for richer aggregate sensor data.

2. Connect the islands and migrate all discrete single-task or device-specific networks into a converged plant-wide network for IoT visibility, real-time operation and cost savings.
3. Deploy flexible multiservice platform across the plant for mobility, collaboration, and fog/cloud computing that is optimized for the next three fast-payback scenarios.
4. Implement a multiservice platform across the network of plants for scale and optimal supply chain and manufacturing operations.

Each of these phases builds on the others, and each delivers a fast payback by itself.

Adding Remote Operations, Monitoring, Control, and Asset Management

Have you faced a situation when your packaging line suddenly stops and you get a safety alert that one of many doors on the machine is open? But since you didn't know which door is at fault, you are forced to send an engineer to the plant floor to physically check all the doors so that you can restart the line. Remote operations delivers a payback the first time it helps you avoid sending a person to see what's going on. In the long run, people always cost more than technology. With IoT, once you've connected your devices on one IP network, adding remote monitoring or asset management capabilities is a logical next step.

The obvious payback is reduced people costs, but there are other benefits, too. For example, from any location on the network, you gain visibility into not only that location but also any other locations you've connected. You also gain insight into device utilization. It will quickly become apparent which devices are over-utilized and which are underutilized, and you'll be able to make smarter management decisions based on that additional knowledge. You might, for example, re-provision a device that's chronically over-utilized by boosting whatever capacities will bring utilization into line.

The trucking industry may be an extreme example of the benefits of IoT-based remote monitoring and asset management, but any organization with dispersed facilities in any industry segment can experience similar benefits. Remote truck management includes a range of functions that allow operators to remove or minimize the risks associated with vehicle investment, improving efficiency, productivity, and regulatory compliance and reduce their overall transportation and staff costs.

In our trucking scenario, the first step is deploying sensors throughout the fleet's vehicles to continually report on the state of each truck, including vehicle maintenance, vehicle telematics (tracking and diagnostics), driver management, speed management, fuel management, and health and safety.

Think of this as a gas gauge equivalent for every component and process in every vehicle. When a sensor indicates a likely problem, such as suddenly dropping oil pressure, the beginning of heat build-up in the engine, or simply a low tire-pressure reading, truck dispatchers see it and alert the driver to the problem. At that point, the driver and the dispatcher determine the appropriate corrective measures and how quickly they must be taken.

From a payback standpoint, with remote monitoring enabled, vehicles spend less time off the road and cost less to operate and maintain. When a truck does have to be off the road, it can usually return to work faster thanks to IoT remote monitoring, which enables the company to avert surprise breakdowns and avoid major disruptions to the delivery schedules customers depend on. So, thanks to IoT, vehicles spend more time generating revenue and less time out for repair. Just the reduction in operational disruption and logistics can pay for an IoT investment.

Davra Networks, mentioned in Chapter 3, is a startup that has been implementing these remote vehicle operations solutions for their clients. Davra's system allows customers to monitor multiple data sources from within a vehicle (telemetry, location, sensor, video, network, and so on). The customers can then log into a centralized management console to have combined views of all elements of a vehicle's health and status. By using the fog computing capabilities onboard the vehicle, customers can react to the data in real time without requiring the vehicle to return to base. Over-the-air software updates, route changes, driver alerts, and even communication with related infrastructure can all be carried out remotely and automated where required. On average, by implementing such capabilities, customers report 15 percent savings in cost of fuel in addition to significant savings in operational and maintenance costs.

"Vehicles by their very nature are mobile and spend the vast majority of their time in locations away from the organizational center, so in order to ensure consistent service availability it is important to have some form of remote access and control over as many vehicle functions as possible," Paul Glynn, the CEO of Davra, told me.

Here's a seemingly very different example: a dairy company in India that operates 150 ice cream stores. I'm particularly fond of this example, because it shows a startup in India successfully applying IoT to address a use case that may not be relevant in the United States or Western Europe but is a common issue in other parts of the world. Power outages happen often in India, leading this dairy company to equip each of its ice cream shops with a backup diesel generator to ensure ice cream remains safely frozen during an outage. Individual store managers, however, would often turn off these generators to try to save money. That worked, as long as there wasn't a power outage. When outages did occur, the company stood to lose what could amount to several thousand dollars' worth of ice cream per outage due to melting and, likely, spoilage—a potential health hazard that puts the company at risk of government regulatory action.

The dairy company turned to Nimble Wireless (Figure 5.3), a local startup, for help. According to Siva Sivakumar, Nimble Wireless's CEO, small-factor multi-sensor devices were deployed in the fridges where ice cream is stored. These sensors automatically connect to the network and can be monitored remotely via software running in the cloud. If the temperature in a fridge goes up 1 to 2 degrees, the system notifies the manager on duty. If the issue isn't fixed within 5 minutes, the system alerts a manager at the next level up. If the temperature in that fridge still continues to rise, alerts will continue to be sent—all the way to the CEO of the company, if necessary. And these are not simply email or text message alerts that can easily be missed or ignored, especially at night. Voice alerts are also generated to prompt someone in the store to take action. Just in case the person receiving the alert doesn't know what to do, the system suggests actions, such as closing the fridge door or turning on the generator. It also runs trend reports showing where problems have occurred, whether they were one-off events or systemic occurrences, and how quickly corrective action was taken.

Within a month of deploying the solution across all of its stores, the dairy company started realizing a payback. Within 13 months, it calculated

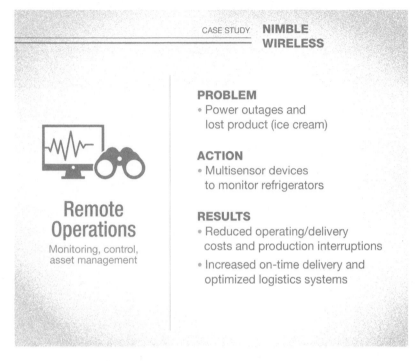

Figure 5.3   Nimble Wireless Case

a return of five times its original investment. Nimble Wireless is now extending the solution originally developed for the dairy company to other food companies that produce cheese, butter, and spices in India.

Here is the last example: illegal pipeline taps or people stealing oil from pipelines. It is a huge multi-billion-dollar problem for the industry. Surprisingly, it happens often—not only in developing countries. The solution: a smart foam pig or a device that you place and push inside the pipeline during its normal operation. Smart foam pigs contain various sensors that can detect and report illegal taps and also issues such as corrosion of the pipeline walls or potential leaks. Combine such a device with the cloud-based analytics and reporting software, and the customer benefits are simply tremendous. "With smart foam pig the customers can reduce the cost of detecting the problems in the pipeline by 95 percent versus traditional inspection methods," said Steve Banks, managing director of i2i Pipelines, the manufacturer of smart foam pigs.

Specific paybacks from these types of IoT-based remote operations include:

- Reduced operations costs, because problems are identified sooner and fixed earlier, before things get worse. Variable operating costs, such as gas consumption, are also reduced.
- Reduced delivery and production disruptions, because companies are better able to meet service-level commitments and avoid any contractual penalties that may apply.
- Increased on-time delivery, which translates to better customer service.
- Reduced delay-based system costs, which helps the company avoid the variety of costs associated with delays.
- Optimized logistics systems, which enable the organization to better optimize its driver, logistics, vehicle, and facility resources for maximum efficiency.

Using Predictive Analytics to Identify, Understand, and Immediately Take Best Actions

As we discussed in the previous chapter, predictive analytics is at the heart of getting the best payback from IoT. Connecting devices and adding a few sensors or meters will quickly generate more information than your staff can handle and comprehend. In fact, your team can be overwhelmed when IoT data starts rolling in faster than they can digest it, even with alerts and other messaging. That's one of the reasons why, according Vernon Turner, senior vice president and research fellow (Internet of Things) at IDC, less than 1 percent of data generated today is being analyzed. You really need predictive analytics to help your staff, at a minimum, sort and understand what's coming in, so they can take intelligent actions. I'm not talking about rocket science here—just recognizing basic patterns and identifying exceptions and deviations will enable you to capture significant value. But that's just a starting point. The benefit of putting all of these smart assets on the same IP network is to correlate and combine the data coming from multiple sources to gain new insights and to take action.

Here's a manufacturing problem: Plants are running at a much higher capacity utilization than ever before. Often facing continuous

24/7 operation at maximum throughput, manufacturers have no time to spare for emergency maintenance, never mind scheduled service. With downtime costing plants up to $20,000 a minute, a manufacturer cannot afford disruption to its processes. In fact, a single such occurrence can cost a plant upward of $2 million when factored for system-wide impact. The same goes for smart grids, smart cities, transportation networks, and other mission-critical systems that require continuous operations and have scheduled maintenance downtime windows that may be permitted as infrequently as once a year. Although in some rare cases full redundancy would be built into the system, in many applications that's neither practical nor economically feasible.

Unlike the Rio Tinto example discussed in an earlier chapter and again below, where problems were sure to occur in nearly impossible locations, the predictive analytics solutions described here can be applied and customized to any location, anywhere, at any time. Even in an urban environment, even if you have a service provider right across the street, when a problem occurs, it still takes time to put the service team in place, diagnose the issue, collect the right parts, and eventually solve the problem. During that time, whether it's an hour or a couple of days, production is impacted. In the meantime, uptime metrics are missed, customer deliveries are in jeopardy, and, ultimately, both the top and bottom lines suffer. The figures below don't show a pretty picture, but with IoT-based predictive analytics you can improve many of these stats.

In his article titled "The real cost of downtime,"[2] published on DevOps.com in February 2015, Alan Shimel said: Downtime has significant impact on a wide range of industries. At a Fortune 1000 company, for example:

- The average total cost of unplanned application downtime per year ranges from $1.25 billion to $2.5 billion.
- The average hourly cost of an infrastructure failure is $100,000.
- The average hourly cost of a critical application failure ranges from $500,000 to $1 million.

I can't imagine any business willingly absorbing such losses, especially if a proven solution is available. Let's look at an example of a fix. Founded more than 50 years ago, FANUC (Figure 5.4) provides a wide range of automation equipment for automotive components and the general industrial market. The company struggled with a lack of visibility into how

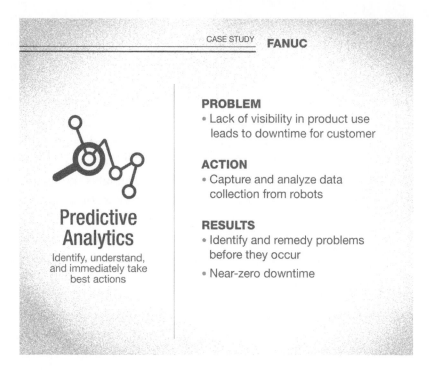

Figure 5.4   FANUC Case

its customers leverage its equipment on the factory floor. FANUC only gained the necessary insight after a problem had already occurred and resulted in costly downtime for its customers. Then, by partnering with Cisco and Rockwell Automation, FANUC found a solution it calls "near-zero downtime."

With near-zero downtime, FANUC has started to capture operational and diagnostic data generated by its robots operating on manufacturing floors (with customer permission, of course), store that data in the cloud, and then leverage predictive analytics to remedy any potential problems before they can negatively impact customers. And it works! FANUC has convinced its customers' OT and IT departments to share their data. By analyzing that data in real time against past history and metrics and by improving its response time to potential incidents, FANUC leverages IoT to deliver a proactive solution—one that, given the stakes (remember, things invariably fail), would be priceless.

Remember the comment from Sujeet Chand in the previous chapter about the huge potential of energy savings. Here is how the Cisco supply chain team is using predictive analytics to accomplish just that. "We manage every aspect of the cost of production in our factories, down to the penny. . . . At least we thought we did," said John Kern, Cisco's SVP in charge of Supply Chain Operations. But until recently, one area Cisco did not manage or have visibility into was the cost of energy. In one of Cisco's contract manufacturing plants in Malaysia, the supply chain team deployed a network of 1,500 sensors across the factory floor and used Cisco energy analytics software to capture the energy consumption data. This information gave them amazing insights into energy efficiency of individual machines, systems, and production processes. For example, they looked at burn-in chambers and discovered that even for similar models the energy use was radically different. So they dug deeper: they replaced underperforming equipment and adjusted the operation of chambers for optimal combination of efficiency and energy use. The result: 15 to 20 percent reduction in energy consumption across the entire plant, which amounted to $1M in cost savings per year. But Kern's team is just getting started. They are already working on taking the energy savings a step further, down to 30 percent and implementing these energy-cutting improvements in more than 20 other factories across the globe. "These results were eye-opening for us. We saved money and reduced our carbon emission footprint," commented Kern.

Once you've linked machines, devices, or things, and their associated sensors and meters, to each other on a single network and captured the resulting real-time data, predictive analytics is the logical next step. There are many predictive analytics solutions and algorithms, several of which focus on specific industries, use cases, or environments. All of these solutions look at the data as it comes in; compare it to what has already been seen; correlate the impact of multiple variables, including environment, weather, materials, or operations; and predict trends with statistical precision. You'll know that a particular problem has X percent chance of happening within this or that timeframe, which is enough time for an alert to go out and the right people to take appropriate corrective measures.

This isn't magic; it's just solid, proven statistical and probability science. The longer the history and the more data you have, the more precise your predictions will be. With the right rules-based software on your end, the predictive system can tell you what's likely to happen and when, as well as suggest a prioritized list of remedies to take. Then you or your people can quickly make the best decision. As with each of the fast payback scenarios, predictive analytics is just a first step on the IoT journey. Once you have deployed predictive analytics in your production environment, your organization can start scoping and implementing more advanced analytics capabilities, including prescriptive analytics and even machine-to-machine learning.

Adopting Predictive Maintenance to Increase Uptime and Productive Hours

The previous payback solution focused on what typical companies in any industry can do to create a fast payback. But some special cases require a separate mention. One of my favorite IoT fast payback stories isn't about a typical company or a typical industry. It's Rio Tinto's mining operation (Figure 5.5) that I described in Chapter 3. But it's worth emphasizing

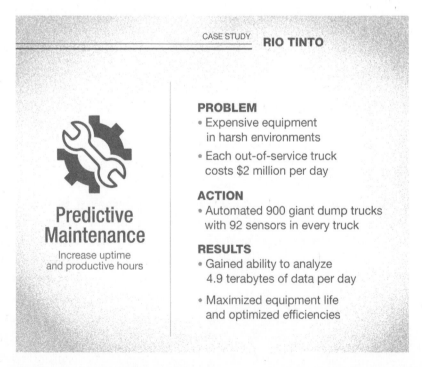

Figure 5.5 Rio Tinto Case

here. It's what you can do even under extreme conditions and still achieve a fast payback. The predictive maintenance Rio Tinto implemented delivered an immense payback. And any company whose business and mission-critical systems face extreme conditions can similarly benefit.

Rio Tinto's goal was to network its processes and equipment to increase efficiency, maximize safety, minimize staffing, and optimize output. A key part of the project involved automating its fleet of roughly 900 giant dump trucks with some 92 sensors divided among the engines, drivetrains, and wheels. The sensors track condition, speed, location, and more, and actually enable the trucks—which travel only on private land—to operate without human drivers.

In aggregate, Rio Tinto's fleet generates approximately 4.9 terabytes of data per day. The information not only controls vehicle operation but also enhances efficiency. Preventative maintenance ensures the company gets maximum life out of its equipment. The position sensors on its trucks can also ensure each vehicle takes the shortest possible route to minimize fuel consumption. These little gains, surprisingly, add up to big benefits.

Most of the required technology to accomplish something like this already exists in the form of smart sensors, intelligent components, connectivity protocols, and software expertise. Let's revisit Rio Tinto. As we've seen, Rio Tinto operates extremely expensive equipment in a very demanding and remote environment. All of that equipment is likely to break down; when it does, it's better if that doesn't happen at the very bottom of a deep, open pit mine. The time and cost of getting service resources to Rio Tinto's disabled equipment is too great to even contemplate—about $2 million per day for each out-of-service truck. Now you need to double that cost, because the company also loses the service of a comparable working vehicle just to tow out the damaged truck. (You're not going to simply call AAA to come and tow one of these behemoths.) So Rio Tinto's cost is already closer to $4 million per day, and it hasn't even fixed the damaged equipment yet.

Do you remember the solution I described in Chapter 3? It's predictive maintenance. Things (equipment, vehicles, machines, resources, whatever) in every industry break down, often at the worst possible times or in the most inconvenient places. It must be a corollary of Murphy's Law. If you can anticipate these breakdowns, however, you can prevent them from occurring at inopportune times and in awkward places. In effect, you can avoid having the production line go down in the middle of, for instance, Christmas holiday order production, because a sensor got covered with dust or a motor needs rewinding.

Predictive maintenance depends on IoT-enabled resources to capture and communicate information about these same resources. That information can then be analyzed in near–real time using predictive analytics to anticipate when the next failure will occur or, preferably, when your company needs to fix a problem *before* the next likely failure. That will give you the necessary time to schedule production, materials, and spare parts—whatever it takes to maintain production schedules without incurring the unnecessary costs that result from not being able to plan ahead.

That's four fast payback scenarios and a few customer implementation examples. Still want more? Here is how your peers are implementing IoT across many industries to accomplish fast paybacks. Try adapting one of these scenarios:

In Agriculture

- In Tasmania, Australia, an oyster farm turned to IoT and predictive analytics to optimize its operations. An IOT system and it sensors monitor conditions through the farm. Oysters are very sensitive to changes in water temperature and can only be harvested when their environment is free from pollutants. IoT generates alerts if the level of contaminants in the water prohibits the harvest or when conditions start to deteriorate and potentially impact the well-being of the oysters. Similar solutions have been implemented in the United States. By helping the companies save their oysters, IoT literally saves their revenue streams.
- In Napa Valley, California, IoT systems monitor and alert the vineyard staff about any issues with the vines and use contextual information to recommend actions, including optimal time for grape harvest.
- In many locations around the world, farmers of water-intensive crops are starting to install sensors and cloud-based systems to help them perform automated field testing and reduce water use.
- Let's add to this list laser guided harvesting systems being piloted right now, "connected cows," including cattle birth monitoring and even bee hive monitoring and predictive solutions, and you start to get a picture of how IoT is beginning to revolutionize agriculture.

In Health Care

- A facility serving the elderly adopted IoT through a combination of wearable devices and cloud software. The system identifies signs that could bode poorly for patients, monitors each patient's vitals, and even alerts staff about likely accidents or falls. It's proved so useful that the facility now allows patients' families to remotely monitor the well-being of their loved ones.
- Other efforts include smart beds, systems linking ambulance and emergency response systems to accelerate patient diagnosis and treatment when seconds count.
- Remote patient care is being adopted for rural patients in both developed and developing economies that allow patients to gain access to specialists located hundreds of miles away. Of course, security and privacy issues continue to be huge focus in these applications.

In Retail

- Many retail chains are conducting trials and implementing omnichannel solutions (another industry buzzword), which basically means providing superior customer experience by combining both online and in-store capabilities. When a preferred or VIP customer enters the store, he or she is greeted by the store manager; if the VIP lingers in the aisle for a few minutes, an associate is sent to help out. If the consumer who bought shoes in the store online before enters the shoe aisle, he or she is presented with an instant coupon for the brand of shoes previously bought.
- Stores are experimenting with smart shelves that complement the smartphone-based customer experience solutions or robot store assistants that help you find products and answer any questions about them.
- Retailers are also testing predictive analytics systems that would allow them to manage the flows of customers, based on the number of customers entering the store and their shopping patterns. They can anticipate how many check-out stations need to be open so that customers do not stay in line for more than five minutes. Many start-ups and large vendors are now working on such solutions. However, they are still fairly immature from both the technology (e.g., location accuracy), and from the business model perspective, and will take time to develop, but if you are in retail or provide B2B2C capabilities, you should become involved in such efforts. I don't even have to mention it by now, but many such functions also require opt-in from customers.

In Sports and Entertainment

- There are many systems (including the one developed for the teams by my employer) that enhance spectator experiences by allowing the attendees to use their own tablets or smartphones to watch replays or view stats, while providing the abilities for the venue operators to manage their operations dynamically from menu and prices of concession stands to seating (Hey, if you are a sports fan with the season ticket, would you want to be given an option to upgrade to a better seat that is now available?)

In Utilities

- If you have been around the utilities industry ten years ago, you remember the excitement about smart grids. The good news is that IoT in the energy sector is finally starting to happen with the accelerated deployments of smart meters and smart grids bringing real cost and energy savings to both utilities and consumers. Some of the utilities are now experimenting with the use of blockchain-based systems to dynamically integrate solar energy into the grid.

In Building Automation

- Smart lighting solutions, physical security, office customization, and office personalization use cases are being implemented in new buildings, increasingly through the retrofitting of existing office buildings. The landlords are finding that such IoT capabilities are attractive to tenants. They produce higher occupancy rates and higher rent.

In Education

- Massive open online courses or MOOCs are all the rage, but we also see the adoption of remote education, allowing students in rural villages to take classes taught by specialist teachers in real time that are not offered locally. Add to it IoT applications on school campuses such as physical security systems, including emergency alerts, energy monitoring and control solutions or smart city applications such as parking systems, and you start to get the picture.

In the Airline Industry

- IoT is helping the airlines and airport operators reduce the time the airplanes stay at the tarmac and reduce the weight of the airplane and thus the cost of fuel. Some of the most efficient airlines have now found that downloading the data from the plane has become the critical time barrier for the planes to stay at the tarmac. Thus, high-speed networking options are now being implemented to reduce that time. In an average airplane, there are several tons of wiring that link multiple sub-systems, but also link video and entertainment systems. The industry is investigating which of these wired connections can be replaced with wireless technologies, effectively eliminating the need for at least some on-board wiring and thus reducing the weight of the plane. The estimated savings per pound of airplane weight vary widely, but a ton of weight saved would definitely make a financial impact.

In the Military

- Even in the military, IoT is being adopted across all the branches. The use of robots, drones, and artificial intelligence there are highly controversial and may still be fiercely debated. The connected battlefield, however, already has become a reality. Connected soldiers wearing 360-degree cameras are being directed by mobile command and datacenters in Humvees. The contextual information from soldiers, drones, satellites, and sensors is allowing soldiers to see and identify dangers on the other side of the hill. Smart clothing monitors health and conditions of the soldiers and can even provide initial diagnostics in case of injury. Submarines now run connected systems that can withstand a torpedo attack. Predictive context systems are becoming available on warplanes.

I can continue to list scenarios and fast payback opportunities in other industries, but I think you can see the point: there are fast payback opportunities in every industry. Some industries are starting to implement connected operations, while some are already successfully adopting predictive maintenance. But I can't think of any market where IoT is not being adopted today.

IoT and the Environment

I recently met with a water utility company providing water and waste-water services for a major metropolitan area in the United States. We discussed their comprehensive approach to ensuring a clean water supply for the city, starting with source protection, water treatment, and the distribution system. Think of their challenge: Regardless of the mix and concentration of pollutants or microbes present in the source of water (a river), they must ensure that they deliver a consistent supply and quality of water leaving their system for consumers. By the way, since the creation of the utility some 80 years ago, the number of people they serve has quadrupled. No surprise that they turned to IoT for help. The utility started with the deployment of a variety of sensors testing physical, chemical, and biological parameters. They partnered with a startup to connect legacy sensors and to collect the data these sensors generated real time. Then they moved to implement diagnostic, predictive, and prognostic analytics that help them manage assets, assure water quality, quickly identify water leaks, and also anticipate the quantity of water required in the city the next day. They are now looking into adopting an augmented reality system for emergency management preparedness.

We are all aware of the environmental challenges facing both the developing and developed world. Polluted air in cities, lack of potable water, industrial waste, dirty and inefficient energy sources, to name a few. The good news is that IoT is starting to help in many of these areas. Cities are deploying systems that monitor air quality and noise levels and can recommend actions as simple as regulating traffic and vehicle access to the city center. Governments and cities are installing tsunami, flood, earthquake, or wildfire warning systems. Select farmers from India, Sri Lanka, China, Kenya, South Africa, the United States, and Italy are already benefiting from smart irrigation systems that reduce water consumption, increase yields, and improve predictability of crops in the fields and in greenhouses. Several cities in California are using smart water meters to monitor and reduce the water use by households during drought. We all know how much food is being wasted and spoiled during improper transportation and storage in both poor and rich countries. When entrepreneurs combine the power of IoT telematics- and cloud-based systems with micropayments and with modern supply chain best practices (replacing traditional and highly inefficient informal distribution networks), the resulting market structure transformation can dramatically reduce both spoilage and the cost of food to the consumers.

Entrepreneurs, governments, non-government organizations, enterprises, and research institutions are increasingly adopting IoT technologies to the realities and cost structures of the developing economies. The Nimble Wireless implementation of remote monitoring I mentioned earlier in this chapter is just such an example. A key to the success in these efforts has been not to blindly implement solutions from the developed world, but instead to identify specific issues or use cases particular to a given country or a region and to leverage IoT technologies combined with creative funding and business models to address them. As a result, potable water and air quality testing tools, animal protection, or deforestation control systems and even clean indoor cooking solutions are being piloted in Africa and Asia.[3]

One of my favorite examples was a pilot of Smart Handpumps by Oxford University in Kenya.[4] Since the majority of people in rural Africa get their water from wells using handpumps, making sure that such pumps work is a key concern. To help with this issue, the Oxford team came up with a simple yet ingenious solution. They installed motion sensors in the handles of these pumps and connected them to the cellular network. When a pump stops functioning, a repair team, who is incented to make timely repairs, is alerted. The result: dramatic increase in uptime of pumps and wells. In parallel, the system also collects the actual water consumption data that can be used for water system prioritization and planning.

In the spring of 2016, Germany reached the milestone of providing almost all of its energy needs from wind and solar power at least for part of the day. Portugal ran four days entirely on renewable power. Denmark set similar records. Wind power has increasingly been a key component of energy strategy for many countries driven by their carbon footprint and sustainable development initiatives. A wind farm is a perfect example of a sophisticated and highly complex IoT system in action that incorporates all four fast payback scenarios. It is a combination of sensors, predictive analytics, predictive maintenance, remote monitoring, fog, and cloud, plus a myriad of wind turbines connected into what functions as a single integrated organism tightly coupled with the power grid. Jorge Magalhaes, senior vice president of engineering and innovation at Vestas, one of the leading manufacturers of wind turbines, summed it up perfectly: "IoT allows us to not only combine but correlate multiple inputs such as weather and wind predictions, expected demand for electricity, current dynamic performance and usage of component and materials to make decisions ahead of time about how best/how hard to run which turbine in the system, when to plan and schedule maintenance when it is most economically viable."

We are just getting started. From tsunami or wildfire warning, air pollution monitoring and prevention to smart agriculture, food management and safety and finally to clean energy, I am optimistic that IoT-based solutions can help address key environmental issues across the globe. The key to their success is that they make both economic sense and help the environment. However, as we will discuss in more depth in Chapter 7, it is critical that these technical solutions be both grounded in hyper-local business and cultural realities as well as accompanied by business process and market structure innovations sorely needed in many countries.

Aspirational Payback

The initial four situations described earlier in this chapter deliver fast, immediate paybacks—the type managers need if they're to build a case for an investment in IoT. Almost any industry can generate similar paybacks by connecting devices to the network, each other, and the rest of the enterprise, and then analyzing the data these devices generate in real or near-real time.

These four use cases often result in tactical paybacks that are quickly accomplished. By starting your IoT journey with small projects that bring in immediate results, you can prove the benefits of IoT to your company and convince any skeptics to invest in the next step of an IoT transformation, both organizational changes and technology solutions. More strategic (aspirational) paybacks take more time, planning, and investment. The payoff, however, can be bigger. In many cases, these paybacks are transformational for your business and the industry as a whole. They often take the form of new business models or new go-to-market strategies and may completely disrupt a market segment.

But you don't need a strategic payback to profit and benefit from IoT at the initial stage. If you focus on the fast paybacks described above and adopt the solution patterns presented in Chapter 4, IoT can transform your business and your career. Here are some steps to consider:

1. *Adopt, modify, and customize proven patterns.* Feel free to adopt and modify them as needed to meet your specific needs.
2. *Connect and instrument basic infrastructure.* This is the beginning of how you collect your IoT payback.
3. *Initiate practical use cases.* Start small, with the low-hanging fruit every business needs. Think remote monitoring.
4. *Optimize a decision engine once everything is instrumented.* With everything connected and generating data, you'll want a decision- or rules-engine to help you organize and understand the data pouring in.
5. *Build IoT around data collection and analytics.* This is how you generate the best payback.
6. *Automate processes intelligently.* Use analytics to guide the automation of business processes (if they aren't automated, human staff may be quickly overwhelmed).
7. *Deploy predictive analytics.* This is the key to maximizing the impact of steps 4, 5, and 6.

Here's an example of a company that started by implementing the first two steps described above. Remember Nimble Wireless, the Indian startup? It also helped a heavy equipment leasing company in India. That company leases equipment for 30 months. When the 30 months are up, it wants the equipment back promptly. The company attaches IoT sensors to equipment before it is leased and ensures those sensors are operational for at least 30 months. This enables the leasing company to monitor its very pricey pieces of equipment wherever they're located. If the equipment isn't promptly returned, the company can retrieve it directly. The cost of the sensors and the monitoring system is peanuts compared to the value of the leased equipment and is trackable on almost any smartphone or

Internet-connected device. The payback is a no-brainer. Going forward, I wouldn't be surprised to see companies everywhere put sensors like this into every piece of expensive machinery. Now that the leasing company has gone through the first two steps, it's working on implementing more advanced use cases.

The use of predictive analytics (step 7), in particular, has the potential to elevate whatever instruments you connect to a strategic level. Predictive analytics can draw insights from patterns that human managers may easily miss, turning a tactical effort into a strategic initiative.

Researchers everywhere are projecting IoT to exceed trillions of dollars in economic impact within a few years. They differ only in how many trillions and over how many years. As a business manager, you need to answer what I call "the trillion-dollar question": How much of that massive amount might come your way and how fast? The second part is straightforward: As soon as you start linking IoT devices over the IP network you will start collecting your payback (see Figure 5.6).

Figure 5.6   How Far Along Are You?

The first part is trickier. The answer depends on the problem or problems you're trying to solve and how ambitious you are in solving it. Based on the examples cited in this chapter and throughout this book, I can assure you of this much: You will experience payback as soon as you begin linking IoT devices. But don't forget that fast paybacks do not mean *easy* paybacks. IoT is not that easy. So please read the following chapters, especially Chapter 8 about common mistakes, and truly internalize and operationalize the recipe for IoT success from Chapter 1 before proceeding to implement any of the fast payback scenarios.

You can't do IoT by yourself. The next chapter looks at the need for people, and where and how to find them. As IoT ramps up, you'll be competing with Silicon Valley, Boston, New York, and other technology hotbeds for many of the same skilled people. The jobs I'll talk about—data managers, process coordinators, change management managers, and such—will be in high demand.

Making IoT Work for Your Organization

6 | Generation IoT Goes to Work

What would the adoption of IoT feel like in your organization? Even though it's hypothetical, the scenario below is based on the real-life experiences at many of the actual companies I've met with over the years.

Whether you have been doing your job for 30 years before IoT arrived, or you're newly hired and learning about your job and IoT simultaneously, IoT will require training in new skills and, most importantly, new ways of thinking and working. So, in that sense, everybody is a newbie and we're all equals. Only the trainers are experts. So here we are, a roomful of newbies trying to understand this thing called the "Internet of Things" and how to make it work as expected. We're a motley assortment of people; some have an operational background and others have a technology focus, not that it matters. IoT is about thinking and doing things differently.

The group's diversity is striking. This isn't just IT or OT or any one department. We bring a breadth and power of backgrounds and skills: geeks from IT, control engineers from OT, and, of course, process people—some with clipboards and checklists. Our efforts encompass

Figure 6.1   The New Journey

legacy knowledge, which continues to be critically important, as well as analytics, new application software and middleware, and new additions to the network—especially fog computing. We're all learning not only the new IoT approach but also how to integrate IoT into legacy systems, combine IT with OT architectures, and blend old skills with new skills. It's exciting, and everybody is working on it—albeit a few more grudgingly than others. It's fun watching the IT and OT people feel each other out. It takes a little negotiation here and there, but we eventually make it work.

By now we've all realized that the people in the group who know the old ways of doing things, the old processes, have no real advantage over anyone else. Because IoT enables the creation of new business models in new ways, we must follow particular IoT-driven business processes. So we're all learning to do things differently together (Figure 6.1). For example, in the past, when we had to find and retrieve data, it could be very tricky. Now, with the new process, the IoT device already knows what data we need and where to find it, and it then communicates that information to us. It also quickly becomes clear what we're supposed to do with the data, because the analytics software tools—which are part of this IoT process—suggest several good options. We just have to decide which one makes the most sense in our current situation.

As it turns out, everybody in the group can pick up the new business processes, as well as the other new processes that will follow, pretty quickly. IoT not only gives us the opportunity to do things differently, but it enables us to do them more simply. Smart IoT devices integrate into smart IoT systems, which can reduce manual processing and, in turn, reduce errors and complexity. With IoT, anyone who is generally aware of the capabilities and tools at their disposal can figure out what should be done when an opportunity presents itself. We all agree: We think we'll like this IoT stuff.

More and Different Workers

As it rolls out, IoT will require a lot of qualified workers. Many will be existing employees, particularly those who embrace change and can be retrained for IoT. There will also be a demand for new roles and new skills, especially those involving data and process. However, even with retraining or reorienting for IoT, a few roles will be rendered obsolete. Some standalone and manual tasks that don't require teamwork and collaboration, for example, are prime candidates for automation. Manual data collection tasks won't be needed if IoT devices generate the data and deliver it for processing to the analytics engines running in the fog and the cloud. Similarly, where analytics are built into an IoT process, the old ways of number crunching and analyzing data won't be necessary. As a result, we will also get by with fewer specialized experts and less on-site technical expertise. No matter where on the spectrum they fall, all workers will need orientation and at least some training in the new IoT-based thinking and processes.

Finding enough IoT-capable workers is the challenge. This is why the second item on my recipe for IoT success in Chapter 1 was *"Attract and train new and existing talent."* Whatever your industry, and no matter what service or product your company delivers, you will find yourself in global competition for talented workers. As the IoT-based economy drives trillions of dollars in economic growth, there will be a worldwide scramble for the same IoT-capable staff. These workers:

- Can handle IoT-based business processes
- Are data- and networking-aware
- Are comfortable with agile operations supported by data-driven decisions and business processes
- Are attuned to the API-, mobile-, and data-driven economy that was already emerging even before IoT began gaining traction and building the momentum we're witnessing today
- Have essential "soft" skills or emotional intelligence. They can:
  - Work across the organizational boundaries
  - Build and effectively execute within diverse virtual team environments
  - Influence agile thinkers to embrace new approaches rather than resist them

Competition for these workers is already fierce, and it will only grow more intense going forward. The industrial segments, including manufacturing, are seeking the same type of workers as Silicon Valley. In fact, some manufacturing segments are desperate for the right workers right now.

In the manufacturing and industrial commerce segments, for example, an overall efficiency trend is driving demand for more intelligent strategies and the people who can execute them. This, in turn, is driving the growth of connected devices—another way of saying IoT.

Manufacturers' investments in IoT will translate to billions in spending. According to John Greenough's March 11, 2016, *Business Insider* article,[1] analysts estimate that global manufacturers will invest $70 billion on IoT solutions in 2020. That's up from $29 billion in 2015. What they're doing with IoT initially is tracking assets in their factories, consolidating their control rooms, and increasing and enhancing predictive maintenance, which drives great payback through forward-looking real-time analytics. While many IoT solutions are still basic, analysts expect manufacturers to eventually implement more complex technologies, such as autonomous robots and augmented reality tools. These trends should excite potential new recruits.

"Pressures on manufacturing workforces are continuing to force companies to evolve. Some are looking to reduce fixed costs, such as headcount; others are struggling with a loss of expertise, with experienced operators retiring. Alongside this, the need to reduce downtime and improve supply chain visibility is ever present. As the current cycle of technology innovation progresses, companies are increasingly focusing on deriving value from collecting and analyzing data from their machines and plants. However, as machines themselves learn and gain their own experience, the dependency on unexperienced workers is reduced," commented Alex West, principal analyst at IHS, a leading provider of global market, industry, and technical expertise.

Although the growth of IoT may complicate recruitment, it's clearly aiding the adoption of automation in various forms. We've already touched on that in regard to more efficient manufacturing and commerce. But automation also includes new demands for remote communications, as well as remote monitoring and control. According to Mark Watson, associate director at IHS, "As manufacturers are being challenged to do more with less, the opportunity to bring together centralized hubs of expertise to support remote workers is well received. IoT-based solutions are also helping to bring customers closer to their suppliers, as service and support tasks are increasingly outsourced." All of this is further fueling IoT's growth and simultaneously boosting—in a directly related trend—the growth of

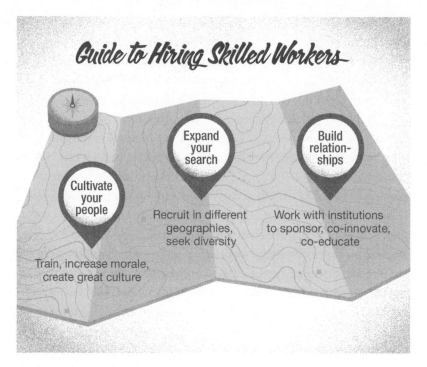

Figure 6.2   Hiring Guide

integrated intelligence, sensor networks, asset tracking, Internet connectivity, M2M communications, and energy measurement and management.
That, in turn, is driving an increase in IP connectivity for this sector.

Taken together, the projections of growth in just the industrial and
manufacturing segments suggest what promises to be an almost insatiable
need for IoT-savvy workers. Where companies will find them—especially
if they aren't located in the glamorous IoT hubs like Silicon Valley, New
York, Boston, and Houston, among a handful of others—will pose a se-
vere challenge that calls for creative solutions (Figure 6.2). The usual recruitment strategies simply won't suffice.

Finding Workers

The easy solution, the traditional solution, is to pay more. Publicize higher
salaries and attract more people. It's a good idea, but it doesn't appear to be

working. Silicon Valley companies already offer top salaries, and they still struggle to attract enough qualified candidates.

As I speak with companies around the world that are wrestling with this issue, the answer comes from an oddly quaint approach: Go back to the basics. Start by cultivating your own people. That means training them in IoT-related skills—not just the technology and processes but also soft skills such as virtual teaming and collaboration. Yes, you risk the possibility of another desperate company quickly wooing them away for these very same skills. And yes, a few of them probably will go elsewhere. You simply need to build that possibility into your model. In most cases, however, it's still easier and more economical to train and motivate your own employees than it is find, hire, and retain outside workers with the same skills.

If you establish a good relationship with your employees from the outset and further that relationship by being responsive to their interests and needs, you'll win. This is especially true when it comes to the current generation of workers, the much buzzed about Millennials. They want workplace input, flexibility, a better work/life balance, and opportunities to make public service contributions, among others. If your company provides such things, they're more likely to work hard and stay put. And because these are the same types of things most employees want anyway, providing them means you would be improving employee morale across the entire company.

The good news is that many traditional training companies, as well as some specialized IoT training organizations and some vendors themselves, are not only adding specific classes around IoT technologies, use cases, and business models but also creating comprehensive curricula that include soft skills and best practices in change management. That means you won't have to reinvent the wheel, just leverage what they've already started.

Next, expand your search. Engage with four-year colleges and universities, but also check out junior or community colleges and even high schools. Rockwell Automation, for example, runs a summer internship program for high-schoolers to extend its reach. Boeing, Northrop Grumman, and other manufacturers run similar programs. Look at the science, technology, engineering, and math (STEM) disciplines for sure, but don't ignore other areas such as communications, healthcare, and retail.

By the way, don't assume that it's sufficient to simply show up at the open-house day or recruiting event. Engage early and comprehensively; sponsor research; offer internships and, especially, joint projects between your company and the colleges. Such opportunities give students a first-hand, and one hopes positive, experience while working with your organization and employees, one that may make them more likely to join your team. "I loved the project I worked on with company X. People were smart, we had fun working together, and I felt we were making a big impact" is the type of statement you want to hear from participants. And you will hear it; I've heard it myself more than once.

Also, consider co-developing curricula with these institutions. If you need more data scientists, partner with the college to develop such classes, and then sponsor them, the accompanying labs, etc. Be creative; don't shy away from unorthodox and novel approaches. Take Siemens, for example. The company needed experts in mechatronics in its Charlotte, North Carolina, facility, according to a company press release from August 12, 2015.[2] Instead of taking the traditional hiring route, Siemens created an apprenticeship program in partnership with a local community college. Modeled after German-style apprenticeships, this four-year program offered a unique combination of on-the-job training and structured curriculum. Siemens was so pleased with the quality of the graduates that it decided to expand the program to several other locations throughout the United States. Paid apprenticeships are gaining traction again in the United States after years of decline. Companies from industry giants like Alcoa to small and medium-sized specialists such as Oberg Manufacturing have embraced this model. Many states and community colleges are starting to offer similar programs. To support these efforts, the U.S. government has recently earmarked $90M of grants as part of the Apprenticeship USA program. Another interesting approach to engage with the IoT community is to offer online courses in IoT technologies. I've seen IBM and other IoT players delivering these courses either by themselves or in partnership with the various massive open online course (MOOC) companies.

An additional area to explore is location tradeoffs. You will face fierce competition for talent at top colleges in top locations, such as Silicon Valley or Boston. But if you choose to work with colleges in, for example, Eastern Europe—which are well known for providing a quality education—you may get top students from this area clamoring to join your company. I've seen it happen.

According to Chris Lewis, industry analyst founder of Lewis Insight, "There are roughly a billion people in the world with different sorts of disabilities. IoT, coupled with smart devices and ubiquitous broadband, is opening up employment opportunities for people who would have previously been excluded from the workforce. Accessible technology will help everyone, not just the disabled. Those who want or need a location-independent lifestyle or one that is more flexible than the traditional nine to five will be able to participate and benefit from this IoT-led economy. All organizations can benefit from taking an accessibility-led design approach and having a more open attitude to let the world's disabled billion benefit from the technology, employment and the benefits of the digital environment in which we all live." Bottom line: Be inclusive and creative; consider how IoT broadens your candidate pool to encompass those whom Lewis refers to—the world's "disabled billion," military veterans, caregivers, parents, and others requiring greater flexibility and who can, and will, be huge advocates for you.

You also need to plan for continuing education and to redefine job requirements to include learning and relearning as mandatory skills. We'll discuss change management in the next chapter, but the point here is this: Don't assume that retraining your workforce is a one-time event or that you're done when you hire a data scientist. This is true for two reasons, the first of which is that you need your workers to internalize and adopt IoT, not just learn about it. That takes time and focus, so don't declare victory too soon. The second reason: IoT is a series of waves of changes that will impact your organization over the next 10 plus years. The capabilities, tools, and outcomes will continue to evolve rapidly. That's why whatever you're teaching your staff today will most likely be obsolete three years from now. Think of it like this: Your entire company needs to go back to school—regularly. As we discussed in Chapter 1, your mindset needs to be total reinvention every three to seven years and continuous learning. As an organization, either you learn and adopt or you die. That's the nature of transformative change.

With all of these possibilities, you should be able to find IoT staff. It may take some extra effort, but if you apply the best practices I discussed above, people should be willing to work with you. By adopting IoT you're giving employees an opportunity for today and astounding growth potential for the future. You're offering them a place in history, as well as an exhilarating experience. Who would turn down a future talked about in terms of trillions of dollars?

New Positions and Old Positions with a New Twist

The activities associated with IoT—cloud and fog computing, analytics, predictive analytics, remote monitoring and control, remote asset management, augmented reality, 3D printing, drones, and more—will involve a wide range of skills. Some will be new and some pre-existing, although even those skills are sure to be impacted by the new IoT-driven economy based on cloud computing and APIs. Out of necessity, this economy will be agile and require collaborative partnerships with a variety of organizations.

In that regard, we can expect to see the emergence of a specific type of organization: I call them IoT solution integrators. These companies will pull together the various pieces that comprise IoT and make it work as a seamless, fluid process or initiative. Integrators may be middleware developers, API creators, custom application developers, systems experts, and value-added providers of all sorts. By the way: They, too, will be hiring people and contributing to our trillions-of-dollars IoT economy. They will be part of the IoT ecosystem we previously discussed, and a few of them may even be part of your own IoT ecosystem.

After that, the first thing you'll notice about your IoT-enabled business is the increase in data flowing to and around the operation. Of course, you'll need people who can handle all of this data as it arrives; they'll know what to do with it and how to manage it efficiently and effectively. And they'll understand it. Some of that data may involve urgent alerts or signs of problems that need immediate attention. Other data may simply be informative and not require any immediate action beyond alerting the people who are interested in knowing it. To handle the systems responsible for all of this data, however, your team will require skills far beyond those of a traditionally trained database administrator (DBA). You'll need people who know your business processes and your product environments, as well as the technical aspects of data analytics. These are people who can learn how to store this data to ensure not only its security, availability, and integrity, but also that it meets your privacy guidelines. They will be able to create the rules and policies that will guide the analytics and intelligent processes behind IoT.

For example, someone at your organization will need to develop a rule or policy for what to do when an IoT message reports a problem with a critical device. This individual will have to define which person or thing receives the first-, second-, and third-level alerts, as well as what should happen when that person or thing receives the alert. Many such tasks require highly skilled, technical data gurus, but many may require just common sense and business sense. In fact, your employees will increasingly write these policies in plain, declarative English or as a list of simple steps. This could be an ideal role for process people.

Other job titles might be data flow organizer, device orchestrator, data manager, and data analyst. At the top of the data hierarchy may be the data scientist, the person who makes sense of the disparate data flowing in and out. In this emerging age of analytics, however, a data scientist for every organization may not be necessary. I expect all sorts of analytics applications to be developed, some horizontal or general purpose, but most vertical and specialized. These apps will have rules and policies to guide them. They will be intuitive and easily customized by simply tweaking a few parameters or inserting a couple of rules in plain declarative language; no special programming required. Alternatively, one or another of the IoT solution partners from your IoT ecosystem may bring in the desired analytics or build such intuitive human interfaces for you. (That may be why you selected them as partners in the first place.)

This isn't to say that you won't want access to programmers or various application developers or coders. You certainly will. As the data flows in, you'll have ideas—especially innovative ideas—of what to do with it to improve operations, better satisfy customers, or generate additional revenue by leveraging the data in a different way. For this, you'll want to work with people who can create the desired apps, APIs, and middleware to make it all work. Again, they can be in-house hires or, more likely, someone from the outside with whom you partner as part of your solution ecosystem.

You've heard me say this before, and I'm sure I'll say it again in many different ways before the end of this book: No organization can do IoT alone. Cisco and Rockwell Automation couldn't do it; I doubt you can, either. It will take a solution ecosystem of partners, contractors, freelancers, consultants, and specialists of different flavors to get the most out of IoT in your particular industry and for your specific situation. You may hire some of these people; the rest will be partners, either individuals or organizations. What form those associations take will be worked out among the team, because every situation is different and each player brings a select set of skills and talents.

Some of these people may form what amounts to a virtual team. You'll have direct hires, as well as partners' employees and/or independent contractors. Whatever the composition of this team, you manage it to work on your IoT solution. Modifications may have to be made to your standard business practices around hiring and contracting, and lawyers may be called in to address any intellectual property rights issues that arise. You may even have to rethink how you measure performance and what key performance indicators (KPIs) you use. These issues aren't in any way showstoppers. I've been working on them with Cisco and many of our partners for years, and they turn out to be surprisingly straightforward in the end.

IoT will change your IT staff, too, starting with the networking department. Traditional IT networking experts will have to learn new skills to accommodate IoT. Fog computing is just one piece. You do need people who are skilled in network architecture and design, network availability, network performance, and much more. IT people already know how to do these things. What's new is designing and implementing them consistently across your production or operational environments, your enterprise IT environments, and the cloud, as well as integrating legacy environments with new IoT capabilities—and doing all of this at IoT scale. Think about it: You'll have a growing collection of new intelligent devices on your IPv6 network, each of which will be collecting, sending, and receiving information 24×7.

The network will eventually have to be prepared for continuous IoT traffic and to handle that traffic while ensuring performance, high availability, and security. And that's just the beginning. There will also be different applications with different performance, processing, and real-time requirements. Your virtual organization and virtual teams will include multiple in-house departments, integrators, partners, contractors, and solution providers. These new architectures and systems will need to accommodate all of these models and scenarios in secure ways.

Your current networking people may be capable of much of this. However, the volume and variety of the traffic, as well as the speed at which data are coming and going will quickly grow beyond what a human staff can handle manually. It's no longer a question of recruiting and hiring more IT staff; that isn't a practical way of solving these problems. You'll need to deploy automation, analytics, and predictive analytics to avoid being overwhelmed by the flood of traffic and data and to truly make such data useful for your business. We discussed the business benefits behind applying the right analytics to data in Chapter 5. I'm not talking about the vast flood of global IoT traffic—the trillions and trillions analysts predict. I'm only talking about the IoT traffic centered around your operation. Even this relatively low volume of activity will overwhelm a human staff if it isn't automated, architected at scale, and supported by analytics. Thus, your IT staff will face a dilemma: ignore the data coming their way or build automated policy-based systems to harness it to benefit your operation.

In addition, you'll need to think about all of the work involved with your business processes, as well as the changes to those processes and workflows that IoT will necessitate. You will, of course, want to change those processes, and change them again and again and again, as your business, your operations, and your customers change in response to what will likely be a rapidly evolving business environment. Remember, one of the main reasons we are attracted to IoT in the first place is to streamline operations, which entails continuous business process change and improvement as business environments and technology tools evolve. Another reason is to find new go-to-market strategies and new business models. These, too, will require massive changes to existing business processes or, more likely, the adoption of entirely new business workflows.

You probably already have at least one person or even a few people who focus on maintaining and managing workflows and business processes. Now, with the IoT wave coming, you may want to invest in business process orchestrators and coordinators, along with business process designers and developers. This is just to keep up with what will likely evolve into highly dynamic IoT-driven environments that need to be continually monitored, maintained, and updated if you want to achieve the full payback you envisioned at the outset.

Then there are the process designers, who used to be called efficiency experts, who study business processes and figure out the best ways to implement them. What we require now, however, addresses more than just conventional efficiency. Today, process designers look at the entire workflow of what amounts to multiple compounded processes. They then find the most efficient and cost-effective way to both handle these processes end-to-end and ensure each process delivers the quality and service customers will demand. In effect, with IoT you have an opportunity to reengineer large swaths of your business to improve quality, customer service, efficiency, and productivity, all while saving money through automation and process redesign. That's the payback we've been discussing.

At this point, I could go on and on, but let's stop here with security, privacy, and compliance. We've touched on security a bit, and we'll get into it more later. For now, I just want to note that you'll need expertise to handle the new security challenges IoT poses. Putting up and maintaining a firewall in front of a PC on the manufacturing floor won't be enough. It's insufficient even today. Imagine what could happen when hundreds or thousands of devices are continually communicating and exchanging information.

So you'll need to recruit and hire and/or partner with security people who will be responsible for identifying and authorizing the good guys while intercepting and deflecting the bad guys looking to sneak in and wreak havoc—from either the outside or the inside—among your approved traffic. You'll need to deploy systems that quickly identify both hacks and attempted hacks, as well as what data has been compromised. And you'll need to deploy systems that minimize the damage. While you're at it, you'll need to set policies and monitor what's happening in terms of privacy and compliance.

The industry is actively involved in bolstering IoT security. This field will continue to evolve rapidly, and there will never be enough security experts for hire. So in addition to an in-house security staff, plan on building a security ecosystem, as well as partnering with your peers and others. Don't think of security as a competitive advantage. Think of it as the area in which you and your entire industry, including your competitors, work collaboratively. We're all in this together against the bad guys. If it isn't done right, security concerns may prevent you from opening up your systems and implementing IoT solutions—and thus prevent you from achieving IoT's benefits. In the end, security shouldn't be a showstopper. It is, however, something you'll want to stay on top of. You need to be prepared to devote your own people to security, even as you leverage your ecosystems and continue to discover and implement automated tools and analytics to address the various related issues.

Interesting IoT Careers

Everything and anything is possible when everything is digitized and communicates over IP (Figure 6.3). In fact, one of the first positions your company will want to fill is that of "IoT visionary." This person will follow IoT and think about what might be possible with it and what it could mean to your organization. Perhaps the candidate for this position is you;

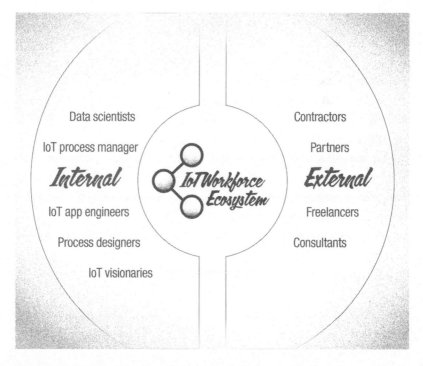

Figure 6.3   Internal and External Career Choices

by reading this book, you've obviously been thinking about IoT and your organization.

The IoT visionary need not be a scientist or an engineer. He or she isn't being asked to invent, engineer, or build IoT. What this visionary really needs to be is inquisitive, thoughtful, and something of a maverick, because the business and its processes need to be looked at in new, possibly unconventional ways. Of course, the visionary also needs to be well versed in the company's current business processes but not so familiar with them that he or she can't introduce changes—and be willing and able to take flack for those changes, if necessary. Every organization has its "sacred cows" and these, too, will be subjected to the IoT visionary's rigorous appraisal. This person must be attuned to the advancements in not only your industry but other industries affected by IoT. The goal is to spot a trend or use case being implemented or solved in one industry, and then determine whether such a solution can be adopted or adapted to address your company's challenges.

What the IoT visionary will need most is executive support, trust, and willingness to build relationships—and to know where the skeletons are buried—while remaining objective. When everything is digitized *and* can communicate with everything else, anything can change. Although not everything will change, much of it might and probably should. Ultimately, IoT will become synonymous with change.

IoT will also provide an opportunity for the problem-solvers in your organization. First, they should focus on old problems that can be solved now that things can collect data, communicate, and follow directions. This step applies to the vast number of problems that can benefit from the four categories of use cases we discussed in the previous chapter, beginning with remote operations. You can then move quickly beyond those low-hanging fruit, the easy pickings.

Take, for example, the emergence of drones. (Picture drones as IoT devices that can fly and communicate interactively.) Amazon is thinking of drones as inexpensive vehicles with which goods can be delivered to buyers. This might or might not be a smart move, but if you think about drones as something that can go places humans can't easily access, from cell towers to pipelines, then you can imagine a number of interesting use cases—many of which may also entail remote monitoring and control. Others may involve public safety or health.

The point is that IoT offers the opportunity to think about your organization in new and different ways. For instance:

- What could I do if I could put a smart meter in a hazardous site and it could alert me if a measurement is too high or too low?
- What could I do if I could put a controller in a remote location and it could turn a particular piece of equipment on or off under certain conditions?
- What could I do to improve my customers' experiences with my product if I could know what each customer does with it and how it's working, and then make adjustments on the fly?

OK, these aren't exactly earthshaking ideas, but that's part of the point of IoT. It doesn't have to be momentous to deliver an initial payback. Think about the earlier example of predictive maintenance deep in a mine. That application was about as mundane as it gets, yet it saved a couple million dollars a day when something went wrong. Maybe it is mundane, but who wouldn't take that result in a flash?

Government's Role in IoT

Government has a clear role to play in IoT. We discussed smarter cities through the example of Barcelona and the positive impact IoT implementations can have on the environment. The success there was driven extensively by the government. Increasingly, governments around the world are beginning to realize that IoT adoption will be one of the key factors defining the competitiveness of their cities, provinces, countries, or regions and that IoT can help solve many of the chronic problems plaguing their economies and their environments. Thus, governments at various levels have a number of key roles to play:

- **Regulators.** There will be competition for bandwidth and other resources; there will be ideas that may conflict with public policy; and there will be dubious IoT-based ideas that may present a public safety threat or privacy concern. Think drones.

These devices will need to be regulated and mediated in a variety of ways. On the other hand, government regulations can help direct and align the industry. Here are a few examples of U.S. legislations and the impact of each:

- The Energy Act drove the need for energy monitoring, including smart meters.
- The Rail Safety Improvement Act specified the requirements and the deadline (since extended) for adoption of Positive Train Control on main U.S. railways.
- The Food Safety Modernization Act drove the requirements for IoT-based systems, including quality control and source tracking, across the food supply chain to prevent food safety issues.
- Then there is the most recent Drug Quality and Security Act, which requires the adoption of a system to identify and trace prescription drugs.

Government agencies play a part in these efforts, as well. Take, for example, compliance with standards. The U.S. government recently mandated adoption of version 5 of the North American Electric Reliability Corporation (NERC) Common Industrial Protocol (CIP)—I know, not a very user-friendly name!—cyber-security standard in the energy industry. For these and other laws and actions to be effective, the government and its agencies need to work closely with the industry.

- **Agenda setters.** Who represents the public's interests in the rush to IoT? Say the government decides it has a vested interest in getting private cars off the road to reduce congestion, save energy, and lower pollution. It must, in turn, encourage the development of autonomous vehicles and other energy-saving initiatives. We've seen plenty of positive examples of government involvement in such efforts, including co-funding autonomous car research and industry test beds as well as issuing new policies aimed at accelerating the adoption of such vehicles. Another example is privacy, where governments help explore various models, boundaries, and best practices associated with sharing customer data, as well as with customers' control over their data. The January 2015 Federal Trade Commission (FTC) Staff Report on the Internet of Things, Privacy, and Security in the Connected World, recommended that the U.S. Congress "enact broad-based (as opposed to IoT-specific) privacy legislation. Such legislation should be flexible and technology-neutral, while also providing clear rules of the road for companies about such issues as how to provide choices to consumers about data collection and use practices."[3] Similarly, governments are increasingly advocating for public health. Because IoT has the potential to monitor individuals' health through a variety of wearables, the government—in conjunction with hospitals and a variety of healthcare providers and insurers—clearly has the public's interests in mind with these types of efforts.

- **Adopters.** Through their spending power, governments can drive the focus and accelerate the adoption of IoT technologies and solutions. In aggregate, governments represent a huge global market. Their priorities, what they choose to buy, and what problems they choose to address can drive the roadmaps of IoT technology and solution providers. Military requirements, for example, have accelerated the technology development and adoption of drones, wearables, sensors (especially bio-sensors), and many IoT communication technologies.

Other government roles include:

- Supporting training and education
- Supporting development of startup ecosystems
- Supporting standards efforts
- Supporting basic research and development
- Enabling competitiveness and openness of the country's markets
- Promoting best practices and modern business models

Globally, governments are already becoming involved. According to Bettina Tratz-Ryan, research VP at Gartner, "Making sound technology investments is a key responsibility of senior government officials, whether they came into their roles prepared to do so or not. Government leaders who assume their roles with a 'digital first' mindset intuitively understand how making significant investments in IT is key to optimizing the costs of program operations, and they are prepared to do so."[4]

In Germany, Industry 4.0 implementation is addressing intelligent manufacturing, that is, applying the tools of information technology to production. In the German context, this primarily means using IoT to connect small and midsize companies more efficiently in global production and innovation networks so they can not only more efficiently engage in mass production but just as easily and efficiently customize products. Similar initiatives sprang up in many countries from Made in China 2025 to Turkey 2023. We also increasingly see private companies and governments forming private/public partnerships. Country digitization initiatives, such as those signed by Cisco and the governments of several countries in Europe, are good examples. Global organizations like the World Economic Forum are becoming involved, too, as both enablers and environments in which many complex topics can be discussed, debated, and agreed on among the government and for-profit and non-profit institutions.

Private enterprise, driven by market needs, is certainly in the best position to spearhead the development of IoT and the continuing innovation that will be required as it evolves and changes. But governments and public interest groups have a valid place in the development and adoption of IoT, too. Let's welcome that.

IoT Visionaries—Yes, This Will Be a Career, Starting Now

Do you think you're ready to be an IoT visionary for your organization? Try this fun mind exercise (mind exercises are homework). Just relax, pour yourself a glass of wine, and think through these points:

- What can change when things communicate with other things via the cloud and the fog (enabling real-time analytics)? How would you re-envision existing processes, business strategies, and customer relationships?
- What are the problems that you know have to be solved and the processes that you know should be improved or fixed?

- What are the problems that you haven't been able to solve because you didn't have the right tools (technical or organizational)?
- How would you solve old problems in new and better ways (start by thinking remote operations and predictive analytics)?
- What new operations, new processes, and new strategies would you like to see?
- How would you solve new problems or take advantage of new opportunities that arise from IoT (think new business models, disruptive practices, and go-to-market strategies)?
- How can you engage with new customers, meet different needs, and work in new ways?

In the process of addressing these points, you've just reimagined your organization and your workforce in the wake of IoT. Now identify one or two that you want to tackle first; these should be the top-priority early wins you know your organization can achieve in the next 12 months. Where would you start?

Let's take this exercise one step further. In Chapter 5, we discussed the immediate, low-hanging fruit categories of use cases that are ripe for implementation today. We also know that IoT isn't a one-time event, from either the technology or the business and organizational perspectives, and that IoT will continue to evolve. Here are a few examples of new capabilities and technologies that, alongside IoT, can position your business for success in the new IoT economy:

- **Remote expertise.** For this straightforward use-case picture an engineer using a tablet or a smartphone equipped with a camera. When pointed at a faulty valve on the manufacturing floor, that device enables a remote expert to see it and diagnose the problem. Yes, we can do that today!
- **Virtual reality (VR).** We've all seen the big VR goggles that are supposed to be the next big thing in gaming, but we can also apply them—together with game engines—in the IoT business world. Think about training your employees and contractors on how to operate a piece of machinery, evacuate a mine, or perform a safety procedure, all from the lab before they go into the field. It is also a perfect tool to train your new hires based on the experience of your long-time employees. Now think about how much faster your employees can become productive and how much safer your operation can be.

- **Augmented reality (AR).** People keep talking about Google Glass and Microsoft Halo, but the industrial, ruggedized AR goggles like those used by engineers on an oil rig make immediate sense. Control engineers can use them to capture cycle times, vibrations, and other operations and maintenance data or diagnose problems without physically holding a diagnostic tool in their hands. For these engineers, AR goggles mean they have both hands available, don't need to carry equipment, and are still able to acquire the data they need. Think of it as having remote experts diagnosing problems, not by using today's remote cameras but by being digitally present on that oil rig, seeing what you see. The AR software can even overlay the step-by-step instructions for you on how to fix the device. Or imagine doctors entering patients' hospital rooms equipped with names, medical histories, and diagnoses all in front of their eyes. But that's just the beginning. The industry is experimenting with AR as a tool for rapid prototyping, accelerating the path from idea to production. Applications are just starting to emerge, but I expect them to be widely adopted and very impactful.

- **Location awareness.** IoT technology can help account for and locate people, animals, and things. Among the many applications are man-down situations in hazardous locations such as refineries, mines, or oil fields; missing children and seniors; endangered species of animals in the national park or cows on the farm; contractors who end up lost while looking for a specific doohickey in one of a home improvement superstore's myriad aisles; and workers trying to pinpoint the tools and other equipment in a massive construction project, across a vast oil field, on a long-haul airplane, or in a container ship. And let's not forget the leased heavy machinery in India described in a prior example. Other applications include inventory management and intelligent manufacturing, where every part has an IP address and can be located and managed in real time. And then there are new business opportunities build on top of IoT and location awareness: Remember the example of Veniam's digital advertising platform in taxis and buses?

- **Robots.** Already moving beyond the manufacturing floor, robots are now being used for inspections and repairs in hazardous environments such as highly toxic tanks. The robotics field is evolving rapidly and new classes of robots are going mainstream. One such example are cobots (collaboration robots) that can feel forces and thus can be hand-guided.

- **Artificial Intelligence (AI).** Now let's give robots more intelligence: Imagine that instead of sending two people to survey and diagnose a potential problem in a mine, you send a robot that not only diagnoses the problem but also makes intelligent decisions on how to fix it—maybe by consulting with a team of experts or using its own judgment. I believe that, over time, intelligent robots will become our co-workers, partnering with us on automated tasks and contributing by making complex intelligent decisions. It's compelling and yet scary at the same time. Intelligent robots are just one of the areas of focus for AI. Machine learning and recently perfected deep-learning techniques are enabling all kinds of new IoT applications from video analytics and self-learning networks to real-time predictive analytics of machinery.

- **Context-aware experiences.** Consumer companies provide such services now. For example, a map app on a smartphone can deduce you're planning to leave for home, so it proactively tells you that traffic is normal and that it will take you around 24 minutes to reach your destination. Now think about all of the amazing applications of context awareness in a business setting. As we discussed earlier, by combining the weather forecast, wind history, energy requirement patterns, characteristics of the materials used, and so forth, a wind farm can make intelligent decisions about which units to turn on and where to point them ahead of time, thereby optimizing energy generation while maximizing the life of the equipment.

- **Mobile experience (anywhere, anytime).** I don't know about you, but I'm addicted to my smartphone. And then I show up on a manufacturing floor and have to use a stationary HMI device attached to a robot. I and many others, including the Millennials who have grown up with these tools, want to use tablets and phones as HMIs. The good news is that the industry is moving in this direction.

- **Autonomous vehicles.** Although getting to a complete (level 5), passenger-ready autonomous vehicle capability may take a while (despite the fact that all major players from Ford, Tesla to Uber are rushing to test, pilot and enable such functionality), autonomous trucks are quickly becoming a reality. You've probably already seen reports in the news about the fleets of autonomous trucks being tested around the globe. It's simply easier to program and operate a fleet of trucks running on the autobahn between two dispatch and delivery centers than it is to anticipate all of the corner cases for a passenger vehicle. Thus, we're going to see soon autonomous trucks deliver parts and become an integral part of the real-time supply chain ecosystem.

- **Addressable parts.** Think about what your supply chain and your production facility would look like if every part had an IPv6 address.

How would you manage your production differently? How would you streamline your back-end production? Get ready; it's coming.

Can you envision yourself or your organization involved in any of the above? Relax; it might just be as enjoyable as it is exciting.

I've given you a lot to think about in terms of how IoT can change your business and your career. You're probably thinking your organization could never embark on this much change. Fear not: The next chapter takes up change management. And yes, you can do it.

7 | Bringing IoT Into Your Organization— Change Management

People generally dislike change. It disrupts the familiar and the comfortable. Change forces you to rethink what were previously routine actions that required no new thought. It requires familiarizing yourself with new processes and procedures. In many cases, change requires the acquisition of new skills. It is, however, inevitable. Over time, everything changes. By the time we're adults we understand this, even if we don't like it, even if we don't agree with the new direction that results from change. Some people may choose to resist a particular transformation, but resistance to change isn't usually successful. In most cases, change is unavoidable because the world is dynamic.

IoT has emerged as both an agent of dramatic change and the result of global forces that drive change. Think of how the automobile ended the era of the horse and buggy, and then went on to reshape modern society in ways both good and bad, but mainly good. Can you even imagine what your life would be like if there were no automobiles or the automotive infrastructure that arose to support it? Similarly, the cloud and the Internet put an end to the era of proprietary computing, replacing it with Internet/

147

cloud-centric information for everyone, anywhere, anytime. Just try to imagine how you would live and work without the Internet. At best, it would be a big stretch to maintain the same quality of life.

And now IoT has arrived, ushering in yet another era of radical business and social change. I'm sure many people a century and a half ago weren't happy with the arrival of the automobile. But as soon as Henry Ford and a few others pioneered automobiles for the masses, there was no going back. IoT will drive changes of that magnitude, including revolutionizing the transportation industry again, and we have no choice but to adapt. But why settle for merely adapting? Let's make the most of IoT. Let's try to capitalize on it as quickly and as much as we can. That's why I wrote this book.

Exploding ATM Solution

A bank in Africa had a serious problem with theft at a certain style of automated teller machine. Some of the thieves install fake ATMs, some tamper with card scanners, while others use crowbars or jackhammers to dislodge the ATM's facing to reach the cash stored behind it. The money is still gone, but at least the facility is left pretty much intact. One group of thieves, however, took a different approach: They used jackhammers and concussion drills to create space behind the ATM in which to place dynamite, blew up the entire facility, and then dashed back in and grabbed whatever cash they could reach. With this tactic, the bank lost both the cash and the facility, which was a total loss. This didn't have to happen too often before the bank was determined to find a solution.

Can you guess what it was? Here's a hint: This is a book about IoT. So yes, the bank devised an IoT solution. It embedded intelligent sensors, mainly motion detectors, at various places in the ATM facility, along with a camera for full on-demand visibility. Now, as soon as a thief hits the ATM—from any angle and with any type of tool—these sensors detect the unacceptable motion, vibration, sound, or concussion and then generate widespread alarms. Thieves are immediately aware that they've been detected. Lights flash, alarms sound, and voice commands are barked out, generally leading to great confusion and panic. Before they even have time to place explosives and destroy the ATM, most thieves dash out and often are grabbed by the police as officers converge on the location from all directions.

Thanks to IoT, the bank not only prevents a theft, which saves the money, but also preserves the ATM facility intact, which is worth more than any cash that may have been lost. This use of IoT proved to have a very good return on investment.

IoT Solutions

IoT solutions to common and sometimes not-so-common problems you may be experiencing are coming to your industry or area soon, if they aren't there already. These are mainly variations on the four fast payback models that we've previously discussed. The African bank's ATM solution is actually a variation of IoT-based remote operations and monitoring. All the bank needed was the fast, fog-based real-time analytics to translate sensor readings into an immediate realization that the initial stages of an ATM heist were underway and subsequently trigger instant alarms.

But specific IoT solutions or particular IoT technologies like fog computing and machine learning aren't really what this book is about. It's about almost exactly the opposite: business change. With IoT, you aren't implementing a solution or a technology; you're implementing a change in the business process. You have to start and finish by thinking about the business process and the changes to that process. In between there will be technologies, solutions, and ecosystem partners, all of them just a means to the end. What's actually important is the impact delivered by business process change, and perhaps even business transformation. So approach IoT holistically; think about change in a business process, and about the change management required before you implement any technology.

I've seen this point repeatedly neglected, by both customers and vendors. In fact, too often the sole focus of the team developing a new IoT solution is on new technology. When the expected results don't materialize, the answer usually lies in either not thinking through the new technology in the context of the existing business process or not changing the business process to accommodate the integration of a new technology. Consider remote operations. The implementation of such a solution without a corresponding change in business process will lead to disappointing outcomes. You'll have a great tool implemented in your plant, but unless you change how plant personnel manages assets, train them to use the new tool, and enforce the new behavior, you'll just waste your money. If this is your first IoT project, your main hope for an early win, you'll also jeopardize your organization's broader IoT initiative. I know I sound like a broken record, but please think of technology solution and business process as two sides of the same coin. They must be approached together. And yes, as you may recall, *"Integrate technology solutions with business processes"* is one of the critical elements in my recipe for IoT success.

Organizations have faced big change before. Six Sigma asked everybody to change. Business process reengineering asked for big changes or, if not, for laying off lots of people. Managers were eager to let people go and boost their bottom lines, but they never quite followed through on the process changes. Lean manufacturing, integrated supply chain management, and enterprise resource planning were also going to change the organizations. Again, companies chalked up some exciting wins and Harvard Business School professors wrote impressive books, but most managers couldn't realize the gains promised in those books—at least not on their own. I understand if you're skeptical about deep business change and the paybacks possible through IoT. Unlike other books, however, I'm not asking you to do anything radical to start with.

What I'm really asking you to do is execute business change through the vehicle of IoT. Start by recognizing that IoT is neither a one-time event nor a single transition for your business; it's a multi-year transformation that should deliver tangible paybacks with every step. IoT is a journey. As mentioned in the recipe for IoT success, you should *"Prepare for a journey, not a one-time event,"* and then be ready to reinvent yourselves as employees and managers, to reinvent your company, and to reinvent your entire industry every three to seven years. Think about the old computer game, The Oregon Trail, where early settlers packed all of their belongings, loaded them on the wagons, and left their old lives behind to find a better future. In that sense, the IoT journey (Figure 7.1) is a multi-year expedition across many peaks and valleys, and sometimes it may even feel like a rollercoaster

Figure 7.1   The IoT Journey

ride. It will be disorienting and exhilarating, anxious and delightful, scary and thrilling all at once. IoT is different from all of those other business transformation options; it's not Six Sigma or BPR or Lean. Unlike them, you can't ignore IoT and still expect to thrive or even survive.

Think about the fast payback ideas listed in Chapter 5. They focused on improving existing business processes, making them more efficient. And they're likely to be your initial successes, your first IoT wave. Some will be opportunistic; most will be low-hanging fruit. Many will be focused on the B2B impact. But soon enough, these changes will lead to more disruptive ideas with deeper, more transformative impacts. Some of the disruptive technologies, such as machine learning, drones, autonomous vehicles, blockchain, and predictive context, will lead to the next IoT waves. Your business environments and your consumer experiences (also known as business-to-business-to-consumer or B2B2C) will change dramatically. Examples like the mass customization or even individualization of cars or motorcycles or enhanced shopping experiences will place consumers in the driver's seat and, in the process, differentiate businesses that offer these capabilities. Not only will existing business operations be transformed but so, too, will business models. New value will be created; new business will be generated. Yes, it will indeed be a journey across many hills and valleys, starting from efficiency and leading to new ways of making money and delivering value to consumers. As soon as you conquer a hill in front of you, the next peak will appear, even more exciting and challenging.

With that in mind, the rest of this chapter will focus on change management in the context of IoT. You can expect to see different versions of the IoT-based enterprise coming to your organization or industry soon. For example, data scientists, plant engineers, and remote operators are already teaming up to centrally operate plants. In other cases, organizations are beginning to combine a variety of advanced technologies (like the ones we discussed at the end of the previous chapter). Among these technologies are immersive collaboration tools, as well as high-density Wi-Fi networks to visually captivate an audience and engage them interactively through a compelling mobile digital experience. Customers in every industry are ramping up their expectations, fast. They want convenience, personalization, and new opportunities and experiences. IoT brings the capabilities to deliver on these expectations sooner rather than later.

In every industry, endeavor, or activity, IoT will change how you operate and compete. It will do so sooner than you can undertake a typical three-year strategic plan. IoT will change worker, company, partner, and stakeholder experiences and expectations. As we discussed in the previous chapter, business processes, product development, support, customer service, go-to-market strategies, supply chain management and logistics, and more are changing as you read this book.

Change Management Required

Enough books, scholarly papers, seminars, conferences, conventions, and the like already keep everyone supplied with everything they could ever want to know about change management, so I won't focus on that here. (If you need a tutorial on change management, it's easy enough to find. Start with the Internet and simply search "change management.")

Instead, let's talk about something I said in the very first chapter and reiterated earlier in this chapter: Be prepared to reinvent yourselves as employees, as a company, and as an industry every three to seven years. That has been going on since long before IoT arrived, and it will continue long after whatever follows IoT emerges.

This much is sure: Jobs and work life will surely change. Thus, at this point, what you need to care about change management is three things: communicate, communicate, and communicate. IoT will impact you; your staff, customers, and partners; other stakeholders; and regulators. Don't leave any of them guessing about what will come next; communicate early and often. You want to avoid surprises, especially unwelcome ones. And some surprises will surely be unwelcome; for example, some jobs will change, some will be repurposed, and some will be completely eliminated. If you're planning to let IoT handle remote operations, you'll certainly want to communicate that fact as soon as possible to those people who currently perform such tasks. But, as we discussed in the previous chapter, there will be no shortage of new jobs relating to IoT. You need to give people enough notice and then help them position themselves for new opportunities.

Another intriguing aspect of IoT transformation is that traditional distinctions become blurry. With IoT, every organization can be a product, service, data, or technology company—or some or all of these concurrently. An organization could shift from one to another and back as frequently as needed to meet customer or market demands. It's hard to say exactly what the circumstances would be, but with IoT it's all possible and not difficult to do technically once IoT is in place.

Change as the New Status Quo

Expect technical, workforce, process, and career changes to become the norm. Cultural changes, too, may become a new way of life. In addition, expect changes to salary tiers, seniority, and even pay scales. Is this disconcerting? Probably, but it needn't be.

The IoT environment should be less rigid and more flexible, and it should enable new organizational constructs. Today, for example, a manufacturing plant's operating team is physically located at the plant. With

IoT that may not be the case. High-speed global IP networks mean that the team can be in any location, as well as spread across multiple locations. Where do you want to work and live? You can reside anywhere, as long as you have access to fast, reliable IP service. IoT can end the days of playing location arbitrage when it comes to people in B2B environments.

Remote operation and automation, for example, reduces the need to locate certain facilities in low-wage locations. Along the same lines, Silicon Valley and Rust Belt companies will now compete for the same talent. This is neither good nor bad; it's just what's possible and starting to happen. Employees in B2B companies could reside in low-cost-of-living areas while receiving top salaries. Location becomes a personal choice, not a salary determinant.

I wonder how many startups are now being bought by manufacturing vendors far from their location? How many high-tech execs now work for car and transportation companies in distant regions? With IoT we no longer need to match incentives, expectations, and geography. It enables us to bridge any geographic divide, as well as blur the lines between industries. With so much technology being poured into a modern car, when do we consider it a mobile datacenter and not just a transportation device?

Think about my home, Silicon Valley. Over the past two years, how many technology executives have moved to work for transportation companies both large and small? And can you find a car company that doesn't have a research or technology hub here? Same goes for the venture capital and mergers and acquisitions (M&A) arms of large manufacturing firms— they all set up shops in the valley. According to a February 9, 2016, press release from professional services firm PricewaterhouseCoopers, the levels of industrial IoT M&A are hitting 10-year highs.[1] At the same time, funding for IoT startups is rapidly growing, noted CB Insights in a March 3, 2016, blog post.[2] Increasingly, high-tech companies and industrial or transportation companies co-invest together. I already work with many of them; for example, Siemens and Cisco are investors in Ravi Belani's Alchemist Accelerator and its IoT track.

No wonder so many industrial company CEOs bring their executive teams to Silicon Valley every few months. Their hundred-year-old business models, ecosystems, and go-to-market strategies are being disrupted, and they're trying to figure out how IoT technology and business model changes are going to impact their companies and their industries. What business will they be in, in a few years? Who will be their customers? With whom will they compete? Will their companies survive?

Why is this happening? Because the worlds of high tech and industry are converging. Ten years ago, you would never see executives from Rockwell Automation or ABB and Cisco or Microsoft sitting in the same room. We were operating on different planets. Now, these industries are starting to come together (Figure 7.2). We've already talked about both groups looking to attract the same talent.

These are just a few indicators of the broader trend. In the next 10 years many industries will morph, new industries will emerge, and the missions and scope of companies will expand or shift. Change is the new status quo.

IT/OT Convergence and Other Workforce Issues

The list of workforce issues that require change management is endless, but let's start with one I know best: the convergence of information technology and operational technology. It's almost the first issue to arise in any production situation around IoT.

As IoT multiplies, the networked connections among people, process, data, and things expand exponentially. And as the worlds of IT and OT begin to converge, a culture clash is usually close behind. I highlighted this issue in the recipe for IoT success: *"Transform culture along with technology."* OT leaders, for instance, may be confounded when IT schedules a weekend shutdown to update software without regard for production requirements. IT leaders, meanwhile, view OT as resistant to modern technology because of their use of proprietary, closed and specialized systems. IT is deeply concerned with cyber security, but OT has traditionally relied on the physical isolation of its systems for security.

This does not appear, at least initially, to be a marriage made in heaven. However, both parties will need to work together—sooner rather than later. Too much potential value is at stake. The fast paybacks described in Chapter 5 all rely on the data flowing from the plant to the IT infrastructure and then to the cloud. We can't accomplish these without IT and OT cooperating at the technological, architectural, and, yes, organizational levels.

The worlds of high tech and established industries are converging. Industrial businesses are being disrupted by new IoT technologies.

IT and OT leaders are starting to cooperate at all levels. OT is embracing open, IT-like technologies, and IT is becoming a business and process partner.

Figure 7.2   IoT Driving Convergence

Despite this potential culture clash, over the past decade or so OT and other LOB functions have increasingly adopted IT-like technologies, such as Ethernet/IP and cloud services. At the same time, IT is becoming more of a business partner, with a better understanding of its role in accomplishing key business and operational objectives. As I said earlier, I often compare this situation to the book *Men Are from Mars, Women Are from Venus* by John Gray.

Indeed, the solution is pretty similar to Gray's suggestions on how to improve the way men and women communicate: Get these groups to speak frankly to each other. As the change management agent, you need to urge the IT and the OT people to simply sit down and talk to each other. Then let them argue, hurl accusations, and bring up past grievances from a decade ago; just let it all fly. Eventually, they'll realize that IoT is too valuable to the business and come to a mutual understanding around IoT procedures. Such session have been conducted in thousands of plants and offices already, and any blood on the floor is easily wiped up, so don't worry.

From there on it gets easier. Communication is the biggest obstacle, and you've just started with the hardest part. After that come negotiation, mediation, and conflict resolution. But because people have started talking with each other, anything can be worked out. You may soon be ready to identify and execute a small, IoT-specific projects that can deliver a fast win. (Flip back to Chapter 5 and pick an example that can deliver a quick payback, perhaps something around remote operations.) Once you have a winning project under your belt, people will readily line up to participate in the follow-on efforts.

As we focus on the IT/OT convergence and the adoption of IoT, let's not forget that most of the IoT implementation will happen in the brownfield environments of existing locations or businesses. Similarly, even while many tasks evolve and become automated, it's critically important to capture and leverage the practical knowledge both OT and IT practitioners have accumulated over many decades. I'll use my father-in-law as an example. For decades, he worked as the chief technologist at one of the steel mills. When he retired several years ago, his company asked him to continue as a consultant, even as new generations of managers arrived and implemented automated IoT processes. Why? Because his practical expertise, developed over 40-plus years, was so unique. He knew, for example, how to formulate steel to meet unique specialized requirements.

So the company did the right thing and tapped into his knowledge and experience as the foundation of its automated decision systems.

I can list many such examples. So, as your OT experts approach retirement age, make sure their practical knowledge doesn't disappear when they leave the workforce. Be proactive about documenting and capturing their insights, both in automated systems and by transferring their knowledge to younger workers.

Changing Roles and Golden Opportunities

If it hasn't become apparent yet, people will have new roles. Will the chief information officer become the chief IoT officer instead? Will LOB managers become change agents? How will the plant control engineer's role change in the face of IoT and automation? Will you need a chief supply chain management officer? Can one person handle the information security office? What about the top data administrator? Does he or she become the chief data officer? Who will oversee integration, compliance, and logistics, among other things? These questions don't need to be answered immediately, but somebody—or more likely a handful of somebodies—needs to start thinking about this, talking about it, and eventually making some decisions.

Another interesting area that will change revolves around your products and services and their development. How will your IoT-based products be conceived, developed, supported, priced, and marketed? How many forms will they take? How will customers find them, buy them, and receive them? Remember our earlier discussion about the different ways you can buy a book or a car? This must be thoroughly considered for your company, your products and services, and your industry.

To be clear, IoT transformation creates a golden opportunity, one that doesn't come often—you have the opportunity to completely rethink your products, services, and development from the ground up. What will emerge is the chance to totally reinvent your product, company, industry, and market. Can you use IoT to sell and deliver your product as a service on a subscription basis? If so, what would the economics of that look like? Think about it.

Some industries may be utterly disrupted. Others may experience barely a ripple. The opportunities, however, are there for products and services, the same ones you have today—or different. There will be new ways to go to market and new markets to serve, with new and different products and services delivered in new and different ways. I don't know about you, but for me just thinking about it can be very exciting. With IoT, anything can become a greenfield opportunity ready to be explored anew.

Say your company produces airplanes today. But with the advent of drones, autonomous cars, and the super-fast Hyperloops, will you still be making these aircraft 20 years from now? Will you be in the airplane-making business, the transportation business, or the mobility business? The car industry is already going through this transformation, rethinking its basic value propositions, business models, value chains, and go-to-market strategies. Faced with massive disruption, the industry is rapidly rethinking itself. It isn't too much of a stretch to imagine that the airplane and car industries could eventually converge. If that happens, who will be better prepared and positioned to lead the new mobility industry? After all, in the same way we now talk about the car becoming a smartphone on wheels, it could be argued that an airplane could become just a multi-passenger drone or a car with wings....

One interesting possibility that springs from IoT is the emergence of the converged software and hardware economy. IoT will produce an insatiable demand for software, development platforms, APIs, and even API exchanges to take actions with the various things you've connected. I'm not talking about millions and millions of lines of code. It's more likely those short, fast applets or micro-services that can be cranked out quickly and revised even more quickly. But these capabilities are balanced with similar trends in hardware, with modules, programmability, and rapid development cycles. It is like yin and yang building on each other. The fog computing trend is a perfect example, where the need for real-time analytics meets the need to connect all the devices and capture and process the data in motion they generate.

Learn and Share

In short, don't reinvent the wheel; instead, learn from your IoT peers. Think of this as just another part of the same message I've been sending throughout this book: Don't try to do it all on your own. The entire IoT industry is feeling its way, discovering what works and what doesn't, and learning not only which use cases to tackle but also how to implement them. In the same spirit, you don't have to be a solitary hero. You can learn from the successes and the mistakes of others. Share what works for you and what doesn't. In effect, you're going to be both a student of IoT and a teacher.

You should, of course, attend IoT conferences. A few are held each year, and I expect many more will pop up as industry after industry jumps on the IoT bandwagon and eagerly learns what works. It will quickly reach the point where you'll have to be selective about which events you attend, making choices based in part on the use cases presented. At conferences, seek out opportunities to talk one-on-one with the presenters and either ask questions on site or follow up with them later.

Plan to talk with your peers, but don't narrow your scope so tightly that you'll miss important insights and experience. For instance, if you're in the discrete manufacturing industry, you can still learn from the implementation of a remote operations solution in the banking industry. When I talk with customers about IoT, I often ask them what they would do differently if they were doing it again. You'll be surprised how many people are willing to share their experiences and help you. The same goes for consultants. The experienced IoT firms or individuals could bring a wealth of practical knowledge to you and help you dramatically reduce the learning curve and the project risk.

You'll have plenty of opportunities to join your peers in industry-level test beds, some of which are created by industry members and some co-sponsored by the government. The Southeast Michigan Test Bed for autonomous vehicles or the interoperability test beds run under the Industrial Internet Consortium (IIC) or the ODVA, an industrial automation consortium, are just three examples. This is a very practical way to converge the industry, resolve key issues and accelerate the adoption of technologies and solutions, all done together with your peers.

You can also establish either a formal or an informal external advisory board to support your IoT efforts. The members will automatically become a group of mentors, from whom you can learn and with whom you can share. Remember, all of these conversations are two-way exchanges. By the way, this group doesn't have to be large or highly structured. Your advisory board might get together only every few months. You can hold the meetings on-line or in your conference room and just bring in sandwiches, so it doesn't have to be expensive, either.

The *Co*-Economy

I've talked at numerous points in this book about the evolving and emerging vendor ecosystem. These relationships will have to be cultivated, managed, periodically reviewed and reconsidered, and sustained over the long term. You'll need to do all of this in the face of a rapidly changing economy and business landscape. In some ways, we'll see the emergence of what I'm calling the *co*-economy—in which companies partner on co-innovation, co-development, co-support, co-marketing, co-training, and more—because the economy will simply be growing too fast and too large for any one company to do it all alone. Besides, you don't want to wait. You'll want your complete IoT solution as quickly as possible, so you and your co-partners will work in parallel, with your partners focusing on their side of the problem while you work on yours.

This, in turn, will result in different organizational structures, both within and outside of our organizational boundaries. We're already starting to see the emergence of symbiotic ecosystems of partners who complement each other and are developing IoT solutions together. These new types of alliances, and new cooperative management approaches, are starting to have significant impact on how individual companies operate, as well as how they're adjusting their internal processes to embrace co-development. For many companies, this is unknown territory. But the sooner your organization embraces this model, the sooner it will be able to benefit from the IoT economy. In parallel to starting your overall IoT journey, you can begin building the ecosystem, one co-development partner and one IoT project at a time. Here are nine rules for both customers and vendors (Figure 7.3) I would recommend in this area:

1. **Don't develop custom solutions.** The more standardized the solution, the lower the cost to you and the higher the chances that the vendor is committed to it long term. We've all benefited already from open, standards-based technology. Let's stick with it as long as it makes sense.

2. **Set the right expectations.** Be clear about what you're trying to accomplish, as well as why, when, and how. Understand the "care abouts" of all participants—both individuals and the organizations they represent. Make sure all expectations are compatible, even if they aren't exactly the same.

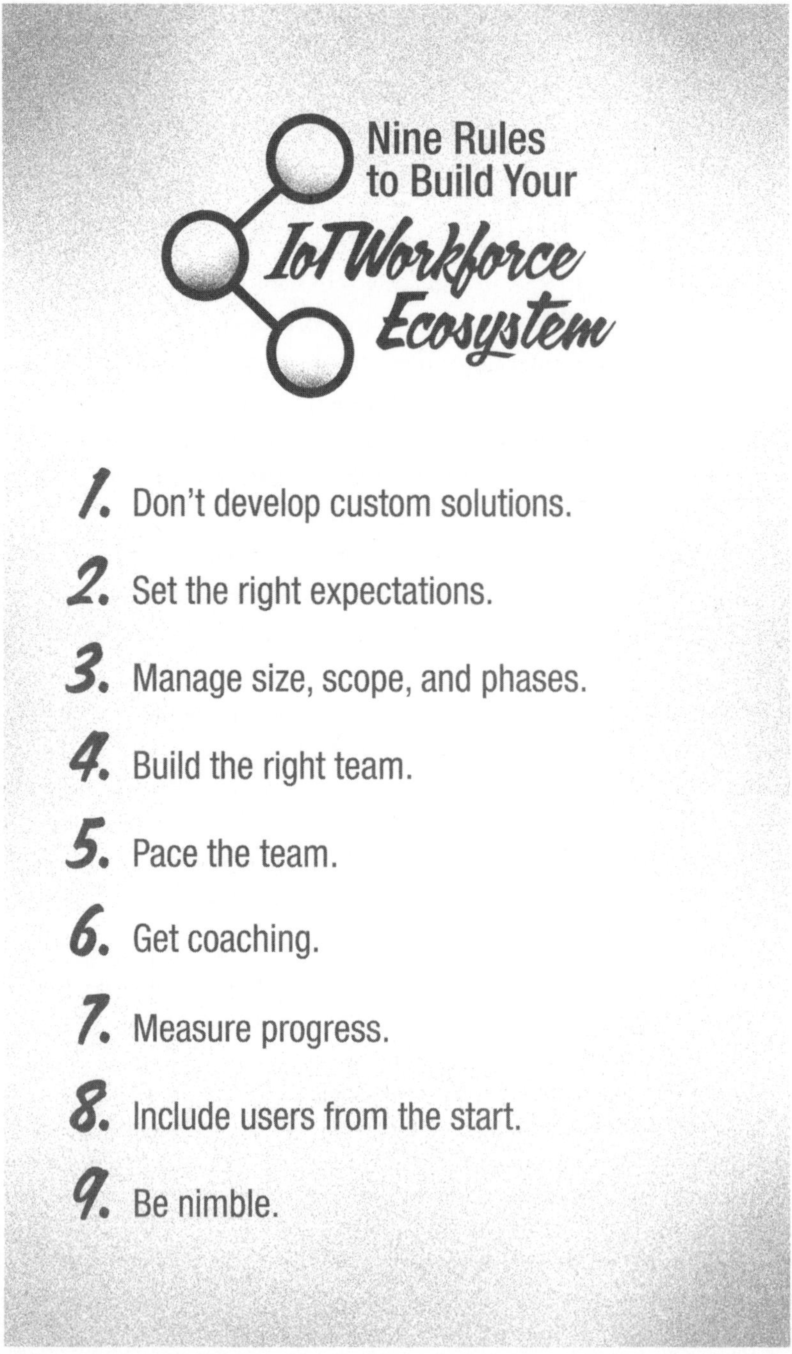

Nine Rules to Build Your IoT Workforce Ecosystem

1. Don't develop custom solutions.

2. Set the right expectations.

3. Manage size, scope, and phases.

4. Build the right team.

5. Pace the team.

6. Get coaching.

7. Measure progress.

8. Include users from the start.

9. Be nimble.

Figure 7.3   Rules for Customers and Vendors

3. **Manage size, scope, and phases.** Like any project, you may split the challenge into several chunks, working on some in parallel and some in sequence. It's a proven way to speed progress.

4. **Build the right team.** Assemble a diverse team with complementary skillsets. If you are co-developing with several organizations, they probably shouldn't be representing directly competing companies. You need the right mix of viewpoints and perspectives, so don't dismiss unusual backgrounds and different personalities. Balance creativity with discipline, and establish guidelines for team communication and dynamics.

5. **Pace the team.** Brand-new co-development teams may want to start small, using the first project as a way to build a cohesive team whose goal is to pick the low-hanging fruit. After an early success, the team may be ready to tackle a bigger challenge, take more risk. If something doesn't work as hoped, plan to regroup and learn from any failure.

6. **Get coaching.** Ask for help from people who have real-world experience in running successful co-development initiatives. You don't want to repeat mistakes when you can just as easily learn from those of others.

7. **Measure progress.** Co-development can sometimes be messy, but that doesn't mean chaos and anarchy. Stay on track by establishing metrics and tracking KPIs.

8. **Include users from the start.** Never assume you know what the user wants. Bring customers into the development process to give feedback on each iteration, and take that feedback seriously. Nobody wants token feedback.

9. **Be nimble.** Don't become too attached to ideas that aren't working. Recognize when you need to make course corrections and move on quickly. In short, don't get married to any particular approach or idea until it has proven itself in practice. In the startup world, we call this notion "a pivot." Most startups would pivot from one idea or business problem to another at least once before they find a winning formula. So, in your IoT internal startup efforts, be prepared to pivot.

Obstacles to Change

Two types of obstacles prevent change: strategic and tactical. Let's briefly look at each.

Strategic Obstacles

The key issue here is a lack of management recognition that a deep and game-changing development is underway. If top managers don't acknowledge that something important is happening, even if they don't understand what it is or its ramifications, then you, dear reader, will have your work cut out to help them see what's going on. (Part of my intent for writing this book was to help you address this exact problem.) If these managers don't recognize that substantive change is percolating all around them, they won't be ready to provide the necessary support to those of you who have caught on and want to start the strategizing, planning, and piloting. At the end, educating and securing their sponsorship will become a critical success factor for your IoT journey. It is worth investing your time and effort to make sure that you bring at least one of the top managers in your organization along with you, starting with your first small IoT project.

The next step is to figure out what business you'll be in when the IoT economy hits its full stride. We've already discussed the transformation going on in the car manufacturing industry. These manufacturers increasingly think they're in the people and things mobility business, rather than the car manufacturing business. As their thinking shifts, many different decisions become possible. They may, for instance, design their products differently, decide to invest in mobility services, or build and operate fleets of autonomous (self-driving) cars and trucks. Similarly, transportation companies—truckers, railroads, and airlines—might consider the impact of drones.

Thinking like this needs to appear in the management suites of companies in every industry. Once that happens, and the related discussions begin, there are many possibilities to consider:

- Data competency and opportunity
- Different understanding of span and control
- New collaborative development environments
- New types of partners, new and/or different relationships
- Customer change management
- Redefining relationships with existing partners
- Reviewing end-to-end proprietary supplier approaches
- Defining looser, nimbler, cheaper, and collaborative relationships
- Seeking multivendor solutions

- Building an IoT ecosystem; joining an ecosystem
- Evaluating global versus local partnerships
- Preparing to adjust relationships and alliances

Tactical Obstacles

I've tried to point out the tactical obstacles to IoT throughout this book, and I hope they're more familiar to you now. However, you'll have to think about them in terms of the bigger and rapidly evolving IoT picture. These obstacles include:

- Security, privacy (refer to Chapter 9 for more information)
- Integration, support, and migration of legacy infrastructure and systems
- Data quality, data management
- Real-time versus batch data, data storage, and perishable data
- Software development, coding, and agility
- Development of workforce skills; acquiring, cultivating, and retaining a skilled workforce
- Change and transitions, the need to continually reinvent ourselves
- Assembling an appropriate ecosystem around your product or solution

Of course, behind all of these issues—both strategic and tactical—is the payback question. It will come up as soon as you make your first IoT suggestion and again at every point that follows. Refer back to the earlier discussions on payback and ROI, and you're also welcome to use any materials from any of these chapters in your discussions.

Exciting IoT Exercise

How do you think IoT will change your company or industry? More importantly, how would you *like* IoT to change them? At this point, nothing is set in stone; you can shape IoT at your organization in any way you'd like. So let's start with two provocative questions:

- How would you like to transform your organization, department, or workgroup?

- What corporate/operational/process information, controls, process changes, and metrics would you need to make this happen?

Now let's envision this as a multistage transition over the course of three to seven years, and then look out further—10 years. Start by answering a few key questions:

- What business do you want to be in; how would you define it; what are the main disruptions, and who are the potential entrants and disruptors in this business; with whom will you compete?
- How might your industry be restructured; who will be the main players; where can you fit in?
- How do you see your organization participating; which control points can you capture?
- Which parts of the value chain would you own versus your partners?
- What will you produce and sell; how will it be packaged and sold?
- Who will be your customers?
- Who will be your employees; where will they work?
- Who could be your partners?
- How will you make money; how would your partners?
- How will you go to market?
- How will you service and support your customers?
- How much can you automate and/or outsource?
- How will you manage and govern the resulting organization?
- What are the key business, technical, and organizational risks you will face?

Get In Front of the Coming Change

Change can be scary. The best way to respond is to imagine repositioning your organization for the most likely future. Of course, none of us has a crystal ball that can predict the future with any certainty. We do, however, have known history that we can use for models of what might happen or what not to do. Here are a few to think about:

- *Horse and buggy versus automobiles*—this pervasive and deep social change brought good and bad, and we continue to live with its benefits and consequences.

- *Plain old telephone service (POTS) versus digital telecom today*—this change enables a wealth of options globally at low cost and provides models for automation.
- *Trains/ships versus airplanes in long-distance travel*—this change brings speed and convenience to transportation as opposed to low cost and a greater time commitment.
- *Paper-based publishing and printing versus electronic, Internet-based publishing and communications*—this change has ravaged the paper-based publishing industry, although signs of a hybrid publishing model are slowly evolving and showing some survivability.
- *Consumer travel industry versus the Internet*—this change really comes down to a preference for personalized and niche services or low-cost, do-it-yourself capabilities, and convenience.

Even a cursory review of historical changes like the five described above suggests some lines of thinking for IoT strategies. One seemingly winning strategy, for instance, might be a or gradual hybrid approach. But how that would apply to IoT in the face of its fast and tangible payback isn't yet clear.

Because of this, I suggest you start a discussion around IoT within your organization. If you can't bring the C-suite into the conversation initially, then start with the LOB and department managers who will be directly impacted by IoT and seek their sponsorship. However, as I pointed out already, you should look for C-suite sponsorship sooner than later. That means you should start talking about the IoT future now and initiate planning for it. You might also suggest an initial project, probably around remote operations or any of the other fast payback items we identified. This approach will let you and your core virtual team test the feasibility of IoT in your organization. Then take it from there.

IoT is not fail-proof, as some vendors and consultants might imply. It is quite possible to make mistakes, both minor and grievous, that will cause your IoT project to come up short of expectations. The next chapter looks at the most common mistakes and problems organizations encounter and how to avoid them. Since you have read to this point, you have heard most of them already. It is convenient, however, to have them consolidated in one short chapter.

8 | Mistakes and How to Avoid Them

Do you want your IoT project to fail? Silly question, I know. But many IoT projects do fail. So how do you ensure that your effort doesn't become a painful "learning experience" and is instead a shining success story? One of the best ways is to learn from other people's mistakes so you don't repeat them. Study their painful "learning experiences," and I hope you'll avoid the pain yourself. That's what this chapter is all about.

Do you remember my recipe for IoT success chart in Chapter 1 that I've kept referring to throughout this book? It was a list of eight items I urged you to consider when starting an IoT journey. Believe me, I don't like creating eye charts. I also don't want to overwhelm or scare you. But, having seen many IoT projects be delayed or fail, I do want to make sure you can learn from these missteps and maximize your chances of success with an IoT transformation in your organization. Just look at the challenges to Industrial IoT adoption listed in the Morgan Stanley-Automation World Industrial Automation Survey "The Internet of Things and the New Industrial Revolution," conducted by the bank's AlphaWise research unit.[1] Among the challenges are cyber security, lack of standardization, legacy installed base, significant up-front investment, lack of skilled workers, and data integrity. It should come as no surprise then that, according to Gartner, between now and the year 2018, the majority of IoT projects will take up to twice as long as planned.[2] This means that IoT is neither easy nor as simple as some pundits imply. But it doesn't have to be a high-risk endeavor either.

We know that IoT doesn't work perfectly every time. An organization's IoT initiatives can indeed fail. Such failures can delay realizing the intended benefits and paybacks, as well as cost precious time and money that the organization may be hard-pressed to lose. Although I don't expect any of you to bet the company on your first IoT project—and I'll repeat this warning several times before the end of this book—the idea is to start with low-risk, straightforward projects and to learn along the way. That way, you put a few successes under your belt while also building momentum, support, and expertise before you encounter an IoT failure. The industry is still young and evolving, so many best practices haven't yet been validated. And everyone—the experts cited in this book, you, and me—is still learning and will continue to do so for years to come. So let's state it here: We're moving into unchartered territory, experimenting, and taking risks. Not every IoT project succeeds the first time, but we can all learn from each other's mistakes and vow not to repeat them.

Some of the mistakes I've observed happened merely because the solutions weren't mature, nor was there enough practical experience in deploying them. As a result, the forecasted ROI proved to be too optimistic. The first generation of vehicle parking solutions is an example. Based on physical sensors inserted into the street surface, these solutions proved to be expensive to install and maintain. Plus, cars and weather conditions damaged many more sensors than anticipated. The next generation parking solutions addressed these problems by using video sensing, which turned out to be much more economical and reliable for both undemarcated and demarcated parking applications. The on-camera processing (think fog computing) implementations also ensure people privacy. Similarly, when smart carparks were designed and deployed in Europe, solution providers didn't anticipate the level of vandalism that followed. People taping over car sensors and resetting them just for fun wasn't considered in the original business case. Once solutions matured, however, and the business cases became more realistic based on practical implementations, the industry learned and adapted.

Another group of common mistakes deals with implementing IoT solutions in isolation (Figure 8.1), separate from the related business processes. Remember when, in the previous chapter, I insisted on considering a technology solution and the business process as two sides of the same coin. This is the reason why. In one instance, a city deployed a state-of-the-art inflow and infiltration detection system in manholes. The solution worked as designed, but the ROI didn't materialize. Why? The technical system installed belowground wasn't integrated with the business processes aboveground, which included the city's sweeping and cleaning practices. Once both elements were combined into one workflow, the expected ROI followed.

A third set of mistakes centers on focusing too much on current requirements, with insufficient consideration given to future needs. "The fundamental mistake I see organizations make today about IoT implementation is lack of planning and lack of architectural approach to scaling

Figure 8.1   IoT Solution in Isolation

the number of connected devices in the enterprise," remarked Dr. Aleksander Poniewierski, partner and IoT/OT leader for EMEIA (Europe, the Middle East, India, and Africa) at Ernst & Young Advisory, which helps companies implement enterprise-wide performance transformation initiatives. "If you do not do the work up-front, defining a standards-based scalable architecture that is flexible enough for your enterprise to add/replace devices and add/diversify services, you will be forced to either keep redoing your architecture for every implementation or you will end up with many incompatible implementations. Either of these scenarios will not bring you the paybacks you planned for," he added.

Let's look at an oil and gas industry example. An enterprise specified and installed advanced process control (APC) systems in its refineries, one facility at a time. All well and good. However, when it later decided to integrate all of these locations into one fully synchronized system to better coordinate outputs and manage the profitability across the enterprise, the company discovered that the individual APC implementations were incompatible with each other and varied in key capabilities. The result: a protracted and costly retrofitting effort to bring all of the APC installations to the same level of functionality, interoperability, and architecture.

In another example, an organization made the decision to adopt a cloud-based platform for transaction processing. Shortly after it went into production, the company then decided to implement predictive analytics capabilities (this is one of the fast payback scenarios, remember). Unfortunately, the firm quickly discovered that the cloud platform it had just installed was incapable of supporting high-volume, real-time analytics processing. As a result—you can guess this, no doubt—the company had to re-architect its platform for real-time use cases, adding significant delay and cost to the project.

Yet another category of mistakes deals with the early identification of science projects versus production projects (another key ingredient of the recipe for IoT success). Because I've used the oil and gas industry as a good example of IoT usage, here's a lesson you can learn from one company's project. In this case, an oil company spent two years working on a project to install a Wi-Fi network in an existing refinery. Refineries are hazardous locations, so from the start the team—a group of contractors—knew this wasn't going to be a garden variety project. Still, the team overcame a handful of obstacles, including obtaining certification for access to the hazardous site, making Wi-Fi work reliably in a site full of metal structures, and integrating this new network with existing technologies and semi-proprietary systems. When the system was completed, the implementation group had a right to be proud of the work they had done. What the team didn't know, however, was that the project hadn't been approved by the business units—the actual customers—and that those units chose not to take it live. Oops. The lesson here: Line up all of the necessary approvals before you start.

What I find most interesting when learning about what has gone wrong with IoT projects is how infrequently the main culprit is technology not working as specified. Rather, the problems more often than not revolve around an inability to pin down the exact requirements, incorrect assumptions, changes to scope and/or requirements midstream, or—to paraphrase a famous line from the classic movie *Cool Hand Luke*—what we have here is a failure to communicate. I've also seen situations where projects were poorly conceived from the start or the problem to be solved wasn't appropriate to an IoT solution.

As with any new transition, especially one of the magnitude of IoT, we've seen and will continue to see many failed attempts and even a few truly spectacular failures. Mistakes and failures can be found in every aspect of IoT, including the technology, solutions, partnerships, business cases, implementations, and more. It's important that we learn from them—as individuals, as teams, and as an industry. The ultimate goal is to not repeat these mistakes at all, but we also need to look for ways to minimize both the reoccurrences and the impact of such mistakes and failures if they do happen.

I know it sounds like a cliché, but I'll say it anyway: We shouldn't be afraid of failure; we should be afraid of *not* taking the risk. We need to be willing to take reasonable risks and to experiment with new technologies and business ideas. But it should be understood that this is a calculated risk. We must do whatever it takes to maximize our odds of success and minimize the risks. I'm definitely *not* preaching the "fail fast and often" mantra. Rather, I prefer the "fail fast/learn together" approach. This is why, as much as we like to trumpet our successes, we should also absolutely share our mistakes and, more importantly, the lessons we learn from them. If you want to learn from your peers' failures, it's important to share yours with them as well.

Table 8.1 below summarizes the most common classes of mistakes and challenges that I've observed over the past few years. They span a range

Figure 8.2   Common Mistakes

Table 8.1 Mistakes and Challenges When Implementing an IoT Solution

Mistake/Challenge	Comments
Starting with technology instead of business opportunity	Focus on a business-relevant problem you want to solve, and learn from others. Remember: The primary goal of IoT is to solve business problems, not enrich technology vendors or excite the company's tech geeks with a cool project.
Approaching a technology solution in isolation without considering integration with the business process and its evolution	IoT projects are rarely implemented in a vacuum. If you don't examine existing workflows and how to change and integrate your IoT solution with them, you'll likely see diminished ROI at best or a complete lack of business impact at worst.
Leading with connected devices instead of data and apps	Applications and data analytics are key IoT solution elements; they drive the need for device connectivity, not vice versa.
Prioritizing solutions implementation without a strategic and long-term focus on organizational resistance and change management	As we've discussed, IoT is a multi-step journey to change how your organization operates and delivers value. You can assume there will be organizational resistance along the way; prepare for an enduring effort to combat it.
Implementing IoT projects tactically without sufficient support by the strategic vision or lack of an actionable vision altogether	Think big, but start small. Be realistic about implementing IoT. Start with a low-risk project that has clear benefits, then become increasingly more ambitious as your expertise and support grow. (For more information, see Gartner's March 9, 2016, report titled "Why Integration Is Critical to IoT Success."[3])
Designing IoT solutions without a proper security foundation	Integrate security into your methodology and implementation from the start, and make it everybody's job. (Chapter 9 has more information on security.)

Table 8.1 (*Continued*)

Mistake/Challenge	Comments
Doing it alone within the company or as a company	Lone wolves, as romantic as it sounds, won't succeed with IoT. This is a team sport. Start assembling your ecosystem of partners from inside and outside the company, and make sure they can work together well. Adjust the processes and KPIs appropriately. Insist on open standards throughout.
Implementing single-vendor solutions (related to the above)	Proactively drive your current suppliers to open up their architecture, embrace open systems, and change their model to co-development with partners.
Taking a grass-roots-only approach	You must have executive support at the highest levels; you're re-engineering the company, organization, culture, business model. You need C-suite sponsorship.
Underestimating the challenge of legacy integration; not migrating to open standards wherever it's prudent	Most IoT projects are implemented in brownfield environments. Pursue an aggressive but thoughtful plan to replace proprietary systems with open standards. Do it based on facts, benchmarks, and empirical results.
Buying versus co-developing; open versus custom solutions	Don't just ask your vendors to develop a solution for you; co-develop it with them—but resist the temptation to develop a custom solution. Insist on an open platform that can be adopted by the industry.
Failing to communicate	Internally and externally, don't sugarcoat communication failures. Do broadcast lessons learned and, of course, successes. Communicate more than you think is needed.
Underestimating the power of established relationships and the installed base	Many traditional industries have well-established long-term sets of ecosystems and relationships. Some of these players are eager and willing to be change agents, but many will resist. Seek openness.

Mistake/Challenge	Comments
Betting on immature technologies	New technologies bring big promises but can also be a gamble. Implement new technologies in phases, and do it together with your peers. Learn and share.
Compromising on interoperability	This mistake will doom your project to a very short life and cost you a bundle. Here are two bywords to live by in IoT: open and interoperable.
Not managing risk vectors properly	Be aware of and thoughtful about how many new variables you're planning to introduce in an IoT project and stage them carefully.
Falling for hype versus building a solid business justification	Resist the hype. If you can't identify the business justification for your IoT project right away, then continue learning, experimenting, and benchmarking your results against your peers' results. At some point, you'll identify a compelling ROI for your first small IoT project.

of categories, from organizational to business and project planning, and from management to partnership, change management, and technology.

As I mentioned at the beginning of this chapter, the good news is that not every mistake is fatal. I can assure you that you'll make plenty of mistakes in your IoT journey. But if you spot them early, you'll be able to recover from and correct them. For instance, I was once involved in a project that required us to access a hard-hat site. The team was initially turned away for lack of permission. After a lot of calls and paperwork, we finally got the access we needed. It wasn't a fatal mistake; it just cost us a couple of days and a lot of aggravation. Similarly, relying on proprietary or semi-proprietary technologies and systems isn't going to kill your project. You will, however, have to go back at some point and convert these to open systems and accepted industry-standard technologies if you want to maximize the benefits and ensure the project will last into the future.

On the flipside, some of the mistakes can be fatal, and we need to watch out for those in particular. For example, failure to limit and control the risk vectors, lack of integration with business workflows, or trying to go it alone are likely to dramatically increase the project's risk level, as well as lead to significant cost overruns, implementation instabilities, and disappointing ROI.

At the same time, overcoming IoT mistakes and problems can be a big boost to your own career. The demand going forward for people with IoT experience is high. A savvy manager could take the experience gained implementing IoT and propel him- or herself into better and better positions. There is no question about it, IoT is the place to be.

Now that you are equipped with key learnings from others, are you prepared to start your first IoT project? Not yet. First, let's get just a bit more technical and look into security, standards, and technology considerations in the next two chapters.

As we have discussed throughout the book, security is the biggest concern that managers have about IoT today. They fear that bad guys will get in and wreak havoc to their data, systems, employees, and customers, steal proprietary information, or even alter product formulas. They worry not only about the short-term damage but also about the lasting negative impact on their businesses and their brands. Many of these fears are valid, but some are overblown. In the next chapter I will offers a factual assessment of the current state of IoT security, where progress is being made and where progress is still lacking—essentially "the good, the bad, and the ugly," but there is a lot of good in the works, and more is coming. Some fear can be healthy, as it keeps us on our toes and steers us away from careless mistakes. Like many other disciplines, IoT security should not be feared, but should be learned and practiced.

Glimpse Under the Hood of IoT Today and Tomorrow

9

IoT Security Essentials

The power of IoT lies, in part, in its ability to operate not only in the physical world of actual things but also in the virtual world, where things are digitized and exist as digital information only. Because it crosses both worlds, IoT can send digital data over the network to a distant controller attached to a physical device, say an important production machine. That data then instructs the machine to turn itself off or on, depending on what you want it to do.

Let's think about this for a moment: You now have a virtual system remotely controlling a physical machine. Can you see why security is so important to IoT? Without an effective security approach, a hacker could turn off an important piece of your production equipment and keep it off, perhaps at some critical point in your production run. You might not even know the problem exists and try to get that machine back online until you discover production has stopped and you physically send someone to the machine to restart it manually.

Ever hear of the Stuxnet attack? The worm initially penetrated an Iranian nuclear facility. The attack drove the machines in such a way that the equipment overheated past the breaking point, effectively shutting down production for months. The worm then spread across industrial operations in many countries, prompting systems people to implement measures to prevent Stuxnet-like incidents. Lacking details about how the attack actually worked, they rushed to quick fixes such as deploying firewalls in front of equipment on the shop floor. The industry has since learned that traditional firewalls, a leftover from the era of perimeter IT defense, would never stop a Stuxnet-like attack.

Physical Separation Provides No Defense

Before IT and OT started working together, OT was fond of separation of systems as a security strategy. Now we know that this isn't the most effective approach. But it is one of the key reasons why, early in this book, I encouraged you to bring IT and OT together.

Security has become one of the leading inhibitors to IoT adoption. I've stopped counting how many conferences and customer meetings I've attended at which IoT security was a top concern, and for good reason. You can no longer rely on physical separation. Everything must be connected. How long would your organization be able to function if email and the Internet went down? Everything, virtually every business process, depends on the ability to connect. Think about the fast payback categories described in Chapter 5. Every single one of them relies on the flow of data from the plant to the enterprise IT network to the cloud. Today, the idea of unplugging your organization from the global network—as comforting as it might seem—is simply absurd.

OK, so retreating from the global network is no longer an option. However, that's no reason to panic. The truth is, not all threats are the same and not all threat targets have the same value to your organization. Your response to different types of threats and different threat targets needs to be measured and proportional (Figure 9.1). This requires risk management.

Figure 9.1   Risk-Based Self-Defense

Security as One More Risk Management Challenge

Today, leading organizations treat security as a manageable risk to be considered and countered, along with all of the other risks they manage. The process for managing IoT security risks is the same as that for any other risk:

- Identify the likely individual threats.
- Assess each threat in terms of its likelihood of occurring and the damage it can cause.
- Identify and deploy defensive measures appropriate to each risk's likelihood and potential damage.

Different vulnerability types produce different threats with the potential for different damage. A threat that can potentially shut down a factory assembly line or an oil rig is of a different magnitude than a threat that can interfere with an inventory stocking process. By assessing the value at risk, you can make informed decisions about how much to invest in defensive measures. In this way, investing in IoT security is no different from buying any of the different types of insurance the organization needs. The investment in all cases should be commensurate with the likelihood of the risk and the potential value of the loss or damage.

As you've read throughout this book, companies have been successfully deploying IoT under various names for years. Yes, there are serious risks, which I'll detail below. But the industry has been busy developing defensive strategies and engaging in collaborative efforts to counter various risks with defensive methods, products, and best practices. Please don't think you can't protect your organization. You can, and it all starts with solid risk identification, assessment, and management.

It is important to understand, however, that IoT doesn't have a magic security bullet. The scope and variety of IoT solutions effectively prevent the emergence of a no-fail security defense. IoT technology is constantly changing, the solutions are continually evolving, and so, too, are the threats and attack vectors. You are dealing with active adversaries who are constantly working to outsmart you and your defenses. Sorry, IoT isn't a one-and-done solution, and neither is your IoT defense. Risk management, as I've said, is an ongoing process that must be revisited at least yearly, perhaps even more often, as different solutions change and new threats emerge. The key for all of us is to be smart and aware of IoT risks—and not to be afraid.

Security and its accompanying risk management should be a top concern for everybody, not just IT or OT, and especially for top management. That's a key task for you and your IoT virtual team—as listed in the recipe for IoT success in Chapter 1: *"Make security everybody's top priority."* A good sign: 82 percent of corporate boards are now concerned about cyber security, according to ISACA and RSA Conference 2016 survey.[1] I'm not sure what the remaining 18 percent are thinking, but everybody needs to get on the security bandwagon now.

My initial thought was to throw some IoT security disaster incidents at you at this point. But you already know about these types of stories—a boy hacking into a local train system and disrupting traffic, or the hack attempts on a nuclear power plant or a public water supply. You don't need to hear any more of these. Anyway, vendors peddle them by the pound to sell their particular IoT security solution.

The only security solution I want to sell is this: informed risk assessment and monitoring, accompanied by an appropriate and proportional security response that accounts for the particular threat level and the amount of value at risk. Once you determine these, you can choose the best vendor option from among the most appropriate IoT security solutions and build it into your IoT ecosystem from the start. Another emerging option worth considering is a cyber insurance policy some insurance companies are starting to offer. After that, there's only one final but important step: Engage your top executives and enlist their support, because none of them would want your company to show up as an IoT cyberattack victim poster child on the front page of the newspaper.

There are many reasons somebody would hack your IoT solution. For some, it's a thrill; for others a political statement; and for a few an act of war or terror. The majority, I suspect, are expecting financial gain by stealing data or trade secrets for competitive advantage, to hobble you as a competitor, or to disrupt your business strategy. A disgruntled employee may also be attempting to exact revenge. The reasons are as numerous and varied as the plots of TV's many police and crime shows. One particular conclusion from years of security studies is clear: Most security breaches take advantage of well-known vulnerabilities that haven't been addressed despite ample alerts, and most attackers are known to you—employees, contractors, or partners of one sort or another. Generally speaking, attacks are neither esoteric nor exotic.

Also remember that security isn't solely an IT or OT problem; it isn't even a technology issue. This is a top management concern. By deploying IoT, your organization is becoming a digital enterprise. Therefore, you need an integrated, companywide security strategy and risk management plan that involves everyone at every level. Security must be a significant part of every employee's responsibilities. Continually emphasize security policies, best practices, and tools as part of everything you do. Build security education into both your organization and your IoT partner ecosystems (Figure 9.2)—make it part of their responsibility, too.

In the end, effective IoT security requires top-down support for a holistic approach that integrates data security with top-notch physical

Figure 9.2   Security Is Everyone's Responsibility

security. Don't think of these as separate domains, and always remember that most cyber-attacks come from inside the organization. Here are three areas of physical security that should be considered as part of your integrated security strategy:

- Focus on addressing top physical security concerns such as tailgating, where unauthorized people follow on the heels of authorized staff as they pass through a controlled door.
- Integrate physical access systems, video surveillance, and the like with digital credentials and permission systems for your entire workforce, including all employees, contractors, and vendors.
- Consider deploying biometric and multilevel physical access systems.

As with everything else I've written about IoT, security is not something you should tackle alone. Find and collaborate with partners inside and outside your organization. Work with the team assembled by your chief information security officer (CiSO). They can help you extend their IT security architecture to OT, and then augment it with your specific security needs, issues, and concerns in mind. Go to IoT security conferences, but pick the events in which your peers showcase the actual implementations they're deploying and share best practices.

Radical New Security Approach

The old way of thinking about security and secure systems was to keep the bad thing out and the bad guys away. This was often referred to as "security by isolation" or a "perimeter defense."

A new approach treats security compromises as a normal part of life. It recognizes that security can't be flawless without completely shutting down the systems, which you obviously don't want to do. Instead, use risk assessments to determine how much risk you can afford to tolerate for each system and business process. Then use policies, analytics, and automation to enable your systems to automatically prioritize, contain, and defeat attacks based on these assessments.

Aim for a proper balance between the benefits of safe, uninterrupted system operation and the risks of any potential security failure. As we said before, not every threat is the same; different responses for different types of threats based on continuous risk management and assessment should be the norm. This new approach applies to both IoT users and vendors. Specifically, users need to take an architectural approach, break the current silos, and not live in denial. Vendors need to take an architectural approach, too, as well as drive industry collaboration and interoperability. Most importantly, they need to design security into everything, right from the start. You can learn more about these topics in the chapter "Securing the Internet of Things: Need for a New Paradigm and Fog Computing," written by my colleagues Tao Zhang, Yi Zheng, Raymond Zheng, and Helder Antunes in the upcoming book, *Fog for 5G and IoT*.[2]

Among the other issues to consider is the fact that physical separation as a security defense practice doesn't work, period. Stuxnet discredited that approach already. Of course, it does not mean that suddenly you need to go to another extreme and open up all your data and move everything to the cloud. Far from it. That's why the industry is implementing hybrid approaches and policy-based data architectures. However, if you choose to continue to follow the "security by obscurity" approach, even if you think your facility is 100 percent detached from the outside world, you're living in the blissful world of denial. What about the contractors, vendors, integrators, and partners with whom you engage? I'll bet there are 10 or more virtual private network (VPN) connections going out of your plant right now.

Then there is Shadow IT, which creates major security issues. The term "Shadow IT" refers to teams or departments making their own decisions about which tools, devices, and connections to implement in their organizations. As empowering as this may sound to a manager who becomes frustrated while waiting for IT to do something for his or her business unit, it clearly compromises the integrity and effectiveness of the company's security system in a big way. So here's a major call to action: Work with your IT and security teams to minimize Shadow IT. This may require easing up on some policies and expediting other changes. External companies may also be of help. One of my friends, for example, runs a very successful operation that assesses how many cloud-based services an organization uses. It's typically dozens, each representing a security vulnerability and a potential point of attack. The operation evaluates every one of these services, and then ensures that only those it certifies as enterprise-class—from both a security and a capabilities perspective—are used across the organization. No matter what you do, it may be impossible and impractical to reduce Shadow IT all the way to zero. Still, the fewer non-compliant tools you use the better security protection you'll create.

The good news is that the security industry has evolved its approach to IoT security. They are increasingly advocating for adoption of a comprehensive before/during/after approach (Figure 9.3):

- **Before:** The objective is to prevent people from compromising your systems and gaining unauthorized access. Preventing both internal and external attacks is equally important—remember, some of the most spectacular cyber-attacks have originated with disgruntled internal employees. Segmentation, role-based access controls, or anti-spoofing mechanisms are some of the most effective tools you can deploy to prevent certain types of traffic from traveling between one type of system (say, your HR system) and another (perhaps your cash management system).
- **During:** The goal is to see how quickly you can identify whether your data and/or infrastructure have been penetrated. It's best if you can do this within seconds and not hours, days, or weeks. Seconds means you can stop the transaction and potentially grab the perpetrator before he or she gets away. How quickly you can see large volumes of data suddenly being uploaded from your organization to an unfamiliar cloud service, rather than a service your organization normally uses, is similarly important. This capability requires intelligent automation and predictive analytics. Fog computing, automation, and analytics can clearly help here. Private blockchain, a highly secure distributed ledger technology just being developed, may prove quite effective in these types of situations as well.
- **After:** Once a hack is identified, your next task is to quickly assess and minimize the damage. This requires tools that document, analyze, and compare information before and after the attack to determine what has been stolen or compromised. You can then determine which data to fix and how, while also mitigating any damage to your infrastructure or processes.

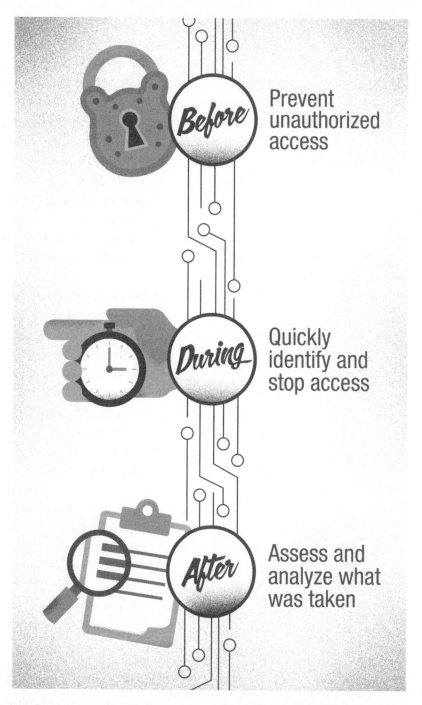

Figure 9.3   A Comprehensive Approach to IoT Security

Some Additional Considerations

As we discussed in Chapter 6, no matter how hard we try, there will never be enough qualified security personnel in the industry. As a result, both you and your peers will likely face a talent shortage in this area. Instead of chasing the latest and most expensive security talent in the market, you may want to implement intelligent systems that actually decrease not only the complexity of your security operation but also the time required to perform key tasks. Such systems effectively reduce the impact of a security resources gap. For example, prestigious tools that give you lots of data sound good and look impressive in theory, but in practice even modest tools that reduce the number of false positives and give you high-quality actionable data are actually useful. In all cases, intelligent analytics and automation can almost always help.

So what should your security product and services approach be? You'll hear different points of view from your peers. Some will recommend implementing the so-called best-in-class products. But such an approach will typically require a substantial investment in the integration of disparate best tools and the commitment of internal resources you most likely don't have enough of already. Others will recommend focusing on suites of products that work well together and offer integrated management, orchestration, visualization, and functionality across the suite's elements. This approach actually can help you reduce the cost of product implementation and integration. Plus, the suites are typically easier to learn and use than collections of disparate best-in-class tools. But too often such suites don't offer best-in-class components, thus forcing you to compromise on functionality and benefits. My recommendation is to look for the best of both worlds (Figure 9.4): architecturally integrated best-in-class offerings with a consistent security policy that gives you the state-of-the-art functionality, simplicity, and automation that will reduce your labor and resource requirements. Yes, they do exist, although you should be prepared to accept that these solutions aren't cheap. (As a side thought, even costly software will be cheaper than hiring experienced security experts.)

Your architecture also needs to be flexible. IoT constantly brings in new use cases (vehicle-to-vehicle [V2V] communication and sensor swarms are just two examples) and new classes of end-devices with distinct capabilities and profiles. More and more data is being encrypted.

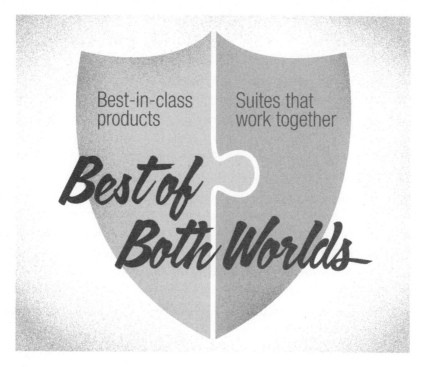

Figure 9.4   Combine Both Worlds

Plus, organizations are constantly implementing new capabilities based on machine learning, network heuristics, segmentation, and traffic isolation. Slowly but surely the industry is moving toward standardization of device classes and profiles. We are also learning intelligent ways to share the encrypted data. Adding to all of that, remember, is the fact that securing your enterprise is not a one-time event. It's an ongoing process, a race between the bad guys and you. Yes, most of the attacks we've seen leverage well-known vulnerabilities. And yes, applying the prescribed fixes is job 1. But you need to have the flexibility to address new security challenges, such as ransomware and other similar new threats, as well. Given the ever-increasing types and variety of attacks, it's important to plan your staffing and tools accordingly. Flexibility turns out to be priceless.

On top of all that, your architecture needs to be comprehensive, policy-based, and protect your data wherever it is. We've talked about your security architecture spanning IT and OT, but that's just a start. Sensitive information can now reside anywhere—the plant floor, retail store, mobile devices, IT infrastructure, local datacenter, or cloud services. So you need to focus on where the data is, and implement data security architectures that cover all of the possible scenarios while allowing you to apply consistent security policies between and among all of these domains. Always keep in mind that data is portable and dynamic. Many of the IoT use cases being implemented are based on data in motion. Basically, this means that the data in your organization is constantly moving back and forth among sensors, fog nodes, datacenters, mobile tablets, the cloud, and so on. It will be streamed, backed up, extracted, and transferred using multiple methods, including those often-prohibited thumb-size storage devices (that's how Stuxnet was spread in industrial networks originally). As a manager interested in IoT, you must now pay attention to both IT and systems architecture. You don't have to design it, but you do need to be informed, because it impacts what you want to do with IoT.

Perspective from the Experts

Christian Christiansen, the program vice president for IDC's Security Products, reports encountering tremendous confusion when it comes to IoT security, according to Sean Michael Kerner.[3] Overall, IDC believes that 90 percent of the current IoT security offerings are just repackaged general-purpose security technologies. Some vendors, for example, offer a generic gateway for IoT with the promise that it will work across a broad range of technologies. Or they offer a generic firewall housed in a ruggedized enclosure with some additional signatures and support for industrial protocols. Such offerings simply miss the point and are ineffective in meeting IoT security challenges.

A large part of the problem, according to IDC, Kerner wrote, is the difficulty in finding experienced security staff. IDC reports that trying to recruit security professionals with five to 10 years of experience is a far bigger problem than hiring entry-level IT security employees. The solution, IDC suggests, lies with meeting the continuing need for more intelligent orchestration and automation to reduce the reliance on and need for more human interactions in the security workflow. I believe that analytics—and especially predictive analytics—incorporated into your orchestration and automation processes can go a long way toward overcoming the shortage of skilled security personnel. At the risk of repeating myself, good software—as expensive as it may seem—is still cheaper than hiring more people.

Meanwhile, an April 25, 2016, press release from Gartner predicted that by 2020 more than 25 percent of identified attacks in enterprises will involve IoT.[4] As a result, the research firm expects worldwide spending on IoT security to reach $348 million in 2016, a 23.7 percent increase from 2015 spending of $281.5 million. Furthermore, this number is expected to reach $547 million in 2018. Although overall spending will be moderate initially, Gartner also predicts that the IoT security market will increase at a faster rate after 2020, as improved skills, organizational change, and more scalable service options improve execution and drive IoT expansion (Figure 9.5).

The press release quoted Gartner Research Director Ruggero Contu, who predicted that despite the fact that by 2020 more than 25 percent of identified attacks in enterprises will involve IoT, it would account for

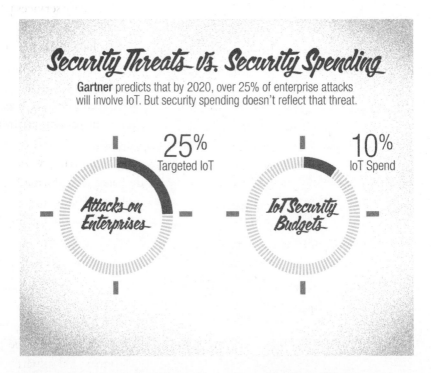

Figure 9.5   Security Threats vs. Security Spending

less than 10 percent of IT security budgets. Such limited IoT budgets, combined with the decentralized approach to early IoT implementations, will prove challenging for security vendors struggling to justify the prioritization of IoT capabilities in their portfolios. Contu also expects many vendors to prioritize spotting vulnerabilities and exploits, rather than, as we discussed earlier, the segmentation and other long-term measures that will provide a more sustainable and architecturally sound approach to IoT security. Contu went on to say:

> The effort of securing IoT is expected to focus more and more on the management, analytics, and provisioning of devices and their data. IoT business scenarios will require a delivery mechanism that can also grow and keep pace with requirements in monitoring, detection, access control, and other security needs.

The future of cloud-based security services is, in large part, linked with the future of IoT. In fact, IoT's fundamental strength in scale and presence won't be fully realized without cloud-based security services that can cost-effectively deliver an acceptable level of operation to many organizations. Gartner predicts that by 2020 more than half of all IoT implementations will use some form of cloud-based security service.

My own experience and observations generally concur with the conclusions of both IDC and Gartner. However, IoT security is not solely a technology challenge. Certainly you should invest in tools to address your specific security concerns. But more importantly, you need to engage the entire organization in the security effort—starting with top management—and insist that decisions be made based on informed risk management, threat assessment, and security policies. From there, you can determine which security technologies you need and which damage mitigation tools to implement.

Best Security Practices

IoT security practices are still evolving. However, based on the many meetings I've had with a variety of customers and experts,

I've gathered a set of practices that will work now and continue to work well into the future. You've read about most of these in the previous chapters, but let's recap:

- **Design (architect) and build an integrated (holistic), enterprise-wide security strategy from the very start.** Don't leave security as a bolt-on at the end. It should be inherent in your IoT process from the beginning.
- **Enlist and engage top management in threat assessment and risk management right away.** Security already puts their jobs and businesses on the line, so make IoT security another business-critical challenge for them. Top management should know how to assess threats and manage risk, and they definitely should worry about these issues as part of their job. You're just asking them to apply both approaches to the IoT risk. (They may need some guidance on the particulars and the scope.)
- **Adopt industry-supported standards everywhere they're available.** Proprietary approaches will cripple your security efforts down the road. Look to standards bodies and trade associations for guidance as needed.
- **Deploy security everywhere—from the central datacenter behind and outside the corporate firewall and all the way to edge devices.** This means insisting that your partners and ecosystem vendors participate and collaborate in your security strategy.
- **Automate and monitor IoT security end to end.** Build in intelligence and predictive analysis, especially fog-based analytics, to keep pace with the volume of events. Alert people to take action as soon as issues become apparent. Manual efforts will quickly be swamped by the volume of IoT activity, even at a small organization.
- **Segment IoT traffic and regular IT network traffic and use a multitenant network infrastructure to isolate problems.** Use segmentation and other well-known processes, but at the same time work with IT vendors to expand their existing software and tools to handle IoT security vulnerabilities. Resist the temptation to deploy IoT-specific tools.

> ▪ **Educate everyone in the organization, as well as all partners across the ecosystem, on security practices.** Plus, regularly update and refresh the IoT security message. In effect, as I've said before, make security everybody's top priority.
>
> I could go on, but that would take us too deep into the security weeds. To find more information on IoT security best practices, talk with your designated CiSO or check with your industry association.

Challenges of IoT Security

The number-one challenge in risk management and threat assessment is the expected vast scale of IoT. We discussed the billions of connected devices earlier in this book. Of course, many organizations *won't* have billions of connected devices. Still, you don't have to be a very large business to find yourself with a million connected devices, especially if you include partners. Even if you have just a few tens of thousands of connected devices, that still amounts to way too many to try to handle the security challenge without automated tools for analytics, orchestration, monitoring, and more. Just one thousand connected devices can generate massive streams of data 24×7, as well as huge numbers of alerts that will overwhelm anything but automated, intelligent (rules- or policy-based) scalable tools and technology.

Compounding the security challenge is the wide variety of devices, including different types of controllers, monitors, meters, and appliances. Many of these devices will belong to your partners, so you'll probably have limited knowledge of what they are and what they do—not to mention how to understand and communicate with them. Even if you're the most extreme control freak, I can assure you that you won't be able to monitor every device in your organization all the time.

The solution is straightforward, but it is also not trivial to implement; you need to orchestrate ecosystem collaboration. If your ecosystem is set up with collaboration in mind from the start—and it absolutely should be—it becomes natural to implement collaborative communication and security cooperation based on common architecture and policy.

Privacy

By now everyone is aware of the concerns surrounding consumer privacy. In the B2B world, privacy may be a slightly less visible issue at the moment, but ignore it at your peril. Along with several data scientists, I recently sat on a panel discussing these issues in the B2B2C markets. One of the hottest topics was permissions/opt-in issues—specifically, how and which data is shared, how to minimize the damage of data leakage, as well as how to randomize and anonymize the data—at what level user data can be analyzed to make it useful without compromising an individual's privacy. The industry is debating various approaches to these concerns, including techniques such as de-identification and pseudonymization. They won't be fully resolved until long after this book is published (if ever), so at this point, just stay tuned.

In the B2B world, key privacy considerations tend to be different. They fall into a few categories:

- **Employee data.** The general rule I've seen companies adopt is, whatever information users put on company-owned devices or infrastructure is under the organization's control. Employers have a right to access and/or monitor that data; this assumes, however, that employees knowingly allow or intentionally put their data on these devices and networks. Because of this assumption, the privacy issues tend to be focused more on clear communication of the rules—employees need to be aware of the policies and the consequences.
- **Location of the data.** Increasingly, where data reside—both physically and geographically—is a big issue for not only consumer-focused companies but also B2B companies and event governments. One of the hotly debated topics centers around the data that cross international borders and if different rules should apply to such movements. Your security architecture should be flexible enough to address such requirements.
- **Protection of sensitive employee data.** As much as you don't want your credit card and other personal data stolen and/or exposed, you and your employer also don't want your sensitive and confidential employment-related data stolen or exposed. Thus, some of the

consumer world's rules and tools regarding your data, such as regulating access to it and using it, are implemented in the business world, too. If you use your company's devices, network, and infrastructure, your activity and data on these are fair game. However, organizations will have to determine and communicate a wide range of issues relating to personal and personnel data—from how much they, as an employer, can monitor their employees' data and limit access to it to how sensitive employee data for example, compensation, should be protected. These have been tricky issues for years, and organizations now need to start thinking about them in the context of IoT. This is primarily a more detailed and elaborate take on the general rules concerning employee data on the corporate network.

The good news is that the IoT industry is increasingly coming together to drive common security standards and best practices. I'll cover the confusing world of standards in the next chapter, but here are a few examples: Horizontal standard bodies such as the Internet Engineering Task Force (IETF), the Institute of Electrical and Electronics Engineers (IEEE), and the National Institute of Standards and Technology (NIST) have kicked off efforts focused on key IoT security use cases in several current and new vertical markets. In addition, ODVA, the International Society of Automation (ISA), and other vertical standard bodies have expanded their security tracks to include the adoption of modern IT security protocols and best practices, as well as their integration with legacy systems and IoT. These organizations also focus extensively on education, training, and sharing best practices. Recently, the Industrial Internet Consortium (IIC) has released an Industrial Internet Security Framework that provides a set of best practices and guidelines in the areas of endpoints, communications, monitoring and configuration. Let's hope that this announcement, the result of two years of hard work by the IIC members, will become a tipping point for the security efforts in the industrial IoT community.

The newly formed OpenFog Consortium (OFC) is prioritizing the use of fog computing as a key security element as well. Just think about the real-time analytics tools running on the fog node in a vehicle or oil rig. These tools can identify security threats and problems as soon as they emerge, and then take the appropriate actions on the spot. As a security measure, this is starting to happen now. By the time you're ready to deploy IoT, it should be ready for use.

Last, the industry is finally working together to drive interoperability and accelerate the implementation of security standards. In the car industry, for an example, the U.S. government is joining research institutions and leading automakers in Ann Arbor, Michigan, to develop, test, and train on new standards and best practices for connected and autonomous vehicles.

Security as Your IoT Foundation

Security has emerged as one of the most important areas in IoT. Yet, despite it being a constant topic of heated discussion, many concerns and honest misunderstandings remain. It does generate one of the most important revenue opportunities for vendors, in addition to giving them opportunities for innovation around new security use cases.

IoT security is more distributed, more heterogeneous, and more dynamic than IT or OT security. It involves multiple organizations and roles, as well as your entire assembled IoT ecosystem. The challenges are different, too. As a result, IoT requires a new approach to security that focuses on not only preventing intrusion but also quick detection, damage assessment, and remediation.

At least we now know that the physical separation of the plant from the enterprise and the Internet has been proven *not* to work. A holistic/architectural approach to IoT security including physical security is required. Every time I meet with CiSOs, I urge them to take ownership of the security architecture for their entire organization, including OT and physical security. Some listen, some don't; some want to do it, but are prevented by internal politics and non-invented-here syndrome. So if you plan to drive IoT in your organization, make your company's CiSO your best friend. Both of you will benefit in the long run.

Still, new types of IoT applications, such as V2V or sensor swarms, create new security challenges. What can you do? Here are a few recommendations to get started:

- Augment perimeter defense by deploying resilient systems that can absorb attacks and keep functioning.
- Similarly, provide alternative fault-tolerant devices and systems that continue to operate, even during attacks.

- Track compromised systems, data, and devices for later remediation.
- Keep track of latest IoT security research and startup activates—they tend to focus on new IoT security use cases and technologies such as blockchain.

In the past five years, the state of IoT security has evolved dramatically: From the archaic approach of security by obscurity in the OT environments to Stuxnet-stricken panic to frantic patchwork and Band-Aid approaches. Now, finally, organizations are starting to take a more mature approach, with comprehensive and flexible security architectures. Even though in aggregate—as an industry, as customers, and as vendors—we've become more advanced when it comes to security, I still meet many customers who stubbornly cling to pre-architectural approaches. A lot of organizations resist IT/OT integration and avoid developing and implementing joint security architectures. Some CiSOs don't believe they're accountable for OT environments. Some customers, meanwhile, continue to live in denial, deploying inadequate security solutions, or reinventing the wheel by solving problems their IT counterparts successfully tackled years ago. On top of that, I still see many vendors trying to hold onto their legacy approaches, offering point products or IT products augmented to imperfectly fit into increasingly architected and standardized industrial environments and protocols. What's definitely required is more education, training, awareness, and sharing. Remember, we're only at the beginning of the IoT security journey.

"Security is a linchpin to successful outcomes, financial gain, opportunity, confidence, and loyalty for individuals, organizations, and governments alike. Conversely, security weakness at any level siphons resources and breaks down trust. Consequently, organizations must recognize that security is a business enabler that they must embrace if they wish to compete and differentiate in a market driven by IoT. They should take a business perspective to security strategies and operations and approach it comprehensively, including the architecture, analytics, governance, privacy, and data sovereignty. Equally importantly, the teams across the functions must have the right levels of skills and training to meet the demands of a connected world," summarized Bola Rotibi, research director and founder of Creative Intellect Consulting, an analyst research, advisory, and consulting firm.

If you're reading this book and thinking about becoming an IoT advocate in your organization, you'll also need to support and drive adoption of a comprehensive, policy-based IoT security architecture. If you proceed with IoT implementation without addressing the security requirements, you're asking for trouble. Don't think of security as a separate task; integrate it into your solution design from Day 1. The good news is that you can get help in many ways. As I said earlier, start by talking to your CiSO and persuade him or her to partner with you. Once you've done that, as I indicated in Chapter 1, there are a few immediate steps I recommend every organization take:

- **Adopt a single security architecture built on an open, unified approach and automated, risk-based self-defense and self-healing capabilities.** That type of architecture is flexible and comprehensive; spans OT, IT, and the cloud; and allows you to set security policies once and implement them across multiple domains. It also integrates into your IoT architecture, infrastructure, and solutions. The architecture addresses before, during, and after attacks, as well as enables you to implement additional capabilities in the future. Remember: Security is an ongoing challenge, one that requires a long-term scalable approach.
- **Converge around standards.** Standards are there for a reason, so insist that your technology providers support and use them. Consider becoming involved in standards bodies such as ODVA or ISA—they have a good mix of vendors and customers already collaborating on standards development, interoperability, training, and adoption.
- **Collaborate and co-develop.** Build your coalition inside the company with the CiSO and the IT security team, as well as with vendors and consultants. Work with your industry peers to learn together. Remember, security isn't your differentiation; it's your foundation. Don't be shy about sharing your best practices and learning from others.

Bottom line: Don't panic and don't be scared. Do use risk assessment and management, embrace a policy-based architectural approach to security, and make security part of your IoT implementation decision criteria from the start. All of that will give you the best chance for success and allow you to confidently move along your IoT journey.

The next chapter discusses standards, which go hand-in-hand with security.

10 | Standards and Technology

Did I say this chapter was about standards and technology? Oops, sorry, I misspoke. This chapter is actually about making technologies work together for business benefits, which is IoT's sole raison d'être. Without seamless interoperability and integration there's no reason for IoT. All of those rosy projections—billions and billions in revenue created by millions upon millions of connected devices, communicating across vast numbers of networks, generating seemingly endless data for countless vertical applications—were based on the assumption that all of these elements, once they could communicate, would interoperate in a smart way. If they can't, who needs IoT at all? We'll just go back to the 20th century single-vendor-does-it-all custom solution models. This chapter will also take a closer look at a few key game-changing technology shifts we've been referencing throughout this book.

So this chapter is about standards, to the extent that only through universally accepted, efficient standards do all of those myriad things and parts and pieces and networks, both new and old, have any chance of communicating sufficiently up and down to exchange data, integrate, and provide the right capabilities for the apps to generate business insights in open, interoperable, and industry-accepted ways. The standards efforts around IoT have been going on for many years now, beginning with the push to adopt and adapt to open networking technologies even before IoT came into vogue. Some of these standards have now reached the point of maturity and, yes, interoperability to enable the use-cases I've been citing in this book. Going forward, the industry is determined to evolve and improve standards within the next few years to keep pace with technology changes and enable more advanced use cases, applications, and value propositions.

The Case for Standards

With IoT, the technology situation is already much more versatile, complex, and fluid than the IT or OT scenarios with which you're now probably familiar. The number of legacy, proprietary, quasi-standard, and specialized technologies is simply mind boggling by itself. At the same time, the industry has begun to cull the traditional market structures of vendors out pushing end-to-end, proprietary, single-vendor solutions. If your company is one of those, become involved now in industry standards workgroups and learn how to thrive in an open world if you want to have a shot at thriving in the IoT-driven economy.

Let's add to that list the duplication of vendor ecosystems even within the same vertical. Just compare the tier-1 supplier ecosystem for German and U.S. automakers, and you'll start to see the picture. Further complicating the IoT standards are the sheer diversity of end devices, sensors, actuators, meters, controllers, appliances, and more that today have varied capabilities and proprietary device, management, and data interfaces and formats. And I haven't even started to count the number of embedded OSes, chip suppliers, and so on that further increase the complexity. This is one of the reasons why an entire industry of IoT platforms—the companies that connect and integrate with proprietary third-party end devices—has sprung up. They've resorted to creating their own abstraction layers and development environments through which application developers interact with these devices and the data they generate. While such an approach is needed today, it is inefficient and redundant. Yes, there

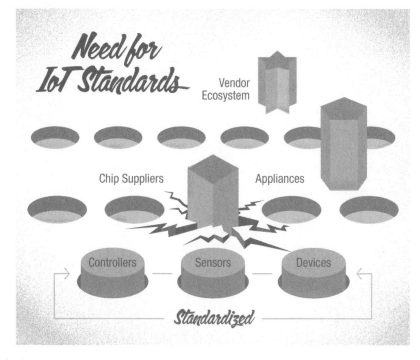

Figure 10.1   Need for IoT Standards

will always be a need for middleware to support legacy devices. However, getting the industry to standardize and adopt common data formats and APIs for new devices will be a big step forward (Figure 10.1). We urgently need to do just that.

Imagine how expensive such an approach is for each of these platform companies to undertake on its own. Even worse, you don't do it only once. Every time one or another of these devices or interfaces changes, you have to revisit it. That's why even the biggest players in the industry are willingly joining standards development teams. As much as each would love its own approach to become the accepted standard, it's too costly to develop and, most importantly, maintain by itself over time. The economics of doing this kind of standards work as an industry-wide collaborative effort are just too compelling to ignore.

But wait, there's more. As we've said throughout this book, we already have billions and billions of connected devices—including cars, buses, trains, office buildings, factories, oil rigs, homes, and entire cities.

Some are stationary, some mobile; some have IP addresses, others don't; some are always on, some intermittent; some are clustered together, others geographically dispersed. And that's just the beginning. The solution requirements vary vastly, as well. Some require devices to transfer megabytes of data every second, some just a few bits every few days; some want data to be analyzed in real time, some don't; some can be powered from the grid, some need to operate 20 years on a single battery. I hope you get the picture.[1] All of these variables are driving an interesting phenomenon. Unlike in the original Internet, we're actually seeing a proliferation of access or "last-mile" technologies. (Last-mile refers to the final leg from the network to the device.) No longer limited to Ethernet, Wi-Fi, and 3G/4G, IoT deployments today also include satellite, Bluetooth LE, low power wide area network (LPWAN) technologies such as LoRa, power line communication (PLC), and various wireless personal area networks (WPAN) such as Wi-SUN and ZigBee NAN, among many others. Which technology is best for each situation depends on several criteria, which we'll discuss later in this chapter. My first point here is to simply convey the complexity and vastness of the IoT world as it stands today at this early stage of maturity.

My other point is that, right now, you'll want to start the migration from proprietary and semi-proprietary technologies to open standards. And I mean tomorrow, if you can. That involves addressing where and when data should be analyzed, security concerns, and the evolving relationship between the central IT function and OT roles within LOBs. Equally important, however, is to encourage your vendors, suppliers, and ecosystem partners to adopt open standards, participate in standards efforts, and do whatever you and they can do to stimulate and embrace standards-based technologies. That will do the most to save you money, headaches, and time when you begin to deploy IoT in production environments and provide you with a scalable foundation that will benefit you long term in your IoT journey.

This state of IoT creates something of a conundrum. On the one hand, we have a desperate need for technology convergence, simplification, and interoperability. We also need to rationalize disparate technologies around open standards and integrate them with legacy systems. On the other hand, IoT requirements and use-cases are diverse and still rapidly evolving. New devices, technologies, and methods are introduced daily for which there may not yet be a standard. How would you resolve this conundrum?

Overabundance of Access Technologies

As noted above, we're all facing an overabundance of access technologies. This is further complicated by disparate devices and the tasks we want our various IoT solutions to accomplish. To even begin to decide among this variety of access technologies, you need to answer these basic questions:

- How many and which types of devices are in your network?
- Are these devices mobile or fixed, and how geographically dispersed are they?
- In which type of physical environment will these devices operate?
- How much data is being transmitted, and what bandwidth is required?
- How time-sensitive are the data transmissions?
- For battery-powered devices, what likely duration of operation is required, and how long should the battery last?
- What are the cost constraints?

Notice that these aren't technical questions, just basic business questions any LOB manager would want answered. Deciding on the right access technology is only the first step in designing IoT capabilities that will drive efficiency and yield actionable insights and better decisions. Before you have a working IoT solution, you'll also want to address the migration from proprietary technologies to open standards (yes, I know I sound like a broken record here), where and when data should be analyzed, security and risk assessments, and the evolving relationship between the central IT function and OT roles within LOBs.

Common IoT Framework

Are you overwhelmed yet? Fortunately, the industry quickly recognized that we can't go through each building block in a solution and ask basic questions like those above without a decoder ring. Thus, we've started to converge on a common IoT framework.[2] That IoT framework is not just a slick marketing gimmick. It actually represents the way serious IoT players think about issues such as architectures, terminology, and logical blocks. Put another way, it's about using common designs, described in the same terminology, to refer to the same things. This isn't cast in concrete yet; it's only a starting point.

Such a framework can guide us on how to reduce the complexity of IoT technologies and solutions. It helps us determine which layers to abstract, where to focus on interoperability, and where to create open APIs as well as common and open standards. Since IoT is still evolving and will continue to evolve for years, we want a way to accommodate new innovations while ensuring that any new things can work with existing things. Otherwise, we'd all be in the position of reinventing everything anytime something changes. The IoT World Forum Reference Model is a good example of such an effort. (The IEEE IoT Architectural Framework is another example.) Its common framework drives interoperability across all IoT components: devices and controllers, networks, edge or fog computing, data storage, applications, and analytics. The model (Figure 10.2) organizes these components into layers and provides a graphical representation of IoT and all that it entails.

Equipped with such a reference model, the IoT industry has been focusing on three different standardization thrusts:

1. **Evolving existing horizontal standards.** As has been the case with many previous technology transitions, the robust standards of the IT world are now evolving to include requirements from OT and IoT. Dozens of interest groups in the IEEE, IETF, and other standards bodies are working on requirements for IoT, including time-sensitive networking (TSN) for cars or industrial control systems and safety; high-speed mobile communications among diverse things such as cars, trains, and other vehicles; or high-coverage low-speed networking technologies for low-power low-bandwidth sensors.
2. **Migrating specialized, proprietary, and semi–standard technologies to open standards.** As we've discussed, major industry players in manufacturing, transportation, and other verticals have historically implemented proprietary technologies or established standards around their own protocols and technologies. This often created conflicting standards, thus inhibiting interoperability and adoption. The IoT industry is working with the major industry standards bodies,

Figure 10.2   The IoT Technology Stack
Source: IoT World Forum Architecture Committee, 2015.

including ODVA, to avoid this issue by migrating to open standards while ensuring interoperability with legacy protocols.

3. **Creating consortia to address key pain points.** Major industry players are joining forces in new consortia, among them the Industrial Internet Consortium (IIC), the Open Connectivity Foundation (OCF), the OpenFog Consortium (OFC), and the OPC Foundation (for open platform communications).

IoT technologies are organized as a technology stack that moves up from physical devices at the bottom through data and applications, and finally processes. As I've mentioned, data analytics and vertical applications are key drivers for IoT. Most recently, I've seen an increased interest in data-in-motion and real-time/near-real-time data capabilities (think predictive analytics and fast payback scenarios), which are driving the latest interest in fog computing. One big challenge with such data is that the data streams tend to age, which drives down their value very quickly; thus, the need to implement real-time analytics capabilities at the edge. Think about using data to identify and stop fraud as it's occurring. This isn't something you want to do hours, days, weeks, or months later. Besides the growing interest in fog-based analytics, the good news is that the industry is quickly adopting an open-source innovation model for both data storage and data governance, which should also speed data processing.

Finally, many of the challenges with IoT aren't technology-related but instead come from the industry's slow adoption and, often, resistance to change. One example of why creating common standards is so important: Wireless HART and ISA100, two different wireless standards focused on connecting sensors to the network. Both were derived from the IEEE 802.15.4 protocols, but each was created by a separate ecosystem of industry players and, as a result, is incompatible with the other. When my team came across these standards a few years ago, we thought we could help the industry converge on a common open standard for the wireless connectivity of sensors. That way, customers could easily choose among many sensor vendors and infrastructure vendors and not be locked into buying devices that only support a given standard. We went to both camps and proposed that we work on a plan to converge Wireless HART and ISA100 into one new open standard. Unfortunately, the idea was dead on arrival. I still hope that someday both standards will converge, but I don't see it happening in the near future. It will only happen when customers demand it and vote with their purchase orders.

Business-Relevant Standards Activities

I recently spoke with Max Mirgoli, executive vice president, World Wide Strategic Partnerships at IMEC, a world-leading research organization in nanoelectronics. He sums up the current standards situation this way: "With the advent of fast and simple connectivity, improvements in image sensing and other advanced sensing capabilities which can be tied together with simple yet powerful algorithms and apps, the IoT revolution has already began. We are starting to see early successes in smart manufacturing, autonomous connected cars, and smart grids, but the lack of convergence on standards can slow the adoption. The good news is that pretty much all the major industry players recognize that without common standards, none of them will fully realize the economic potential of IoT. Thus, with the emergence of standards such as 5G, I am optimistic that the industry will band together to solve key technological and architectural challenges of IoT via common standards and interoperability."

I couldn't say it better myself. Standards efforts are important. With so much at stake in IoT, we want to avoid standards chaos and standards wars whenever possible. Remember the video industry's Betamax and VHS wars in the 1980s and 1990s? Or, even before that, the audiotape recording wars, when audio cassettes and 8-track tapes fought it out? Standards invariably benefit everybody. The same will be true with IoT, but even more so.

What follows is a brief summary of the main standards initiatives that are important to businesses embarking on IoT. This is by no means a comprehensive list. It's also subject to change as standards efforts emerge, depart, and evolve.

Horizontal Standards Efforts
- IEEE has kicked off a specific IoT initiative (see http://iot.ieee.org/). "IEEE has a long-standing track record of driving technology transitions through standards and interoperability. IEEE IoT Initiative is a multifaceted undertaking that brings together industry, academia, entrepreneurs, and investors," said Oleg Logvinov, who leads the industry engagement track for the initiative. He went on to tell me that "from the creation of the standard for an IoT Architectural Framework (IEEE P2413) to closing the gap between policy and technology development (IEEE Internet Initiative), IEEE is taking a very comprehensive and ambitious approach to fostering the creation of an IoT ecosystem based on open standards."
- International Telecommunication Union (ITU) Study Group 20 is developing IoT standardization requirements that will initially focus on smart city applications (see http://www.itu.int/en/ITU-T/studygroups/2013-2016/20/Pages/default.aspx).
- oneM2M Consortium (http://www.onem2m.org) is defining standards for a common M2M service layer to connect devices with M2M application servers. It targets business domains such as connected transportation, health care, utilities, and industrial automation.
- In both the AVnu Alliance and the IEEE, the industry is developing a set of standards around Time Sensitive Networking (TSN). "Time Sensitive Networking aims at building a foundation for more open,

easily accessible, and highly secure real-time control systems for the IoT," explained Georg Kopetz, member of the Executive Board at TTTech, an early pioneer of TSN. "For customers with mission critical applications, TSN offers real-time guaranteed latency, low-jitter and zero congestion loss for time critical traffic in converged networks," he added. As I discussed before, real-time analytics and apps are one of key drivers of IoT. That's why guaranteed network latency or delay that TSN offers is so important. TSN is enabling a standard-based approach to many use-cases from connected vehicles to the motion control applications on the factory floor.

Industry Consortia

- IIC (http://www.iiconsortium.org/) is working to accelerate IoT development and adoption in the industrial sectors to interconnect machines, business flows, intelligent analytics, and people at work. It has created reference architectures, established a range of innovation test beds, and is now identifying core standards, as well as gaps and requirements for future work. "The IIC has become the global consortium for Industrial IoT collaboration. With the membership of over 250 companies and 20 testbeds, the Consortium is evolving its Industrial Internet Reference Architecture and forging close collaboration with the Industrie 4.0 consortium," Paul Didier, Cisco's representative to IIC told me.

- OCF (https://openconnectivity.org/) is defining connectivity and interoperability requirements for connecting billions of devices. It is driving interoperability for device-to-device, device-to-infrastructure, and device-to-cloud communication by defining specifications, as well as creating open-source code and a certification program. This is a must-do to integrate billions of devices, sensors, and the data they generate into IoT solutions in a scalable way.

- OFC (https://www.openfogconsortium.org/), mentioned earlier, is developing an open-fog computing architecture for distributing computing services and resources close to users and endpoints to meet the growing demands for local computing in IoT. It will be releasing its reference architecture as this book reaches bookshelves.

- OPC Foundation (https://opcfoundation.org/) is leading the efforts on data interoperability, manufacturing processes, and equipment in the automation domain via its Unified Architecture. Thanks to its track record as an industry neutral forum, it is attracting new participants and expanding its scope across the entire technology stack. I expect it will continue to strengthen its role as the place where the industry gets aligned.

Industry-Specific Standards Bodies

- ODVA has been working tirelessly since the 1990s to champion open standards in the automation world and to migrate existing industrial automation standards to IP and Ethernet while ensuring interoperability with legacy protocols.
- ISA is tackling a wide range of standards issues, certifications, education, and training for the automation industry.
- PI, the umbrella organization for PROFIBUS (Process Filed Bus) and PROFINET (Process Field Net), is driving both sets of technologies.

It may seem as if we're sometimes taking two steps forward and one step back in terms of standards, but in general I'm very optimistic. The proponents of open standards clearly have momentum. Just visit the Hannover Fair, the largest industrial trade show on earth, and you'll see all of the devices proudly displaying their new standard Ethernet or wireless interfaces. The next step is for the customers to actually turn off the I/O interfaces and proprietary/specialized networks on their smart devices and start using such standards-based connections. So it's only a question of when, rather than if, open standards will become the norm in IoT.

New Technology Arrivals

Even as I was writing this book, new technologies emerged—and they will continue to do so. It also quickly became apparent that I could never include all of them and still finish the book. Instead, I decided to highlight a few that I consider the most important and far enough along to write about. What comes after, you'll have to discover on your own. That shouldn't be too hard. Just stay involved with your industry association and/or check out industry and IoT conferences and trade shows once a year or so.

Fog Computing

You've read my prior references to fog computing. Specifically, fog computing creates a platform—comprised of what we call a fog node—that provides a layer of compute, storage, control and networking services, and event stream processing between end devices on the ground and in cloud computing datacenters. Fog isn't a separate standalone architecture;

instead, it extends and scales the existing cloud architecture all the way to the edge of the network, as close to the source of the data as possible. The purpose is to enable real-time data processing and analytics of either large amounts of data or data in motion. The objective of fog computing isn't connecting devices differently. Rather, it's analyzing the data from the devices faster, with less latency and more efficiency. In effect, with fog computing we're putting data processing closer to the devices that generate or collect that data (Figure 10.3), and then analyzing it right there in real time.

A few years ago, Flavio Bonomi—founder and CEO of Nebbiolo Technologies, which focuses on the application of IoT technologies in industrial automation—led the definition (and naming) of fog computing with his team. When I asked him about fog, he summarized it well: "As we started to work on projects such connected vehicles, smart grids, and smart cities, we identified a common set of requirements for compact, scalable, well-managed, secured, and integrated networking, computing,

Figure 10.3   Fog Computing: Bring the Cloud to the Edge

and storage resources between the endpoints on the 'ground' and in more distant clouds. The term 'fog computing' was, in fact, naturally motivated by this need to bring more cloud-like capabilities 'closer to the ground.' In time, it became clear that fog computing actually facilitated the convergence of OT and IT and enabled new IoT use cases that required real-time capabilities, deterministic performance, physical security, and safety. Since it inherits elements from both IT and OT, fog computing naturally mediates between both domains at the various levels of the stack, from networking to security to the data level to the application level."

So what's the big deal about fog computing? At first glance, it doesn't appear to be all that different. In truth, however, it amounts to a distinct innovation. Fog computing (Figure 10.4) brings analytics and processing to the data. That's the difference, and it's a big difference. In the past, we always brought the data to where the processing occurred. That generally meant sending information to some distant central datacenter, which

Figure 10.4   Fog Computing: The Ultimate IoT Enabler

added cost and significant delays. Now, with fog computing, we can scale the cloud and make it viable for real-time use-cases—the cloud and the edge can work together as an integrated system. Cloud software can send a policy to the fog node, requesting only certain types of data or only the exceptions to, say, a temperature threshold. The data is processed in the fog node based on this policy and only these exceptions, and the specific data requested is sent back to the cloud. The rest of the data is either stored locally in the fog or discarded.

As a result, we can convert the raw data collected from connected devices into useful information that can be acted on immediately—often in real or near-real time. When fog computing removes the latency from an IoT transaction, things can happen that fast. From there, we can also convert that information into valuable business insights through new applications, including real-time analytics and predictive context.

In short, fog computing brings:

- Near-real-time or real-time processing and analytics capabilities to the edge of the cloud
- Processing and analytics closer to the data and where they are used
- Much faster and more efficient analytics via a policy-based edge-to-cloud-to-edge system

Consider that the first stage of the Internet focused mainly on batch processing, wasn't time sensitive, and didn't use machines that consumed a lot of bandwidth. Now consider that even a single automobile can generate a huge amount of data and requires serious bandwidth—especially because that data is more time-sensitive and, therefore, even more important. (As an example, ask yourself how long you have to react if your car starts to overheat.)

Enter fog computing, which solves some of today's most common challenges, including:

- High latency on the network
- End-point mobility
- Loss of connectivity
- High bandwidth costs
- Unpredictable bandwidth bottlenecks
- Broad geographic distribution of systems and clients

As we've discussed throughout this book, fog computing is a key enabler of IoT, and it's driving an array of new use-cases in every area of life and industry—from retail to healthcare to oil and gas exploration and production. Preventive vehicle maintenance is one example. The sensors in each new connected vehicle generate up to two petabytes of data each year. It would be impractical and prohibitively expensive to send all of this raw data over the mobile network to the cloud for real-time processing. Fog computing turns these vehicles into mobile datacenters that can sort and index the data in real time and send alerts when action is required—for example, checking an overheated engine or filling an underinflated tire.

The industry has recognized the transformational capability of fog computing to enable a new wave of use-cases that weren't possible with cloud-centric implementations—hence the November 2015 creation of the OpenFog Consortium. "We formed OFC to accelerate the adoption of fog computing to solve pressing bandwidth, latency, and communications challenges associated with IoT, artificial intelligence, robotics, and other advanced concepts in the digitized world," OFC Chairman Helder Antunes told me. "Our technical workgroups are creating an OpenFog architecture that enables end-user clients or near-user edge devices to carry out computation, communication, control, and storage. And we plan to accomplish these goals in a collaborative manner, where interoperability between technology vendors is also ensured."

Blockchain Opens New IoT Possibilities

Blockchain has emerged as a technology that allows a secure exchange of value between entities in a distributed fashion by maintaining a continuously growing list of data records that are protected from tampering and revision. The technology first appeared on most IT radar screens a few years ago in the form of Bitcoin, a virtual currency that relies on blockchain technology to ensure its security and integrity. Although Bitcoin's future is uncertain, blockchain is a different story.

As the currency's underlying technology, blockchain is attracting considerable attention for its ability to ensure the integrity of transactions over the network between any entities. For example, I spoke with an energy company looking at blockchain to manage the interactions between solar panels and the power grid. Automobile companies are considering the technology to authenticate connected vehicles in the V2V environment. Among the many other uses of blockchain being considered are the ability to trace the sources of goods, increase food safety, create smart contracts, and perform audits. Blockchain, it turns out, is a natural complement to IoT security in a wide variety of use cases.

Blockchain IoT implementations are still at a proof-of-concept stage, but standards are already starting to emerge. The Linux Foundation set up the Hyperledger Project, a partnership with several dozen major technology and financial players, to hammer out an agreement on open-source blockchain standards. For now, blockchain is presented as a sort of distributed consensus system ledger or database where no one person or entity controls all of the data. In effect, blockchain creates and stores a permanent or immutable log record of every transaction. As an emerging open standard, compliant variations of blockchain could enable products or solutions to offer different levels of control and programmable business logic via smart contracts. We'll just have to watch and see what happens.

According to Martha Bennett, principal analyst at Forrester Research, blockchain could be a transformational technology that changes the game in banking, IoT, and beyond. "Long-term, blockchain has the potential to revolutionize distributed computing. Looking at it purely from a technical perspective, many of the projects currently underway are laying the foundation for new ways of approaching distributed computing inside and outside of banking—doing for the storage and application layer what the Internet did for the communications layer. It's early days yet, and it will take time for all of the security, privacy, and scale issues to be addressed,"[3] Bennett commented.

This much we know now: Blockchain, which produces and saves a distributed log of any type of transaction activity, enables people to put their trust in a "trustless" transaction environment. It essentially eliminates the need for a central trusted intermediary between buyers and sellers or, in the case of IoT, between communicating things. In fact, blockchain could potentially eliminate the need for any intermediaries in most transactions. For those who want open, trustworthy IoT communications without having to rely on intermediaries, blockchain, especially "private" blockchain, could provide the answer and enable the type of distributed IoT exchanges people have barely begun to imagine could be possible.

Machine Learning Enhances Real-Time Analytics

Like blockchain, machine learning is another important technology for IoT. It delivers a critical technology behind real-time predictive analytics, one of the key IoT use-cases. Machine learning has been around for years, but the recent advances in deep learning, especially supervised learning, have made it more valuable to IoT. Basically, with supervised learning, you can train the analytics system to improve its predictive accuracy—the more data on device operation, failure, and maintenance you feed into it, the more accurate the predictive analytics system becomes. Furthermore, although unsupervised learning has not evolved at the same pace and still has many open issues, it, too, is proving to be an invaluable capability for IoT. Think about zero-day attacks, where the hacker is exploiting a vulnerability in the software that is at that time unknown to the software provider. In such a scenario, since no data is yet available to train a classifier, such as a neural network, advanced unsupervised learning is starting to be used to detect such attacks.

Self-learning networks (SLN) are a great example of disruptive power of machine learning in IoT. In short, SLN is an architected solution combining powerful analytics with a wide set of machine-learning technologies (including cognitive learning from machine to machine) that enables networks to become intelligent, adaptive, proactive, and predictive. SLN has been architected with high scalability in mind: To that end, a wide set of machine learning algorithms are used at the edge of the network, which constantly learns network traffic patterns in order to build mathematical models.

Such models can then be used for a variety of purposes:

1. Prediction of application performances: by predicting the level of quality of service that IoT applications will receive from the network, it becomes possible for the network to anticipate and adapt accordingly.
2. As we discussed, security is known as one of the main challenges of our industry, with constantly evolving attacks that are becoming more and more pervasive and sophisticated. SLN makes use of

machine learning to compute highly sophisticated models capturing normal baselines. Such models allow for the detection of advanced attacks, such as data ex-filtration, and denial of service attacks against the IoT network.

The SLN gets smarter as more events occur: Each node in the network performs modeling using machine learning, and learns constantly. Hosted on network edge devices and connected via advanced networking, SLN enables the network to both detect and respond much faster to problems.

"The concept of self-learning networks was born in 2012 while we were working on highly challenging problems for the IoT. Over the past few years, we faced a number of fascinating technical challenges, which led us to develop a highly novel and disruptive architecture and technology. We just announced the first product of a family of SLN portfolio called Stealthwatch Learning Networks for the detection of advanced threats. Without a doubt, many more SLN innovations applied to the IoT will emerge over the next few years that will considerably impact the IoT architecture, enabling a wide range of new services and capabilities," commented JP Vasseur, Cisco fellow and inventor of SLN.

Fog computing, blockchain, and machine learning are just three of the myriad technological and architectural shifts emerging around IoT. Stay tuned; many more are incubating, driven by the new challenges and the new opportunities IoT creates.

With its combination of open standards, interoperability, and new technologies, IoT is gaining powerful new capabilities and business models that will define winners and losers across industries. Already, savvy LOB managers are asking for open, IP-based IoT architectures. And companies like Cisco and Rockwell Automation are working with an increasing number of partners that have made the strategic decision to embrace open standards and evolve to the open IoT model. The paybacks are real; I saw them firsthand at last year's IoT World Forum in Dubai, where IoT early adopters presented their results.

The next chapter, "IoT State of the Union," definitely is not a recap of everything you have read so far. I bring in some new ideas and provide a glimpse into IoT's future, although I am not a futurists in any way, shape, or form.

11

IoT State of the Union

Remember the exercise we did in Chapter 7? It centered on the question of what you'd like your business to look like in 10 years. Now let's try a different exercise: How big a financial impact do you want IoT to have in your organization?

Have you been excited by the analyst and pundit projections of billions or even trillions of dollars in top- and bottom-line impact resulting from IoT in the coming years? These figures are, without doubt, tempting. How much of that impact would your organization want? This is the proverbial how big a piece of the pie question. (Since they are projecting trillions and tens of trillions of dollars, even the tiniest slice amounts to millions.) Before you answer, let me caution that the projections below are based on statistical formulas you don't want to bank on, at least not until some of the returns actually trickle into your pocket.

The best you can count on is either what you're likely to save or recoup, initially anyway, by piloting some of the fast-payback models described in Chapter 5 or whatever you estimate the payback to be on your pilot project. Take remote operations. If it enables you to avoid sending one person to check a monitor at one remote site once each week and that saves you, say, $200 per week times 52 weeks a year, then you'll recapture $10,400 every year. Now push that example to five people and five different trips each week, and you'll save five times that amount. If it's 100 people or 1,000 people ... well, you can do the math. In any case, that's not a bad return for what amounts to the cost of one meter-reading device and a few bits of network bandwidth. It's a real payback, both immediately and over the long term. How much you really save, of course, will depend on your particular use case.

Now let's take the conversation on IoT's impact in a totally different direction. How engaged would you like to be in your customers' organizations? Do you want to be partners with them? Will your customers be co-developers of your products and services? How much will they be worth long term as both customers and partners? What's the lifetime value of this or any customer or, for that matter, this or any partner? Again, the answer depends on you, the customer/partner, and the use case.

What happens when we look at this discussion from the customer side? How will your organization make major purchases of equipment, machinery, and supplies in 10 years? Remember, your organization not only *has* customers, it *is* a customer of others for all of the things you buy. So will you try to partner with one, some, or all of your suppliers? Are you prepared to do the work and make meaningful contributions to their products or services? How will you expect to be compensated or rewarded for co-innovation or co-development?

Clearly, IoT touches all aspects of the customer/partner relationship. In the IoT economy you won't always be either the provider or the customer. The bi-directional nature of IoT impacts the buying as well as the selling, the using as well as the making and/or distributing of products and services. In effect, IoT impacts the entire value chain.

Now think again about what problems you would like IoT to solve for your organization right away. How much is it worth to you to resolve any of these challenges—one of which might be your first IoT pilot project? Then try to imagine what problems you might want to solve in 10 years, when IoT will be much more mature and you'll be more experienced with it. I don't expect you to know all of the answers immediately. Rather, these are simply the questions you'll want to consider as you move forward. Ultimately, every project needs to be cost-justified and present an ROI. IoT is no exception. (As a reminder, Chapter 4 described approaches to cost-justifying IoT through ROI.)

New Economy

IoT is bringing about a new economy. Now that you've reached the end of this book, do you have a better sense of what that economy will look like? It will, of course, be completely digitized and connected. People and organizations will work together differently, too. Specifically, IoT will emerge as the first step in bringing about a co-economy where:

- People and organizations cooperate and collaborate in more and different and deeper ways.
- Devices communicate with any devices.
- Openness rules.
- Proprietary becomes a temporary experience.
- Customers are free to choose on the basis of what they want and need, rather than being constrained by the attributes of the thing—be it physical, logical, or virtual.

So we'll collaborate and cooperate with our customers, and they'll do the same with not only us but also the rest of our IoT ecosystem. Our traditional roles will quickly evolve from buyers and sellers to co-creators, from competitors to collaborators, from technology providers to business value creators, and from resellers to solution integrators. We'll all be part of multiple ecosystems, because we'll all play multiple roles—expert, partner, collaborator, service provider, supporter, integrator, customer, and more—among multiple partners.

It sounds a little overwhelming, doesn't it? How am I going to keep all of this straight, you ask? You are right to ask. It won't happen all at once, that's for sure. Intelligent management, orchestration, configuration, analytics, and process tools, along with equally intelligent delivery, development, and deployment systems, should help keep us not only sane but also more productive than ever before. We shouldn't even have to commute to an office or a production facility if we don't want to. With IoT remote operations, there will be almost nothing we can't access virtually over the network (as long as we have the right authorizations, of course). Just imagine unmanned production sites with remote operators sitting in headquarters and running oil fields or assembly lines halfway across the globe. Our biggest problem may be resisting the temptation, or the pressure, to work 24×7.

By the way, this isn't just a "work" thing. In 10 years IoT will be poised to have a deep impact on our personal lives, too. It will change how our families do things as profoundly as the way the first wave of the Internet changed how we relate to the larger world. IoT is about how we control and automate the environment we live in, as well as how we shop, find healthcare, and more. It's sure to redefine many aspects of our day, both personally and professionally.

All of this contributes to why it's so important for us to get IoT right. We need to build the appropriate foundation with best practices in security, open standards, architectures, processes, policies and regulations, culture, and business (Figure 11.1). We need to focus on scoping and redefining the jobs for both our current employees and the newcomers to our organizations. We need to set not only the vision but also a realistic IoT roadmap for our organizations, whether they're for- or non-profit enterprises or governmental organizations.

When you're successful in 10 years—and I have no doubt that you will be—you probably won't even be talking about IoT as IoT. None of us will. "We don't talk about ecommerce anymore. We simply do it. The same way in 10 years nobody will be talking about IoT. It will be part of everyday operations," said Paul Glynn, CEO of IoT platform provider Davra Networks, at the McRock IIoT Symposium in Montreal in June 2016. In other words, IoT will go mainstream in the next 10 years. It will have not only crossed the chasm but become standard operating procedure.

Winners and Losers

Who will be the winners and losers in this new IoT-enabled economy? Or, to put it differently, how will you differentiate your company in an IoT-enabled world and the accompanying co-economy?

Let's start with what we know: By 2020, according to industry experts, IoT will make up almost half of IT budgets as organizations scramble to

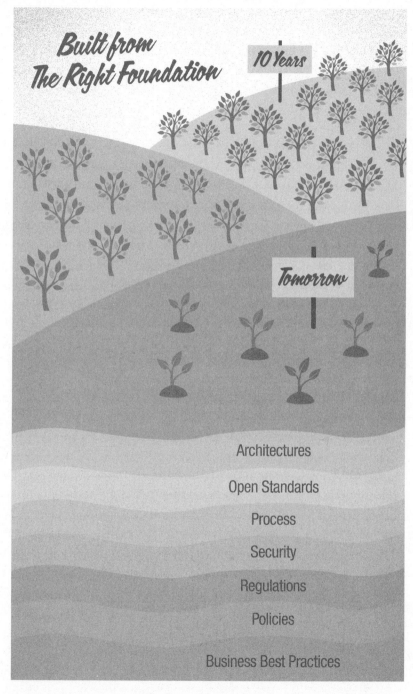

Figure 11.1 Projecting the Future: Built from the Right Foundation

digitize and connect things, wrote Chloe Green in a June 8, 2016, article in *Information Age* magazine titled "The IoT to make up almost half of IT budgets by 2020."[1] It won't just be IoT and IT, either. LOB units and OT will play key roles, too. This isn't going to be an IT thing or an OT thing, nor will it even be an LOB thing exclusively. IoT is going to change the organization from top to bottom, so plan to get the C-suite sponsorship as early as you can.

For the near term, IoT is primarily a B2B thing—even more specifically, an industrial B2B thing. B2C activity is currently focused around shopping and personal health and fitness, with some attention paid to home security—but even that hasn't taken off as fast as initially anticipated. Eventually, however, I expect most disruptive implementations of IoT to come from B2B2C. Although we haven't seen them yet, they will start percolating to the surface soon.

Beyond the industrial and transportation industries, healthcare should emerge as a big winner in IoT. That industry can use IoT to monitor patients remotely and even potentially intervene in certain instances. Whatever IoT can do to reduce physical visits to doctors' offices and emergency rooms could also reduce the cost of healthcare delivery. Beyond that, combining the plethora of microscopic sensors embedded in clothing or edible sensors ingested into our bodies and connected to personal area networks is likely to revolutionize diagnostic and preventive care.

Retail also promises to be an IoT winner. Already running omnichannel programs and using other tools to enhance and ease the shopper's buying experience, retailers also use IoT to streamline supply chain and inventory processes. Further in the future, IoT will combine with rapid systems retooling, 3D-printed specialized and spare parts, and just-in-time delivery via drones both to drive the convergence of production and retail and to enable the sale and delivery of mass-customizable and individualized products on demand. The entire retail value chain will be disrupted in the long run: Food will be cooked or "printed" in your home, along with clothing and other goods. It will take quite a while before such capabilities prove to be more than science fiction, but eventually you'll even be able to use IoT to control a variety of robots—it's just more things connecting to other things.

The financial services industry, meanwhile—mainly in the form of banks—currently operates huge networks of connected ATMs. Banks

already leverage these machines, along with their websites, to enable truly personalized, face-to-face remote banking to reduce costs, increase revenues, and achieve higher customer satisfaction. This can be done today. Tomorrow, blockchain and IoT are likely to revolutionize both financial and non-financial transactions even more.

And then we have the other winners—you, the readers of this book. As early adopters, which I hope you either are or will become, you stand to gain valuable experience before many of your competitors. Tomorrow, you can have your IoT projects underway. They'll begin to revitalize and re-energize your business. You'll win praise, speak at conferences, and receive awards at trade shows. Then, within 10 years, you'll have new and different business processes, go-to-market strategies, pricing and delivery models, support and service models, and staffing and employment models—all due to IoT. But by then you won't even remember these early efforts. They'll just be the way your digital organization does things. That's what I mean when I welcome you to Generation IoT.

State of the IoT Union Today

As I write this, mid-summer 2016, the state of IoT is mixed. It's gaining traction and experiencing great success in the industrial segments, logistics, transportation, and smart cities. Other segments, such as healthcare, retail, and agriculture, are just starting to pilot IoT projects. According to The MPI Group's "The Internet of Things Has Finally Arrived" study, "most manufacturing companies have limited understanding of IoT or how to apply it to their businesses," but "roughly two-thirds of manufacturing executives believe that IoT will increase profitability over the next five years."[2] Translation: Business leaders expect IoT to have an impact on their enterprises, but right now they're confused and don't know where to begin. That's exactly why I wrote this book, to get you and your peers started with IoT and to maximize your chances of success.

The fact is, IoT remains vastly overhyped. Technology providers both large and small, solution developers, and integrators—some consciously, some not—have all played a part in promoting, publicizing, and, yes, overstating where IoT is today. I have to admit I've done my fair share of that, too. We all saw the transformational capabilities IoT could deliver for businesses and consumers, as well as the big new revenue streams for the vendors, and we wanted to make IoT a reality tomorrow. But as I hope you've seen throughout this book, IoT doesn't need the hype. It has been steadily advancing for 10 years or more, with new developments and players appearing what seems like weekly. And yet, even though the projected numbers of IoT's growth and impact may be statistically correct, they're still so mind-bogglingly large as to be incomprehensible—it's almost like trying to understand government budgets.

The hype isn't all bad. It has had a positive impact in many areas— from inspiring entrepreneurs to focus on IoT use cases and technology gaps to encouraging vendors to invest in IoT to accelerating the move to open standards and interoperability and, finally, to bringing together many industries to work cooperatively. Negative consequences do remain, however: By over-representing current solution capabilities, over-simplifying the implementation challenges, and over-promising the business impact, the hype surrounding IoT has increased the risks of initial IoT projects.

To paraphrase Davra Networks' Glynn, we'll know that IoT has made it when we stop talking about IoT as a distinct and separate phenomenon and simply absorb it into the fabric of our businesses and our lives, as we've done with the Internet, ecommerce, and other technologies. For example, when was the last time you heard anyone mention service-oriented architecture (SOA) in a business conversation? Probably not for years, but it hasn't gone away. It has simply been absorbed by IT and, in turn, by the way we conduct business. The latest advances of SOA, in fact, will likely be part of your IoT projects in the form of micro-services that are requested when certain actions have to be taken in response to certain IoT events. Although you shouldn't expect to hear much about services at the business level, the experts you bring in to your IoT ecosystem to work with the technical plumbing will make heavy use of an array of services, micro and otherwise.

As I said in the very first chapter, and despite the intense hype, IoT is very real today, and it will continue to evolve and grow for years to come. There are many fast paybacks, almost sure-bet use cases, for any organization eager to move forward with a pilot project, at least. IoT also serves as a catalyst for the long-expected convergence of various technologies and new business models. Just look at all of the new companies popping up and touting myriad "IoT as a service" or "lean" operations or the variety of open and subscription-based pricing models.

Remember the discussion on the different ways you may buy (or choose not to buy) a car in the future? What about the usage-based models for industrial assets and components, such as capacity or energy efficiency leases, springing up around the industry (converting a traditional capital expenditure [capex] outlay into a recurring operational expenditure [opex] charge)? Then there is the adoption of consumer freebie models (think razors and razorblades), where manufacturers monetize the data (for example, charging for alerts and exceptions) but give away the hardware assets, or even the overhyped sharing economy models. Some of these experiments will fizzle, but many will result in substantial new value for both customers and providers. However, in order to properly implement such models, the customers must have an in-depth understanding of their IoT business processes and be equipped with the TCO data based on their actual operations. Armed with facts, they can then intelligently evaluate the ROI tradeoffs between various pricing approaches. While I see many large enterprises experiment with such IoT business models and apply them selectively (for example, some high-ticket items in health care or transportation), I believe that the enterprise-wide IoT implementations need first to reach the level of maturity and scale before such models can be adopted comprehensively. Having said that, I do see a lot of interest in "IoT as a service" in midsize and even small companies. So I would not be surprised if the integrators and service providers packaged such offerings based on fast payback scenarios and targeted them at these audiences.

Era of Innovation and Disruption

I've been involved in what we now call IoT since the mid-2000s. I haven't felt as much excitement about being part of the creation of a new industry since the beginning of the 1990s, when the networking industry and the Internet exploded. And now we're building the next wave of the Internet. Although we're just starting the journey, there's already an initial set of fast payback business use cases. We don't have to wait to capitalize on IoT.

You'll often hear people talking about IoT in the context of all the devices being connected, but connectivity is just an enabler and the consequence of attractive use cases. These use cases, and the business value propositions they produce, drive the connectivity, not vice versa. We aren't connecting things just for the exercise; serious value and benefits are at stake. That's why you've read this book this far. That's also the reason for innovation.

When you look at the history of innovation and disruption, neither has been uniform across industries. This is the major flaw in some futuristic movies—the creators assumed, wrongly, that the pace of innovation would be constant, consistent, and simultaneous across many industries. Sorry, but the reality is quite different. In the car industry, for example, we saw a spur of innovation that resulted in the creation of entire industries some 100 years ago, while the follow-on innovations have mostly been evolutionary and incremental. The same thing happened with the airline industry. The PC industry has been floundering for years, waiting for the next compelling innovation and fresh use cases. The mobile industry is starting to plateau, too.

I think, however, that IoT is now providing the stimulus for a new wave of innovations and new value for many old and not-so-old industries (Figure 11.2). The congruence of new capabilities delivered by chip, material, or software industries, as well as the emergence of new use cases, business models, and market structures in vertical markets, are feeding on each other and creating new value in many unexpected ways. Just look at how IoT is transforming the manufacturing, transportation, retail, and health care industries, which until recently have been about as plodding as any industry could be. Better still are the new industries, such as drones, being created—awaiting only the capabilities, use cases, and government regulations to catch up. Banking, finance, and technology converged decades ago. Now high tech and manufacturing are rapidly converging. IoT is behind all of this.

So let's see where IoT stands as we approach the fall of 2016. In general, after a few years of hype, chaos, and experimentation, the IoT industry is maturing and becoming more realistic and sophisticated at the same time. At industry gatherings we're focused less on big numbers and the "IoT promise" types of presentations and more on actual results. We're sharing not only a common vision but also best practices, success stories, and failures. Each industry category reflects this shift:

Figure 11.2   Waking Up Industry Innovation

- *Large and midsize enterprises.* The low-hanging fruit is ready and ripe for picking. Tens of thousands of enterprises have started on their IoT journeys, focusing initially on cost savings, efficiencies, and productivity improvements. If you're one of these companies, please share your experiences and lessons learned with your peers. If you haven't started with IoT, it's time to craft your vision, figure out a pilot project, and build some success and knowledge.
- *Small businesses.* Yes, the initial thrust of IoT focused on and was led by large enterprises. But small businesses can benefit from IoT, too, as they've done with ecommerce, cloud computing, mobile computing, and analytics over the past two decades. Just pick a proven use case—say, remote operations—and try it. Many integrators and service providers with horizontal technology capabilities, vertical solution capabilities, or business process capabilities are eager to help you deploy the most mature, standardized, easy-to-implement, and, thus, cost-effective solutions.
- *Vendors.* These companies are investing in IoT technologies, platforms, vertical go-to-market strategies, and services as if it were the California Gold Rush all over again. The market is starting to consolidate (Cisco buying Jasper or Softbank buying Arm are just the latest examples). Horizontal and vertical vendors are forming strategic alliances, and a few have already created extensive partner ecosystems. I'm very encouraged to see the level of collaboration across a wide spectrum of vendors. One of my early concerns about IoT was that (similar to the fieldbus wars and browser wars at the onset of the commercial Internet 20 years ago) it also would be Balkanized, with vendors focusing too early on differentiation and grabbing market share instead of working together to move the industry forward and make IoT happen for everybody. So far, when you go to major industry events such as the IoT World Forum, you'll see most of the players doing the right thing, contributing their knowledge and expertise, learning and sharing together. Let's hope such attitudes continue.

Although notable exceptions do exist (especially the large, established players in their respective industries, which have chosen to stick to their old business structures, models, and technology approaches), the good news is that over the last five years I've seen the ranks of IoT naysayers dwindle dramatically. Some vendors are joining the IoT revolution through top-down, board-level decisions; some hire external change agents (often from outside their industry); and some start with grass-roots-level projects sponsored by LOB department heads or C-level executives. Some vendors even set up separate IoT units. It definitely isn't easy to transform companies with 100+ years of history and hundreds of thousands of employees. But the established vendors are realizing that they may not have 10 or 20 years to go through such a transition. IoT is starting to disrupt their industries now. So when you think about selecting vendors to work with, you should have many good options. Just be wary of any vendor that isn't truly committed to open, standards-based solutions. If a vendor isn't working with any of the major vendor-neutral standards groups, steer clear.

- *Consultants.* I've worked with many great consulting companies, both large and small, that are taking on different aspects of IoT. (Some have contributed key insights to this book.) The right consultants can help your organization identify the best problems to tackle first, build the business case, assess the risks, assemble an IoT solution eco-system (even act as matchmakers), integrate the solution with business workflows, and avoid major pitfalls in the process. My only advice is to look for consultants who bring real-life experiences to your IoT project and have a proven track record verified by your peers.

- *System integrators and service providers.* Both of these categories have been transforming themselves to become essential players in the IoT ecosystem. Many horizontal technology resellers have built vertical technology, business expertise, and sophisticated integration capa-bilities. They've forged alliances with traditional vertical experts to gain insights into the specific requirements of a given industry, access to the LOB decision makers, and know-how in legacy system inte-gration. The same goes for vertical integrators, many of which have invested in expertise in modern technologies, development tools, and best practices. Some have even embraced open systems, although I've seen a lot of resistance to standards-based approaches driven by inertia, misinformation, fear of opening their customer bases to competitors, and the addiction to high profits awarded to them by custom, one-off implementations. As we discussed in Chapter 3, service providers— after a few years of trial and error—are playing a key role in the IoT ecosystem, not only as connectivity providers but also as integrators offering sophisticated managed services. You should consider them as partners for your IoT journey.

- *Developers.* Until recently, most of the developers participating in IoT were vertical specialists with deep knowledge of specific use cases and legacy infrastructure and deployments. But in the past two or three years, the IoT developer ecosystem has evolved dramatically. IoT's real business opportunities, along with a bit of its hype, have attracted "mainstream" horizontal developers. Some (especially the larger ones) have even set up vertical practices and IoT groups. In parallel, we've seen both the more established and the new device and infrastructure vendors open their platforms, offer modern application development environments and interfaces, and embrace co-economy methodologies. As we discussed in the last chapter, the industry is also working to standardize data formats and interfaces (although we aren't there yet). Bottom line: For your next IoT project, cast a wide net and consider traditional and non-traditional application developers as partners. Some truly will surprise you.

- *Suppliers*. Keep your organization's suppliers informed of your direction and plan to recruit them, if appropriate, as part of your IoT ecosystem. Most are highly motivated to figure out and implement IoT with you. They want to add value and co-innovate, too.

- *Customers*. Whether your customers are businesses, governments, or consumers, don't forget to engage them. IoT value creation today is mostly centered around efficiency and improvements in existing processes. But tomorrow's IoT is about new value propositions for consumers and new revenue streams for enterprises. Customers don't want to simply buy your products and services anymore. They want to have a stake in the outcome and contribute to the success. They want to co-innovate and co-develop their digital future with you. After all, customers know their businesses best. So engage them strategically now, and consider the possibility of bringing customers into your IoT ecosystem as participants in your co-economy (more on that below).

IoT and the Co-Economy

You've read references in the previous pages to the emerging co-economy (Figure 11.3). It's the product of the greatly improved communication capabilities inherent in IoT and the fact that IoT is too complex to be tackled by one organization alone, no matter how big. It's also an essential element of IoT success. The co-economy is the mindset, the process, and the value proposition where companies partner with other companies, combining their skills, talents, and resources for anything from a one-off project to an ongoing initiative.

Think of it as a big folk or square dance where partners come together, twirl around, and then move on to other partners. Some partners

Figure 11.3   The Co-Economy

will come back repeatedly; others will dance once and leave the floor. The co-economy drives things such as collaboration, cooperation, and even co-opetition to the max. Companies that not only take such a model mainstream in their organizations but also integrate such an external web of projects and relationships with their internal processes, culture, and KPIs will be best positioned to thrive in what I'm referring to as the emerging IoT/co-economy.

Some aspects of the co-economy have been around for years. (I remember when the idea of "co-opetition" surfaced back in the 1990s, for example.) Now it's going mainstream, changing our fundamental assumptions about how to get things done. The co-economy is redefining how companies not only build their products but also define their culture and processes. It entails redefining employee skill sets and how we measure success. Finally, the co-economy involves redefining business relationships. It's changing how we think about who is the vendor, who is the customer, and who is the partner.

The skills required to navigate the co-economy are complex. New co-development models are customer-centric. It isn't just customers' IT departments looking to co-innovate; their LOBs also want to partner on solutions that deliver specific business outcomes. Vendors need to form ecosystems of partnerships that focus on customers' business challenges rather than their own technical offerings. We need to co-innovate with customers, other vendors, and startups, each of which brings its own skills, expertise, and relationships to the table. When the customer is at the center, the whole ecosystem benefits.

Entire industries are being reshaped by IoT and the co-economy. Developing a game-changing innovation like the self-driving car, for example, blurs the lines among manufacturing, transportation, and technology. These industries previously existed in separate universes. Now they're chasing the same pools of talent to work on different sides of the same innovation effort. Orchestrating the co-economy will entail a web of relationships, contractual arrangements, and both formal and informal agreements that address a wide range of issues and govern everything from intellectual property to exclusive relationships to the equivalent of marital prenups.

As your organization begins its IoT journey, it isn't too early to embrace co-innovation and co-development. It all starts with an IoT/co-economy champion—in this case, you. Work to change processes and culture around co-development. Dismantle silos and develop strong ecosystems of partners that complement your organization's strengths. And while you're at it, lay to rest the "not-invented-here" mentality once and for all. Companies that work in isolation, focusing only on one-company end-to-end solutions, are in danger of being out-innovated and out-operated. Those, however, that understand the power of the co-economy will be the new winners in a world driven by IoT and digital capabilities.

In 10 years the co-economy will be the way we work. As with IoT, we'll no longer even have to talk about it; it will simply be what business has become. Having various partners and watching them come, go, and return based on each company's changing needs will be the way we do business. (I'm already working on a new book that explores the co-economy in depth, so watch for that next year if you want more information.) Also like IoT, the co-economy will mean a different way of thinking and working. The co-economy has already started to happen in a big way, so stay tuned.

Unavoidable Fact of Life

If you aren't a techie, you can avoid the technology and the more technical aspects of IoT. If you aren't business-focused, you can avoid the business aspects of IoT. What you can't avoid is change. With IoT, change—especially big, disruptive change—is both a given and an unavoidable fact of life.

Florence Hudson, senior vice president and chief innovation officer at Internet2 made an observation that has stayed with me: "The Internet of Things provides the opportunity to disrupt or be disrupted. We each need to decide which it will be for our industry, our business model, our company, and our clients. New business models, leveraging technology in new ways, can create new revenue opportunities." She went on to say, "but, we must also have a plan to ensure trust, identity, privacy, protection, safety, and security (TIPPSS) in the systems we create to protect the things and people in the mix."

Hudson concisely sums up two salient aspects of IoT: the power of disruptive change and the deep concern about security (TIPPSS). Once you start connecting things, you can conceive and execute new processes and innovative strategies that wouldn't have been possible before. This, in turn, enables business creativity and innovation at its best. That's one of the key reasons you'll want to pursue IoT. But you don't have to be the most innovative or creative light bulb on the connected ceiling to fully participate in IoT transformation. Just be as creative and innovative as possible, and then let your other "co-s"—or whatever you want to refer to them as—take over from there and be assured that any resulting value will flow between you. None of these things will happen, however, if we don't take a comprehensive architectural approach to security. So starting with your very first IoT project, security is job 1; it must be integrated into the core fabric of your solution, business process, and job function. The IoT industry has matured significantly in its thinking and approach to security over the past five years, but we're far from achieving an adequate level of security sophistication and pervasiveness. Security is still a major risk to IoT adoption.

"What's real is the huge change IoT already is producing and the increasing pace of change as IoT picks up even more steam. The challenge for observers is that IoT has no precedent either in terms of the opportunities it presents or the risk it creates. With respect to risks specifically, while security and privacy are foremost on practitioners' minds, a more comprehensive risk assessment covering areas like network capacity, data processing locations, data governance, etc., must be part and parcel of any IoT deployment," observes Sanjaya Krishna, digital risk consulting leader at KPMG.

Krishna is correct. With IoT, we are in many ways in unchartered territory. We also won't know the full extent of IoT's impact for 10 years or more. In the meantime, what we do know is the tangible value many companies are reporting from implementing IoT today. It just makes so much sense. And yes, there are serious risks that we all need to consider and mitigate, including both the risk associated with IoT and the risk associated with either not implementing IoT properly or not starting on

Figure 11.4　Welcome to Generation IoT

the IoT journey. I'm convinced that the risk of not preparing for the IoT economy and the co-economy is huge—too huge, in fact, to contemplate. Flip back to the exercise we did at the start of this chapter when we calculated the payback from one simple remote control project that saved $200 a week or $10,400 a year. OK, that's not enough to affect any company's bottom line. But what if we were talking about 35 projects or 173 projects each year and the aggregated savings amounted to $1.8 million or $23.7 million per year or more. Now you're talking about affecting the bottom line. Yes, start with one project, but don't stop there. Just keep it going.

So what are you waiting for? Reread the exercises in Chapter 7 and create an IoT vision for your organization. Use the recipe in Chapter 1 to cover your bases, and then pick one of the fast payback scenarios in Chapter 5, build a business case and your virtual team, secure C-suite sponsorship, and take on your first small, low-hanging-fruit IoT project. Start your IoT journey with open eyes, learning and sharing with your peers and managing risks with clear outcomes in sight.

I firmly believe that for many of us IoT represents a once-in-a-lifetime opportunity to redefine our industries, organizations, and jobs. I can assure you that in 10 years you'll be amazed at how much impact you've had. Are you ready to begin? Good. Welcome to Generation IoT (Figure 11.4).

Notes

Chapter 1

1. Trefis Team, Harley-Davidson's Success Story in the U.S., *Forbes*, December 19, 2014. http://www.forbes.com/sites/greatspeculations/2014/12/19/harley-davidsons-success-story-in-the-u-s/#58c4074550fc
2. Reeves, Martin, and Lisanne Pueschel. "Die Another Day: What Leaders Can Do About the Shrinking Life Expectancy of Corporations." The Boston Consulting Group's *bcg.perspectives*, July 2, 2015. https://www.bcgperspectives.com/content/articles/strategic-planning-growth-die-another-day/
3. Manyika, James, and Michael Chui. "By 2025, Internet of things applications could have $11 trillion impact." McKinsey Global Institute, repurposed in *Fortune*, July 22, 2015. http://fortune.com/2015/07/22/mckinsey-internet-of-things/
4. Vernon Turner, Carrie MacGillivray, Marcus Torchia, Madeleine Cinco, Milan Kalal, Monika Kumar, Roberto Membrila, Andrea Siviero, Yuta Torisu, Nigel Wallis. Worldwide Internet of Things Forecast Update, 2016–2020, #US40755516/IDC, May 31, 2016. https://www.idc.com/getdoc.jsp?containerId=US40755516
5. *Ibid.*
6. LeHong, Hung, Jackie Fenn, and Rand Leeb-du Toit. "Hype Cycle for Emerging Technologies, 2014." Gartner, July 28, 2014. https://www.gartner.com/doc/2809728/hype-cycle-emerging-technologies-

7. Noronha, Andy, Robert Moriarty, Kathy O'Connell, and Nicola Villa. "Attaining IoT Value: How to Move from Connecting Things to Capturing Insights." Cisco Systems, 2014. http://www.cisco.com/c/dam/en_us/solutions/trends/iot/docs/iot-data-analytics-white-paper.PDF
8. *Ibid.*

Chapter 2

1. Surface World 2015. http://www.rosler.com/uploads/media/RoslerUK_OpenDay_2015.pdf
2. Wallbank, Paul. "A geek's tour of Barcelona." *Decoding the New Economy*, November 1, 2013. http://paulwallbank.com/2013/11/01/touring-barcelona-smart-city-internet-of-things/
3. Vernon Turner, Carrie MacGillivray, Marcus Torchia, Madeleine Cinco, Milan Kalal, Monika Kumar, Roberto Membrila, Andrea Siviero, Yuta Torisu, Nigel Wallis. Worldwide Internet of Things Forecast Update, 2016 -2020, #US40755516/IDC, May 31, 2016. https://www.idc.com/getdoc.jsp?containerId=US40755516
4. Manyika, James, and Michael Chui. "By 2025, Internet of things applications could have $11 trillion impact." McKinsey Global Institute, repurposed in *Fortune*, July 22, 2015. http://fortune.com/2015/07/22/mckinsey-internet-of-things/

Chapter 3

1. Cisco Case Study 2015: IoE-Driven Smart City Barcelona Initiative Cuts Water Bills, Boosts Parking Revenues, Creates Jobs, & More
2. Vernon Turner, Carrie MacGillivray, Marcus Torchia, Madeleine Cinco, Milan Kalal, Monika Kumar, Roberto Membrila, Andrea Siviero, Yuta Torisu, Nigel Wallis. Worldwide Internet of Things Forecast Update, 2016–2020, #US40755516/IDC, May 31, 2016. https://www.idc.com/getdoc.jsp?containerId=US40755516
3. Digital Transformations with Internet of Everything, Cisco 2016.
4. *Ibid.*
5. *Ibid.*
6. *Ibid.*
7. "IoT Application Enablement ScoreCard," MachNation, 2015, and "IoT Platform-Enabled Solutions ScoreCard," MachNation, 2016.

Chapter 4

1. LeHong, Hung, Jackie Fenn, and Rand Leeb-du Toit. "Hype Cycle for Emerging Technologies, 2014." Gartner, July 28, 2014. https://www.gartner.com/doc/2809728/hype-cycle-emerging-technologies-
2. PepsiCo Infrastructure as a Service Profile, Rockwell Automation.
3. Macaulay, James, Kathy O'Connell, Chet Namboodri, and Kevin Delaney. "The Digital Manufacturer, Resolving the Service Dilemma, "Cisco Systems, November 2015.
4. Mining Firm Quadruples Production, with Internet of Everything. Cisco Case Study, 2014. www.cisco.com/c/dam/en/us/solutions/collateral/data-center-virtualization/unified-computing/dundee-precious-metals.pdf

Chapter 5

1. Lewotsky, Kristin. Industrial Internet of Things: Sifting Reality from Hype. Motion Control Online, January 15, 2015. http://www.motioncontrolonline.org/content-detail.cfm/Motion-Control-Technical-Features/Industrial-Internet-of-Things-Sifting-Reality-From-Hype/content_id/291
2. Shimel, Alan. "The real cost of downtime." DevOps.com, February 11, 2015. http://devops.com/2015/02/11/real-cost-downtime/
3. Harnessing the Internet of Things for Global Development, Cisco and ITU, 2016.
4. "Smart Handpumps" to bring a reliable water service to rural Africa. University of Oxford, July 2, 2015.

Chapter 6

1. Greenough, Josh. "The manufacturing industry is being revolutionized by the Internet of Things." *Business Insider*, March 11, 2016. http://www.businessinsider.com/internet-of-things-in-manufacturing-2016-2?utm_content=buffer34155&utm_medium=social&utm_source=twitter.com&utm_campaign=buffer
2. Siemens. "Siemens' first class of U.S. apprentices graduates, national model for skills-based learning." Press release, August 12, 2015. http://news.usa.siemens.biz/press-release/siemens-usa/siemens-first-class-us-apprentices-graduates-national-model-skills-based-l

3. Federal Trade Commission. "Internet of Things, Privacy, and Security in the Connected World." Staff Report, January 2015.
4. Gartner Report: The Top 10 Strategic Technology Trends for Government in 2016, Bettina Tratz-Ryan co-authoring with Rick Howard, Cathleen E. Blanton, Rick Holgate, and Neville Cannon, June 2016

Chapter 7

1. PricewaterhouseCoopers. "Industrial Manufacturing M&A Records 10 Year High in Deal Volume Despite Recent Declines in Value, According to PwC US." Press release, February 9, 2016. http://www.pwc.com/us/en/press-releases/2016/pwc-q4-industrial-manufacturing-ma-press-release.html
2. CB Insights. "The New Manufacturing: Funding to Industrial IoT Startups Jumps 83% In 2015." Blog post, March 3, 2016. https://www.cbinsights.com/blog/industrial-iiot-funding/

Chapter 8

1. AlphaWise. "The Internet of Things and the New Industrial Revolution." Morgan Stanley-Automation World Industrial Automation Survey, April 18, 2016. http://www.morganstanley.com/ideas/industrial-internet-of-things-and-automation-robotics?cid=sm_corp_lnk_may_04_2016
2. Press release: Gartner Says by 2020, More Than Half of Major New Business Processes and Systems Will Incorporate Some Element of the Internet of Things, Gartner, January 14, 2016.
3. Gartner. "Why Integration Is Critical to IoT Success." March 9, 2016. http://www.gartner.com/smarterwithgartner/iot-integration-questions/

Chapter 9

1. ISACA and RSA Conference 2016 survey. http://www.isaca.org/About-ISACA/Press-room/News-Releases/2016/Pages/Survey-82-percent-of-Boards-Are-Concerned-about-Cybersecurity.aspx

2. Chiang, Mung, Bharath Balasubraman, and Flavio Bonomi. *Fog for 5G and IoT,* John Wiley & Sons, April 2017. Zhang, Tao, Yi Zheng, Raymond Zheng, and Helder Antunes in the chapter "Securing the Internet of Things: Need for a New Paradigm and Fog Computing."

3. Kerner, Sean Michael. "IDC: Specialized Threat Analysis Is Hot." *eSecurity Planet*, March 8, 2016. http://www.esecurityplanet.com/network-security/idc-specialized-threat-analysis-is-hot.html

4. Gartner. "Gartner Says Worldwide IoT Security Spending to Reach $348 Million in 2016." Press release, April 25, 2016. http://www.gartner.com/newsroom/id/3291817

Chapter 10

1. Kranz, Maciej. "Number of Access Technologies and IoT Deployments Is Skyrocketing." LinkedIn blog post, July 7, 2015. https://www.linkedin.com/pulse/number-access-technologies-iot-deployments-maciej-kranz?trk=mp-author-card

2. Kranz, Maciej. "IoT Meets Standards, Driving Interoperability and Adoption." Cisco Digital Transformations blog post, July 21, 2015. http://blogs.cisco.com/digital/iot-meets-standards-driving-interoperability-and-adoption

3. *Forrester Report,* "Don't Get Confused by the Blockchain Hype in Banking." Martha Bennett and Jost Hoppermann, June 16, 2016.

Chapter 11

1. Green, Chloe. "The IoT to make up almost half of IT budgets by 2020." *Information Age*, June 8, 2016. http://www.information-age.com/it-management/finance-and-project-management/123461579/iot-make-almost-half-it-budgets-2020

2. The Internet of Things Has Finally Arrived. The MPI Group, 2016. www.mpi-group.com/wp-content/uploads/2016/01/IoT-Summary2016.pdf

Glossary

(Definitions Specifically in the Context of Internet of Things)

5G: (also known as 5th-generation mobile networks or 5th-generation wireless systems) is the proposed next generation of cellular networks design to address key IoT use-cases

Actuator: a mechanical device responsible for moving or controlling a mechanism or system

Analytics: the discovery, interpretation, and communication of meaningful patterns in data that provide business intelligence and predict likely future scenarios

Anti-Spoofing: a technique for countering network attacks where a person or a program assumes the identity of another person or program for illegal purposes

Application Programming Interface (API): a set of routines, protocols, and tools used by software applications to interact with other entities

Autonomous Vehicle: (also known as driverless car, self-driving car, or robotic car) a vehicle that is capable of operating and navigating without human input; multiple levels of automation have been defined

AVnu Alliance: a consortium of companies working together to establish and certify the interoperability of open audio video bridging and time-sensitive networking standards

Big Data: extremely large data sets in various forms that require new technics for proper and timely data analysis

Blockchain: a distributed public or private database hardened against tampering and revision that allows a secure exchange of value between entities

Bluetooth Low Energy: (also known as Bluetooth LE or BLE) a short-range wireless personal area network technology optimized for low-power applications of IoT

Brownfield: an environment in which the new technology has to be integrated with legacy systems. Contrast with *greenfield*

Building Automation: the automatic centralized control of a building's heating, ventilation, air conditioning, lighting, security, and other systems through a building automation system

Cloud Computing: a kind of Internet-based computing that provides processing resources and data to devices

Common Industrial Protocol (CIP): an industrial object-oriented protocol for industrial automation applications supported by ODVA

Connected Vehicle: a vehicle equipped with Internet access and connectivity within the vehicle that allows the vehicle, its systems, and devices to interact with each other and the external services

Cyber Security: collection of tools and processes that protect information systems and electronic data against criminal or unauthorized use

Data Processing: a series of operations on data to retrieve, transform, or classify meaningful information

Datacenter: a facility or a department that houses computer systems and associated components, such as telecommunications and storage systems

Drone: an unmanned aircraft guided by remote control or onboard computers

Ethernet: a family of computer networking technologies used to form a local area network (LAN)

Event Stream Processing: a set of technologies designed to process data in real time

First Phase of Internet: initial phase of commercial Internet focused on providing people with access to the information and to each other

Fog Computing: located at the network edge close to data sources, it extends the cloud computing capabilities by providing a layer of compute, storage, networking, and data processing services

Gateway: an interconnection device that links diverse standards-based and legacy access and field networks; often the initial network element connecting multiple sensors and edge-devices to the network where consistent IP services can be implemented

Greenfield: a project that lacks constraints imposed by prior work. Contrast with *brownfield*

Identity: set of attributes related to a person, device, or the combination of both used to recognize them by computer systems

Industrial Automation: use of technologies in industrial processes to make them more efficient and safer

Industrial Internet Consortium (IIC): open membership consortium that sets the architectural framework and direction for the Industrial Internet. The consortium's mission is to coordinate vast ecosystem initiatives to connect and integrate objects with people, processes, and data using common architectures, interoperability, and open standards

Industry 4.0: A German industry and government initiative driving the definition and adoption of smart factory or factory of the future, centered around interoperability, information transparency, technical assistance, and decentralized decisions

Institute of Electrical and Electronics Engineers (IEEE): a global technical professional organization that, among others, drove key connectivity standards

International Organization for Standardization (ISO): an international standard-setting body composed of representatives from various national standards organizations

International Telecommunication Union (ITU): a specialized agency of the United Nations (UN) that is responsible for issues that concern information and communication technologies

Internet Engineering Task Force (IETF): an open standards organization that develops and promotes voluntary Internet standards, in particular the standards that comprise the TCP/IP

Internet of Everything (IoE): brings together people, processes, data, and things to make networked connections more relevant and valuable than ever before (In this book I used IoE as a synonym of IoT.)

Internet Protocol (IP): one of the foundational protocols of Internet, the communications protocol that provides an identification and location system for computers on networks and routes traffic across the Internet

Internet of Things (IoT): the next wave of Internet where every device is connected to other devices and the cloud; the new value is being delivered by solutions that analyze the data generated by these devices and applications optimizing business processes

IPv6: A key IoT enabler, Internet Protocol Version 6 is the most recent version of the Internet Protocol that substantially increased the number of available IP addresses, allowing every device to be connected

ISA100: a wireless networking technology standard developed by the International Society of Automation (ISA) to provide connectivity to wireless sensors and other end-devices. The official description is "Wireless Systems for Industrial Automation: Process Control and Related Applications." One of the standards based on IEEE 802.15.4 radio technology

Line of Business (LOB): a function responsible for operation or "running" the core business within an organization

Long-Term Evolution (LTE): a standard for high-speed wireless communication for mobile phones and data terminals. In this book, LTE and 4G cellular networks are used interchangeably

LoRa: a low power wide area network (LPWAN) standard intended to connect wireless battery-operated IoT devices

Machine Learning: a type of artificial intelligence (AI) that provides computers with the ability to learn without being explicitly programmed. A key set of technologies to provide advanced predictive analytics and maintenance capabilities

Machine to Machine (M2M): In the world of service providers, the communication systems that connect devices to devices other than cell phones

Mobile Network Operator: (also known as a wireless service provider, wireless carrier, cellular company, or mobile network carrier) provides wireless voice and data communication services to customers and owns or controls all the elements necessary to sell and deliver such services

Mobile Virtual Network Operator (MVNO): (also known as a mobile other licensed operator [MOLO]) a wireless communications services provider that does not own the wireless network infrastructure over which it provides services to its customers

National Institute of Standards and Technology (NIST): a measurement standards laboratory, and a non-regulatory agency of the United States Department of Commerce

ODVA: A pioneer of open systems in industrial automation, a standards development and trade organizations aimed at the advancement and promotion of open, interoperable information and communication technologies for industrial automation

Open Connectivity Foundation (OCF): a foundation that is creating a specification and sponsoring an open-source project to enable billions of connected devices to communicate with one another regardless of manufacturer, operating system, chipset, or physical transport

OpenFog Consortium (OFC): a consortium focused on driving industry and academic leadership in fog computing architecture, testbed development, and a variety of interoperability and composability deliverables that seamlessly leverage cloud and edge architectures to enable end-to-end IoT scenarios

Operational Technology (OT): organizations and technologies operating production processes and industrial control systems

Power-Line Communication (PLC): a communication protocol that uses electrical wiring to simultaneously carry both data and alternating current (AC) electric power transmission or electric power distribution

Predictive Maintenance: techniques designed to determine the condition of in-service equipment to anticipate when maintenance should be performed

Programmable Logic Controller (PLC): a digital computer used to automate industrial processes such as control of machinery on factory assembly lines, amusement rides, or light fixtures

Radio-Frequency Identification (RFID): the use of radio waves to read and capture information stored on a tag attached to an object

Real Time (Analytics, Processing): capability whereby inputs are processed or analyzed without delay

Remote Asset Management: a set of tools that enable engineers to control, monitor, troubleshoot, and correct the operation of physical assets remotely

Self-Learning Network: a solution that combines analytics and machine learning to enable a network to become intelligent, adaptive, proactive, and predictive

Service Provider: a company that provides its subscribers access to the Internet

Shadow IT: a term used to describe information-technology systems and solutions built and used inside organizations without explicit approval by the information technology (IT) function

Smart City: a city wherein an investment in technology infrastructure and solutions fuel sustainable economic development and increased quality of life

Sensor: an object whose purpose is to detect events or changes in its environment, and then provide a corresponding output

Uptime: the time during which a machine or a set of machines is in operation

Virtual Private Network (VPN): a capability to connect to a company's private network using public Internet and perform the tasks as if the computer were directly attached to the enterprise network

Wearable: clothing or accessories that incorporate computer and advanced electronic technologies and are typically connected to the network

Wi-Fi: a wireless networking technology that enables devices to connect to local area networks

WirelessHART: a wireless networking technology based on the Highway Addressable Remote Transducer Protocol (HART) and the IEEE 802.15.4 communication protocols used to connect wireless sensors and other end-devices

ZigBee: an IEEE 802.15.4-based specification for a suite of high-level communication protocols used to create personal area networks with small, low-power digital radios

Acknowledgments

This book could not have happened without the guidance, advice, expertise, and support of so many members of the IoT community. I am sincerely grateful to them for encouraging me to put this guide together and for sharing their experiences, examples, and best practices. In particular I would like to thank the following people for their contribution to the content of this book: Helder Antunes, Steve Banks, João Barros, Douglas Bellin, Ravi Belani, Martha Bennett, John Berra, Kevin Block, Flavio Bonomi, James Buczkowski, Lionel Chocron, Sujeet Chand, Paul Didier, Barry Einsig, Wim Elfrink, Rick Esker, Dave Evans, Bruce Frederick, Biren Gandhi, Paul Glynn, Asit Goel, Cheri Goodman, Alex Goryachev, Jos Gouw, David Gutshall, Kathy Haley, Steve Hilton, Richard House, Florence Hudson, Ram Jagadeesan, Tim Jennings, John Kern, Serhii Konovalov, Georg Kopetz, Sanjaya Krishna, Chris Lewis, Oleg Logvinov, Leah McLean, Jorge Magalhaes, James Manyika, Brian McGlynn, Chris Melching, Max Mirgoli, Rama Naageswaran, Chet Namboodri, John Nesi, Keith Nosbusch, Larry O'Connell, Fazil Osman, Aleksander Poniewierski, Balaji Prabhakar, Whitney Rockley, Hilton Romanski, Bola Rotibi, Mark Schulz, Thorsten Schaefer, Tony Shakib, Pavan Singh, Siva Sivakumar, Carly Snyder, Steve Steinhilber, Gary Stuebing, Dima Tokar, Bettina Tratz-Ryan, Vernon Turner, JP Vasseur, C. Prasanna Venkatesan, Paul Verkuyl, Nicola Villa, Padmasree Warrior, Mark Watson, Alex West, Chris White, Zia Yusuf, Arkady Zaslavsky, and Tao Zhang. Special thanks to Alan Radding for content assistance and Alice Shimmin for proofreading and copyediting. Thank you Jo Anne Alvarado

Dominguez for working tirelessly to schedule all the calls. Lindy Bartell and an amazing team from Duarte: Amanda Holt, Nate Hernandez, Ed Jones, Jessica Savage, and Meredith Suarez—a big thank you for your help with graphics. Malee Dharmasena, I really appreciate your help connecting me with the industry thought leaders. And last but not least, I am grateful for the guidance and advice from Richard Narramore and Tiffany Colon from Wiley.

About the Author

Maciej Kranz, vice president, Strategic Innovations Group, at Cisco brings 30 years of networking industry experience to his position. He leads the group focused on incubating new businesses, accelerating internal innovation, and driving co-innovation with customers and startups through a global network of Cisco Innovation Centers.

Prior to this role, Kranz was general manager of the Connected Industries Group at Cisco, a business unit focused on the Internet of Things. He built a $250M business from the ground up in 18 months and relentlessly evangelized the IoT opportunity across Cisco and the market, making IoT one of Cisco's major priorities.

Previously, Kranz led efforts across Cisco to define, prioritize, and deliver Borderless Network Architecture and roadmaps. He also drove business and product strategy for the wireless and mobility business and led product management for the stackable Ethernet switching business unit through its expansion from $400M to $6B in revenues.

Before coming to Cisco, Kranz held various management positions at 3Com Corporation, where he drove a $1B Ethernet network interface cards (NICs) product line. He began his professional career at IBM Corporation.

Index

Page references followed by *fig* indicate an illustrated figure; followed by *t* indicate a table.